Life and Letters of Wilder Dwight
by Wilder Dwight

Address:
HardPress
8345 NW 66TH ST #2561
MIAMI FL 33166-2626
USA
Email: info@hardpress.net

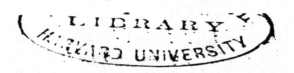

LIFE AND LETTERS

or

WILDER DWIGHT,

LIEUT.-COL. SECOND MASS. INF. VOLS.

By

Mrs. Eliza Amelia (White)

"Do not spend your days in weakly fearing or regretting this or that life, — lives whose whole sweetness and value depend upon their opportunities, not on their length." — LETTERS, p. 214.

BOSTON:
TICKNOR AND FIELDS.
1868.

UNIVERSITY PRESS: WELCH, BIGELOW, & CO.,
CAMBRIDGE.

𝔗𝔬 𝔱𝔥𝔢 𝔐𝔢𝔪𝔬𝔯𝔂

OF

THE PATRIOTS THROUGHOUT OUR LAND,

WHO, IN THE SAME SPIRIT WITH THE SUBJECT OF THIS RECORD,
HAVE FALLEN IN THE SAME CAUSE.

CONTENTS.

CHAPTER I.

CHAPTER II.

CHAPTER III.

CHAPTER IV.

CHAPTER V.

CHAPTER VI.

CHAPTER VII.

CHAPTER VIII.

CHAPTER IX.

CHAPTER X.

CHAPTER XI.

CHAPTER XII.

CHAPTER XIII.

LIFE AND LETTERS OF WILDER DWIGHT.

CHAPTER I.

BIRTH. — ANCESTRY. — EARLY LIFE. — EXETER ACADEMY. — SCHOOL AT WEST POINT. — HARVARD COLLEGE. — CAMBRIDGE LAW SCHOOL. — FOREIGN TRAVEL. — PROFESSIONAL STUDIES. — PRACTICE OF THE LAW. — FAVORITE RECREATION.

WILDER DWIGHT was born in Springfield, Massachusetts, on the 23d of April, 1833. Of English descent, his family, on both sides, were among the earliest settlers of New England.

John Dwight, of Oxfordshire, England, who settled in Dedham, Massachusetts, in 1636, is described, in the quaint records of the town, as " publicly useful, and a great peacemaker." He brought from England a valuable estate, and dying, in 1659, left the same to his only son, Timothy, who, according to the record, " inherited his estate and virtues, and added to both." Timothy, a cornet of troop in his younger days, went out against the Indians ten times, — nine of which he either killed or took them prisoners. He was afterwards a captain of the foot, and then a justice of the peace, and, at his death, in 1717, is described as " a gentleman truly serious and godly, — one of an excellent spirit, — peaceable, charitable, and a great promoter of the true interests of the church and town."

1

Nathaniel, eldest son of Timothy, named his eldest son Timothy, who was the father of the Rev. Timothy Dwight, President of Yale College, — certainly the most distinguished member of the family.

Henry, fourth son of the first Timothy, had ten children. His eldest son, Joseph, was a brigadier-general of militia, and prominent in command under Sir William Pepperell, at the taking of Louisburg from the French, June 6th, 1745, and subsequently raised and commanded a regiment sent for the reduction of Ticonderoga.

Edmund Dwight, brother of Brigadier-General Joseph Dwight, was the fourth son of Henry, and served, also, at the taking of Louisburg, as an ensign. He afterwards became a captain in His Majesty's service, and died in Halifax at the age of thirty-eight years.

His eldest son, Jonathan, settled in Springfield, Massachusetts, and had four sons, the second of whom, Jonathan (grad. H. U. 1793), was the father of William Dwight (grad. H. U. 1825), and the grandfather of Wilder Dwight, the subject of the present memoir.

The mother of Wilder Dwight was the daughter of the Hon. Daniel Appleton White (grad. H. U. 1797), a descendant of William White, of Norfolk County, England, who settled in Ipswich, Massachusetts, in 1635, and in 1640 removed to Haverhill, Massachusetts.

He was one of the grantees of the Indian deed of Haverhill, dated November 15th, 1642, which instrument was, it is said, both written and witnessed by him.

It has been thought worth while to record the purely New England origin of Wilder Dwight; for in him we recognize the principles and habits of thought and life of the New-Englander.

Yet a more noble ancestry was his. In his journal he has himself recorded it, as follows : —

" *Illustrious Ancestry.* He alone has it who has lived a useful, excellent, and honorable life. Then he can look back upon the obedient child, the generous youth, the mature man, — all the ancestors, progenitors of his present self. And they, too, his only ancestry. He began with nothing, he has made everything ; but on dying, he takes his nobility with him, and can never leave it, except as a pleasant mem ory, to his successors."

He was the second in a family of seven sons, three of whom, besides himself, served with credit in the late war.

From early childhood he was esteemed a boy of rare promise. But in this he was not remarkable, — promising children are the rule, not the exception. His distinction as a child was, that he gave promise of exactly what he afterwards performed.

Manly, courageous, self-possessed, acute, original, frank, affectionate, generous, reliable, he was in boyhood, not less than in manhood, one in whom to place an absolute trust. Yet, in less vital points, he was no pattern boy. He had a quick and irritable temper, hard for himself to subdue, and hard for others to contend with ; but there were times when one could hardly regret that which led him to such a manly struggle for self-control. Upon this contest he entered almost in his infancy. Side by side with his repeated outbursts of angry temper are remembered his early efforts to control it.

With high health and abounding animal spirits, a somewhat rude and boisterous manner, added to his constitutional irritability, made him often troublesome as a boy. Yet there was a charm about him which more than atoned for it. This charm was due not only to his true, transparent nature, but also to that in his eye and smile, which, from his earliest infancy to his latest hour, spoke eloquently of the soul within, and was magnetic in its influence upon others. To this was added, under circumstances calculated to call it forth, a gentle consideration for others, which was in striking contrast with his usually brusque and careless manner.

His drollery was irresistible. Many a reproof did he ward off by it in childhood, many a dark hour did he brighten by it in after years.

He was uncommonly clear-headed and strong in intellect, yet he was not a precocious child in the ordinary acceptation of that term. His cleverness was of the kind which has been described as " that of those children who grow up to be clever men ; — a cleverness which, as a rule, furnishes fewest anecdotes, makes least show, leaves boys essentially boys, not at all like men."

His *character* developed early. He had, even as a little child, a sincere love of right and aversion to wrong, though he did not desire to hear preaching on the subject.

It was his delight, from early boyhood, to relieve the wants of the poor and suffering. His " acts of

kindness and charity" at that period are no less vividly remembered than are those of his riper years.

His eagerness for out-of-door life and sport was
never restrained. He grew up under the free air of
heaven, and amidst the most inspiring scenery of
earth. To both these influences may be traced much
that was valuable in his life and character.

In company with a circle of boys from families of
the immediate neighborhood, his playground was re-
stricted only to the beautiful hill upon which they all
lived, where they had the freedom needed for enjoyment, while they were seldom beyond the eye or ear
of some watchful parent.

Probably no set of boys ever grew up under circumstances more favorable to good physical and
moral development ; and, in this connection, the
thought forces itself upon us, with what added interest we should have looked out from our windows
upon the happy, noisy group, had we then realized
for what some of them were in training.

More than twenty years later, when their country's life was in danger, a large portion of them —
true patriots and soldiers — gave themselves body
and soul to her service, thus " doing," as has been
justly said,* " the highest duty man can do," and
alas! too early " dying," some of them,† " the best
death man can die."

* See the remarks of Mr. Ellis, at the meeting of the Suffolk Bar, upon the
occasion of the death of Wilder Dwight. — Appendix III.

† Prominent among the sons of Springfield here referred to is Colonel Everett
Peabody, of the 25th Missouri Infantry. On the morning of the 6th of April,
1862, while commanding a brigade, he fell in the memorable battle of Shiloh,
but not until he had, by personal vigilance and valor, done service of " priceless
value " to the Union cause. " A more gallant officer, or truer gentleman, has
not laid down his life for his country."

Springfield, at the time to which our record carries us back, was not the thickly populated city it now is. The charming old town had all the advantage of a purely country life, with something remaining of primitive simplicity, to suggest a remembrance of early Puritan days.

With the descending sun of Saturday evening, the Sabbath commenced. Then the usual week-day occupations were laid aside, and, for the children, the Scripture print and the Old Testament story were brought forth, as the appropriate recreation for the evening.

Only positive illness or tempestuous weather, on Sunday, prevented parents and children from going in company to the house of God for public worship.

At home, after each of the circle had selected and learned a text of Scripture, the fascinating pages of Pilgrim's Progress, read aloud to the children, made the Sunday hours among the pleasantest of the week.

Driving, on the sacred day, excepting to and from the " meeting-house," as it was called, was a thing unknown, and those who ventured to depart so far from the prevailing custom as to take a sober, quiet walk with their little ones, before sunset on Sunday afternoon, were looked upon by their elders, if not with condemnation, at least with surprise and regret, that they should be willing to take the lead in setting so questionable an example.

The artificial excitements which now wait upon the young in the city and its suburbs formed no part of their life in Springfield at that time. The lyceum lecture, the temperance lecture, the anti-slavery lecture, the town-meeting, the political caucus, these were the entertainments of our future patriots. Upon no one of them did the circumstances peculiar to his native town exert a more marked influence than they did upon the ever-wakeful, earnest spirit of Wilder Dwight.

As soon as he could speak in sentences, he began to plead for the Sunday privileges, which he perceived were a source of enjoyment to the rest of the household, promising, if he might only be allowed to " go to meeting," that, when there, he would " sit still," — a thing he was never known to do at home. Before he was quite three years old his wish was granted. He kept his promise, and was always orderly and even reverent in his manner at church.

The services were short, and in that respect well fitted to secure a child from weariness. The preaching,* to which, as he grew older, his attention was directed, was of no ordinary character. Doubtless it was greatly due to this advantage of his boyhood that the subject of religion was of paramount interest and importance to him throughout his life. Good preaching on Sunday he always esteemed a privilege to be earnestly sought and highly prized.

At the age of seven years and six months, he began to attend political caucuses and conventions with his father, and would give humorous and appreciative accounts of what he heard.

* That of the Rev. William B. O. Peabody, D. D., who died in Springfield on the 28th of May, 1847, after a faithful ministry there of nearly thirty years, in which " he enjoyed the cordial respect and good-will of all his Christian brethren of every name, and the devoted love of those to whom he ministered so long."

At the same age he began to study industriously, and from that time he was a faithful student.

That was a sober day at his home when he first went from under its roof to fit for college, at Phillips Exeter Academy.

He was then thirteen years old, and although faults of temper, already mentioned, frequently called for reproof, he had ceased to be regarded merely as a child.   He had grown to be a confidential friend and adviser, relied upon alike by his parents and his brothers.   When any question arose for decision in the domestic circle, it was to his good sense and good judgment, to his ready sympathy and disinterested effort, that then, — as well as later in life, — all instinctively turned.   The same fidelity to duty which had made his presence at home so important marked his life at the academy ; where, says the preceptor, " from the beginning to the end of his course, he was a pattern pupil." *

The following extract from his diary, kept at this time, shows the character of the boy : —

" December 31st, 1846.

" To-day is the last day of the old year, and in commencing the new I wish to lay out some rules, in relation to myself, which I will *try* to observe.

" In the first place, I will exercise every morning after breakfast until school-time, and after school at night, until supper-time.   Secondly, I will study after dinner until school-time, and I will go to my room after supper, and busy myself in studying or in reading a *useful* book until bed-time.   Thirdly, while in school I will try to busy myself about my lessons, and, at any rate, behave in an orderly manner.

* See Appendix II.

" And I will observe strictly these rules, except when it is right for me not to do so ; that is, at such times as I may think it right, though I may err in that opinion.

" And may I also try to correct my defects of temper. May I watch every word that comes from my mouth ; and may I let my yea be yea, and my nay be nay ; and may I not merely write these things down and think no more of them, but may I always keep them in my mind, and remember them most of all when I am angry, as that is the time to control myself."

While he was at the academy, and indeed throughout his life, whenever he was absent from home, it was his habit to send to his family a letter containing an account of each week as it passed.

He now writes : " I will try to profit by your advice as to my companions, and to associate only with those that are good."   To this resolution he faithfully adhered.   In no way did he more clearly show his purity of principle and purpose than in the choice of his friends.

On being directed to select his own subject for composition, he decided upon one which, as we look back upon his whole course through life, is characteristic : " Confidence is conqueror of men ; victorious both over them and in them."

Not less does the following extract from one of his letters of this period foreshadow the future man. The principles which he laid down so forcibly when a schoolboy of fifteen were the source of his strength and success throughout his life : —

" No man ever did anything in this world, however trifling, unless he felt confident of his ability to do it, and unless he entered upon it with a cheerful and firm determination to accomplish his end, let come what will come."

At the end of two years he was fitted for college ; but, not wishing to enter so early, he passed six months at the private military school of Mr. Z. J. D. Kinsley, at West Point, in order to secure the advantage of the military drill, while at the same time he continued his classical studies and received instruction in French and mathematics. In May, 1849, preparatory to entering college, he returned to Exeter for a review of his studies.   In the following July he writes in his diary : —

" On Monday, July 16th, I was examined for entrance to the Freshman class, and after due trepidation and effort, on Tuesday, at about 4 P. M., I received my ' admittatur,' overjoyed at finding it an unconditional one."

He took high rank as a scholar, and maintained it throughout his college course.   The following extract from his diary shows by what means he accomplished this result : —

" *March*, 1850. —   . . . . I am somewhat of ' a dig,' I suppose ; and though the character is rather an ignominious one in college, it is in so good repute elsewhere, and among wiser persons than Freshmen, or even Sophomores, that I shall endeavor always to deserve the title.

" Natural geniuses — that is, lazy good scholars — are few and far between ; I shall, therefore, estimate myself as a very common sort of a person, and, as I desire to excel, I shall choose the way which seems to promise success."

Among the advantages which he enjoyed in Cambridge, that which he valued most highly was the instruction received, in lectures and recitations, on the evidences of natural and revealed religion, from the Rev. Dr. Walker. Not less did he value the pulpit ministrations of this distinguished preacher, to which, at stated intervals, it was his privilege to listen.

In the journal which he kept during his college life, and while he was in the Law School, a large space is given to abstracts of Dr. Walker's sermons.

In one of the earliest of these occurs the following sentence ; it indicates the influence which these teachings exerted upon his character: " You must lay a foundation of religious feeling and principle, upon which to build, in after years, as long as you live."

At another time he writes: " *Sunday, January 4th,* 1852. Heard Dr. Walker preach from the text, Ecc. 8th, 11th: ' Because sentence against an evil work is not executed speedily, therefore the heart of the sons of men is fully set in them to do evil.' " After a long abstract of the sermon, he says : —

" This is the sermon on which I may well found the first resolutions and actions of the opening year. All my life has been a series of violations of law, though I have ever had a theoretic veneration of it. Memory runs back over a sad list, and time passes on swift wings. To-morrow is to-day ere it is spoken, and yesterday was lost in irresolution and weakness. Now — now — now ! God — God — God ! Eternity — eternity — eternity ! Action in the one, mercy and justice in the second ! Pain or pleasure, joy or grief in the last ! Let me remember, then, that ' though a sinner do evil an hundred times and his days be prolonged, yet surely I know that it shall be well with them that fear God, which fear before him ' ; that no man knoweth the ways of God,

—— they are past finding out.   Then I will trust in the goodness which is inscrutable but inexhaustible.   I will apply
my heart to know, to search, and to seek out wisdom, and
to know the wickedness of folly.   And may these thoughts
glow in my mind ; may they rouse my energies till I seek
to embody them in my actions, and make their spirit felt in
my life, and may not these aspirations be transient and
shadowy."

Although he was eminently practical in the bent
of his mind, he was keenly sensitive to the beautiful.   After writing at length upon the subject, in
his journal, he says : " The true love of beauty, —— let
it be my guide in all my pursuits.   The love of
real and true beauty must excite a love for purity,
excellence, and worth."

In reply to one of his brothers, who had asked
his advice as to a course of reading, he says, after
giving a list of books which it is well to read, if
they relish : " I do not think, so long as one avoids
vicious and immoral books, that it is so much a question what particular books he had better read, as it
is an imperative duty to *read something.*   Read, ——
keep reading, —— and you will not regret it."

He faithfully followed the advice which he gave to
his brother.   His love of books amounted to a passion.   While he was in College and in the Law
School he collected a valuable library of one thousand volumes.   He would deny himself any other
indulgence for the sake of possessing a fine edition
of a good book, or a rare copy of an antique ; and it
was only when the temptation came in that form
that he was ever led to incur a debt.

After a visit to his grandfather's library, early in

his college life, he writes: "I feasted myself on the covers and title-pages of many old books. I could do nothing more, for to select was impossible among so many beauties, so I was forced briefly to admire all. To me there is something pleasant and beautiful in the mere excellence of print and paper. I have a sort of blind veneration for these two powerful agents considered by themselves; and therefore enjoy old books, fine editions, and rich bindings, even when I can go no farther than the outside."

In his journal we find a just tribute to a beloved and revered relative. It is inserted here as indicating the struggle for self-mastery which formed so large a part of his life: —

"I believe that there is more true philosophy in cherishing the agreeable thoughts and fostering an unruffled spirit than in any self-discipline. In some moods, nothing would disturb me; in others, every occurrence is an annoyance. But how can this calm be maintained? It is the fruit of many struggles, — the clear settling of a much-troubled and turbid spirit.

"Never was I more struck by the beauty of such a character than in ——, who has been staying with us. Her life has been one of a great deal of trial and severe discipline. She is now a ministering angel of content and peace. Her presence is a benediction. Her voice, as she utters her simple, plain, sincere words of interest, sympathy, or advice, is a messenger of joy. Hardly a harsh or disagreeable word or act has disturbed our home while she has hallowed it."

The following record, in his diary, contains the secret of his own success in life: —

"The more I read, and the more I see, the more inevita-

bly I am led to the conclusion, that all men who leave anything behind them, and whose lives are, in a true sense,
respectable and successful, are the incessant, earnest work-
ers ; — those who propose an object in living, and whose
aims all tend to the accomplishment of that object."

Not less characteristic of him, from the beginning
to the end of his short life, is the following, on
another page, quoted from Dr. Walker : " Success,
ultimate success, in whatever a man undertakes, de-
pends almost entirely — yes, I believe I may say
almost entirely — on forecast and perseverance ; on
that peculiar constitution and training which dispose
one, in the first place, to mark out for himself the
course he will pursue, and then fire him with a
resolution to follow it up or die."

The year 1853 — the last of his college life —
was full of interesting experience to him ; yet his
journal,* during this and the following year, after
which he ceased to write in it, contains only abstracts of Dr. Walker's sermons, with occasional extracts from books he was reading.   These all indicate the serious thoughtfulness of his inner life, while
memory holds a bright record of his healthy outward progress, during those years, in all that was
needed to prepare him for a happy and useful future.

On leaving college, he entered the Law School at
Cambridge, with ardent enthusiasm for the profession.   There, too, he took a prominent position, re-

---

* It should be said that neither the journal here mentioned, nor that kept
during his boyhood, from which we have quoted, was ever seen by any eyes but
his own, until after his death.

ceiving the first prize in 1855.   On leaving the Law
School, he passed fourteen months in foreign travel.
He sometimes spoke with regret of this interruption
to his studies, because it placed him further from the
attainment of the main purpose of his life.

He first visited England, proceeding thence through
Germany to Switzerland.   There, after some days of
" hard mountain and glacier climbing," he met with
a sad check to his progress, in the misfortune of a
kick from a mule.   Of his characteristic way of meeting this disaster, the friend * who accompanied him
wrote at the time: " Dwight, who bore his accident
with the heroism of a soldier and the calmness of a
philosopher, frequently exchanged expressions of delight and wonder at the wild scenery about us, for
those which disappointment and pain would have
prompted."

A more serious interruption to his travels awaited
him.   While still suffering from lameness, he was, to
use his own language, " thrown violently on his back,
as with the sudden gripe of a strong arm," by typhoid
fever.   When thus seized, he was at a little hotel at
Giessbach, which looked directly out upon the cascade,
whose constant fall was very irritating.   Soon, however, through the generous hospitality of strangers, he
was removed to a quiet and cool apartment in a house
farther up the valley, where he was, as he said, " the
guest of an honorable man and a counsellor." †

* Charles Wentworth Upham, Jr., son of Hon. Charles W. Upham, and
nephew of Dr. Oliver Wendell Holmes.   " Fairest and gentlest of his race," he
died on the 2d of April, 1860, beloved and lamented by all who knew him.

† " Monsieur Von Rappard was, for nearly half a century, Privy Counsellor
of Prussia, and for some years President of the Council, a man of wealth and

There, under the devoted care of three friends *
of his college days, two of whom came most unexpectedly to his relief, he realized that to the darkest
experiences of human life there is a bright side. The
friendships thus cemented, never to be interrupted
but by death, made even this period of suffering a
pleasant remembrance to him ever after.

As soon as his strength was so far restored as to
admit of his being again a traveller, he left Switzerland for Paris, whence he writes : —

" This life abroad is very agreeable, but I am beginning to
have my misgivings about its usefulness. I wish I had more
faith in that ' expansion of mind,' etc., which is to result in-
sensibly from my present life. Perhaps when I begin to
move again my mind will change, but just at present, I am
pining for a quiet settlement in Boston, with my few irons
in my feeble fire, and a professional progress that would tell.
Whole weeks of palaces, pictures, monuments, etc., are agreeable, but is not that all ? "

After repeated visits to the courts of Paris, he
says : —

" It is singular to note the same manners and ways in the
French courts that I have seen at home ; and, also, the same
style and expression of face. I think the Law has an influence upon the features, so that a company of lawyers, selected from all countries, would look more or less alike.

" It seems to lengthen, sharpen, and wither the face ; not
that there are not hundreds of fat, round-faced ones, but

---

high station. In 1848, his family, from their republican tendencies, became fugitives. They came to Switzerland, and made Berne their winter residence,
and purchased the Giessbach for a summer retreat."

* Charles Wentworth Upham, Jr., Grad. H. U. 1852 ; Horace Howard Furness, Grad. H. U. 1854 ; Atherton Blight, Grad. H. U. 1854.

that in such cases Nature has been too strong for the Law, or, perhaps, the latter has never contested the point fairly."

Again, he writes : —

" You would be amused and instructed by the economy of Paris. I used to think that, theoretically, you had something of it yourself, and that, under favorable circumstances, you might develop a system which would render six boys a smaller encumbrance than they generally prove ; but you must come. to Paris to correct the many extravagances of even your theory. Such a thing as a breakfast or a dinner is hardly to be got in Paris, except where foreigners have introduced their own comforts or extravagances. But you can purchase all the component parts of any meal, and regulate the proportions at pleasure. It will come to you with a price affixed to every fragment, and your total, which may be great or small, with your appetite or liberality, will always be composed of an infinity of little items whose separate feebleness is no preparation for their combined force.

" The total, like the bundle of sticks, is strong enough, but one has great contempt for the two-penny twigs which compose it. To a practised eye, the table, as it is spread before one, represents at once a feast and its price. A nation which begins by adopting a currency which divides a franc into one hundred parts, and which thus magnifies small amounts by calling *ten cents* fifty centimes, which goes on to make every meal a sum in arithmetic, and forces economy upon one by affixing its separate penalty to every petty extravagance, may easily become, under the slightest pressure, most accurately and, to an uninitiated eye, rather painfully economical. My landlady rose, last week, a few centimes on the bread, and informed me of it with an orotund emphasis intended to frighten me out of my appetite. I was able, on reflection, to face the total with Yankee equanimity.

" By dividing their money into such minute fractions, they can register every item of expense, affix its value to

2

every article, and speak respectfully of amounts for which we have no name."

When he was about to leave Paris for Spain, he wrote : —

" Leaving Paris calls for the same preparations and effort as leaving home. You get quietly and comfortably settled here, and to recur to discomforts and vexations of a portmanteau and a carpet-bag requires resolution and energy. My French teacher, whose Parisian habits of morning coffee, eleven o'clock *déjeûné*, and evening dinner, leave no want unsatisfied, and no aspiration unattained, cannot understand why Monsieur Dwight, who has such a *joli appartement avec ses bons amis*, and with the facilities and delights of Paris at his elbow, can think of going to seek annoyance and irregularity in inhospitable Spain.

" But he yields gracefully to the separation, and has just been making his profuse and obsequious adieux with endless repetition of ' *bon voyage*,' ' *au plaisir de vous revoir*,' and ' *merci !* ' ' *merci !* ' "

From Madrid he writes more confidently of the advantages of travelling than he did, during the previous month, from Paris.

" What a stimulus being on the spot is ! I long to read a hundred books about early Spanish history, and I constantly feel how little I am prepared for travel. Perhaps I never should become much more so by waiting at home, and it is in this belief that I reconcile myself to staying now. I read and pick up whatever I can, keeping my eyes open, my mind alive, and my body active. There is no discipline better for the development of energy, physical and mental, than vigorous travelling. You have uncertainties before you, are bothered with difficulties, thrown upon the resources of a ready invention, and enticed and rewarded by novelties. Every day furnishes new opportunities, kindles fresh curiosity, and opens further vistas.   The mere routine of living changes with almost every change of place.   The daily walk teaches a thousand things and explains innumerable questions. . . . . This evening, I have been querying a good deal about the wisdom of running away from home, and I incline, now and then, to question it; but, on the whole, I believe the time lost is much more than compensated, and I am quite content that the past is as it is.

" About the future I cannot yet feel entirely decided, but I beg you to believe that, however I act, my good purposes for becoming an active and, in my degree, a useful man are not relinquished, if I allow them to seem slightly postponed."

Of the " mode of life in Spain " he says : —

" They practise a simplicity and severity of economy and abstemiousness in this unhappy country which astonishes a New-England housekeeper.   Take the dinner, for example. I am told that in most well-regulated Spanish families it resolves itself into what we should call soup; that is, a stew is made of beef, pork, beans, and, perchance, cabbage.   The juice of these ingredients opens the dinner, while the viands and vegetables are served up as separate courses. In that way you have the semblance of a dinner, the form of recurring courses, but, in truth, the goodness was all boiled out, and has been eaten in the soup.   This dish of beef which has yielded itself up, heart and soul, to some former pottage, and beans which have exhausted their strength in support of the same alliance, is the invariable accompaniment of every dinner.

" Like many other Spanish institutions, it presents the faint shadow of former greatness, and mocks the senses with a show of nutrition whose substance vanished in some former age.   It is the tattered cloak of some bygone Don, and ill conceals the poverty and rags which remain.   In short, I think that the regeneration of Spain must commence by the introduction of roast beef and boiled mutton.   How low must that nation have fallen which can feast itself upon the degraded and effete shreds of a once rich and juicy roasting-piece, — whose only birthright is a mess of pottage !

"My guide-book — invaluable prompter to astute observations — says that the people of Spain eat to live, but do not live to eat.   I suppose the truth to be, that, except under the pressure of a harsh necessity, they are very much like their neighbors, and love a good thing when they can get it.   The truth is, they are poor."

Of a visit to Malaga he says : —

" I wandered outside the town, and seeing a pretty chapel on the summit of a hill, followed the path, which had frequent white crosses as stations and resting-places for devout pilgrims.   On my way up I met a lady, followed by her servant, who were slowly picking their way over the sharp stones which strewed the path.   My ignorance was attributing their slow and difficult descent to thin shoes, when a close inspection showed me that the evil consisted in a total want of that protection.   They took their penance gingerly, however, and went as lightly and smoothly along the hard path of repentance as its steepness and stoniness permitted.   The atonement seemed harsh, and their poor white feet were well punished for any former wanderings.   They passed me muttering prayers and devoutly watching their steps ; and I thought, as I looked after them, what a coarse and clumsy expedient the poor women had put their faith in."

After leaving Malaga he met "on board the transport ship Sovereign," going to Gibraltar, some Crimean officers, in whose account of their adventures he became greatly interested.   After the pleasant hours passed with them he writes, with no premonition of his own future : —

" It brings one much nearer the horrors of war to meet a few men fresh from its experiences, than to read a great deal of graphic description. And we realized the sadness which follows many of those young officers home, when our Irish friend could not speak, except with tears, of the loss of a brother officer who had been his tent companion."

In looking back upon Spain, where some of the pleasantest days of his wanderings were passed in the renewed companionship of the friends who had nursed him so tenderly in Switzerland, — the " Giessbach Club," as he says Upham calls it, — he writes : —

" It is singular to recollect the difference between my feelings on entering and on leaving Spain. Even its discomforts have lost all their harshness, and many of its annoyances I shall regret."

After an interesting tour through Italy, he joined his friends of the Giessbach Club again in Constantinople. With them he visited Balaklava, Sebastopol, the Malakoff, and the Redan. He speaks of finding himself by the grave of the French soldiers who were killed in the attack on the Malakoff. " At its head," he says, " is a cross bearing the inscription : ' 8th Septembre, 1855. Unis pour la victoire, Réunis par la mort. Du soldat c'est la gloire, Des braves c'est le sort.' "

From Constantinople he went to Athens, and thence, a second time, to Paris, whence he wrote : —

" Time here is beguiled of all its power, and slips lightly away ; at least to that male portion of humanity who are not condemned to an existence of shopping and dressmakers. Ladies work harder here, suffer more, and are still stronger than I could have believed. The choice, too, is so extensive that it ought to be distracting. . I called the other morning upon Mrs. ——. She was seated in the midst of an enormous pile of lace, embroideries, pocket-handkerchiefs, etc.,— in a perfect labyrinth of francs and phrases which my limited French could not achieve. Standing near her, awaiting the exit of the handkerchiefs, was a pliant, plausible, apologetic Frenchman, loaded with black lace, and holding out one piece very temptingly to entice her away from the ' mouchoirs.' On the other side, a nice, natty little milliner, with that marvellous union and harmony of ribbon and lace, called a head-dress in English and a coif — something or other in French, in one hand, and a bewildering array of bandboxes at her side, was awaiting her turn. In a corner was an artist trying to obtain another sitting for his picture, and my own visit concerned a pair of slippers which I had purchased for the fair Mrs. —— in Constantinople. This was the tableau upon which the Doctor entered who has been trying for the last two weeks to restore her to her former health. I thought, from the expression of his face, that if he knew of a purgative which would act upon these various imps of fashion it would have been his first prescription. This is the way people travel in Europe for their health, with the other aggravations of Paris dinners, an occasional theatre, or a tedious reunion. I have been led, in view of all this, to consider how much mental excitement and physical prostration is every day represented by the toilettes of the Boulevard. It is a sad problem, for there does not seem enough domestic tranquillity left after the subtraction to furnish that blessing to more than one family in a hundred, without considering the other and numerous drafts upon the meagre remainder which must result from other causes. Yet those things are vastly pretty. In face of all these drawbacks, I still think that a well-dressed woman is the highest effort of modern civilization."

After a run through England and Scotland, he returned home in the summer of 1856, and resumed his studies in the office of the Hon. Caleb Cushing, Attorney-General of the United States. Soon after reaching Washington he wrote : —

" I have changed my boarding-place during the past week, and I have been very much amused with the politics of my new table. The patron of the establishment is a broken-down judge ; ruined himself, I believe, with copper, has got an amiable, mild wife and twelve children. Under these advantages and disadvantages, having always professed sound Democratic principles, the Land Office opened its doors and received him to a small salary. The wife and children — the latter for the most part daughters — aid the fallen fortunes of the family by keeping boarders. They gather around their board merchants who have failed in everything but Democracy, and are therefore clerks, and young men whose fathers or uncles have aided the cause, and one or two army officers. The table, however, takes its tone from the government clerks, whose life outside of the routine of office is one prolonged echo of ' democratic principles.' I presume there are one hundred tables in Washington which assemble the same motley crowd and are enlivened with the same monotone of politics. . . . . We have several quaint oddities whose conversation is agreeable. They are full of the gossiping history of the past twenty years, — personal anecdotes of celebrated men and famous debates, — so that one picks up a great deal of entertainment ; at the expense, however, of no little loss of time. These fellows are confirmed loafers, and chat away their leisure with great success. I have the example of the Attorney-General as a corrective. He is at his office before seven, and does not see his bed until the small hours of the next morning. I do not see how, without sleep, without recreation or diversion, he sustains the immense labor which he does. He looks young, too, through it all, and is keen and lively as if he were thirty."

At the end of two months, he returned to Boston, and continued his studies in the office of the Hon. E. R. Hoar and Horace Gray, Esq. Here he not only enjoyed the best possible professional advantages, but he had also the happiness of forming friendships by which his after life was greatly enriched.

In January, 1857, he writes to his friend Furness : —

"If you could see a young man getting up under the first faint symptoms of dawn, breakfasting, and rushing to town by steam, sitting down in an office in Court Street, and wearing through the days of preparation with no definite idea of what he is preparing for, — rushing off again under cover of twilight, and dining after his labors, from a habit formed *abroad !* — if, I say, you could observe this phenomenon daily, — if you could see him moving in obedience to an impulse which knows no relenting, you might have the friendliness to hope that he was on the way to something good and desirable, but you could not help shivering at the thought that ' the way was long, the night was cold.'

"My dear fellow, the law is the perfection of human reason when you begin to read it, while you keep away from men and affairs. But the closer you come to men and things, the less perfect it grows to you."

Again, two months later, he says : —

"If you have any curiosity about me, I can say for myself that I am learning to labor and to wait, in true lawyer-like fashion."

In his diary of the summer of 1857 are the following records : "*Saturday, July* 18*th.* Took office at No. 35 Court Street." And, again, "*Monday, September* 28*th.* Sign up. Office open."

In January, 1858, he writes to an absent brother : —

" My business swells by little rivulets and drippings, and I am exceeding my expectations of success."

Again, he says : —

" It so happens that my practice gets on swimmingly. I am afraid of a lull, but the wind holds remarkably."

His early success was, doubtless, greatly due to the confidence in his ability with which he inspired his friend Judge Abbott, who at once employed him as junior counsel in important cases, and of whose generous kindness he never ceased to speak with gratitude.

In addressing the Supreme Judicial Court, upon the occasion of the death of his departed friend,* Judge Abbott says : —

" I can say in reference to my appreciation of him what I know you will appreciate as the highest evidence in my judgment of his qualifications as a lawyer, that I have come up before you and your associates, — the tribunal which I most respect above human tribunals, — depending entirely upon briefs furnished by my associate, this young man.

" I have trusted, — beginning with the first cause he ever had occasion to try after being admitted to the bar, — trusted, what I should rarely do, the entire preparation of causes to him, and sat down to the trial of them without any personal attention to the preparation myself. That, Sir, is the highest possible testimony I can give, as to my own belief, as to his qualifications and prospects."

In the spring of 1859 he became the partner of Horace Gray, Esq., in whose office he had formerly been a student.

* See Appendix III.

The relation which Judge Gray held to him, affording opportunity for intimate acquaintance, gives peculiar value to his estimate of him, both as a lawyer and as a man. From the warm tribute paid him by this valued friend, at the meeting of the Suffolk Bar,* upon the occasion of his death, we extract the following : —

"My acquaintance with him began when, introduced by the gentleman who has just spoken, he applied to enter my office as a student when I was about to form a connection in practice with the present Mr. Justice Hoar. I had occasion to hear all his arguments upon questions of law before the Supreme Court.

"And after he had become my partner, it was in his room that the first steps were taken toward getting up the Second Massachusetts Regiment, of which so much has been already said.

"And I can truly say, that, from the beginning of our acquaintance, my love, my respect, and my admiration for him went on increasing to the end.

"If I may be permitted to judge, from the assistance I derived from him, first as a student and afterwards as an associate, and from having been present at the argument of nearly all the questions of law which were argued before the full bench of the Supreme Court while he was at the Bar, I should find it hard to name one of his age who was better grounded in the principles of the law. And I think I may say, that I have never known any young man who combined, in such just and equal proportions, the theory to be learned from the books with a readiness of practical application to the facts of cases as they came up.

"It has been said here to-day, that his judgment was uncommonly mature for his years, and that is true. But it is

* See Appendix III.

not all. He did not rest satisfied with what he had attained. As he grew older, he improved, not only in experience and in soundness of judgment, but in breadth of view and height of aim, and in generous consideration of the efforts of others not so high in their aims or so fortunate in their faculties as himself. He had no mean spirit of rivalry. He ran, not to pass others in the race, but to reach the goal ; and he would have run the same race if no others had run with him. . . . .

" To those who really knew him, his warmth of feeling was not less remarkable than his purity of principle and his strength of character. None but his intimate friends knew how much of his time was taken up in acts of kindness and charity."

The " acts of kindness and charity " here mentioned were the most interesting feature of his professional life to those who watched his progress with something like solicitude, lest the practice of the law, so often believed to exert a hardening influence, added to the success which seemed to attend everything he undertook, should induce a spirit of selfishness in place of the readiness for disinterested effort which, from early boyhood, had been one of his greatest attractions.

This anxiety was relieved, as it was seen that his very profession led him to "weep with them that wept," and to " rejoice with them that did rejoice." Most precious are the memories of him at that period ; when, his heart full of generous impulse and kind affections, he went forth on his errands of mercy, to " feed the hungry, to clothe the naked, to visit the stranger, the sick, and in prison."

One of the most beautiful traits of his manhood,

which greatly endeared him at home, was his sympathy with the youngest members of the household. Whatever were his own occupations and pleasures, he was never unmindful of theirs. He entered into their feelings, and made their interests his own. Especially did he enjoy doing everything in his power to make their childhood happy.

When the annual festivals came round, it was for their sakes that he welcomed them. No one now remaining in the once unbroken family circle can ever forget how on Christmas Eve, after " the little boys," as they were called, were safely in bed, he would appear in the parlor, his face bright with smiles, his arms laden with gifts which it had been his pleasure to procure, and which it was then his pleasure to arrange for them in anticipation of the coming day.

Throughout his life he took delight in children. When, after a fatiguing day in the practice of his profession, he returned home worn and weary, he used to say that nothing so rested and refreshed him as a good frolic with a child.

There are others, besides those of his own family, whom he left in childhood and youth, — some since grown, others fast growing, into womanhood and manhood, — who remember him as one to whom they looked up with respect, yet who never felt too far beyond them in years to join in their sports, and to sympathize in their interests and pursuits.

In one household, where he was most familiarly welcomed, it was said, after his death : —

" Everything we do seems to have some association with him. To-night we are reminded of the interest he showed in the children's recitations of the catechism.

"One Sunday evening is particularly remembered, when, in the absence of their father, the children brought out the big Bible and laid it before him, and told him he must be father; and he sat down and read with them all the Sunday evening chapters, with as much interest and earnestness as if it had been his own family circle."

His favorite recreation — to which, from the time he entered college, he gave some weeks of every summer — was found in camping out for hunting and fishing among the forests and lakes of the Adirondacks or the White Mountains.

His high enjoyment of this rough life in the woods is characteristically expressed in the following extract from a letter written in the course of an expedition on foot through the White Mountains: —

"I do not propose to give you anything more than a glance at ten days very full of work and play, and very rich in adventure and bracing health. There is a vital cordial in this northern air which justifies almost any amount of panegyric. Think of toiling seven or eight hours through the woods, over what is called a *logging* path, — leaping over stones, avoiding, or failing to avoid, stumps and trees, undergrowth and overgrowth, up over hills, down through swamps, wet by showers, drenched to the skin at the very moment when the dinner, trout, just caught from the brook, was beginning to bubble and sputter over the fire, eating it, at last, half-cooked and wet, sleeping in the open air on hemlock-boughs, before a fire glowing and crackling through the night with all the glare and sparkle of birch and oak, waking to a bath in the brook, and an expedition, in pursuit of breakfast, to some stream before the mists of morning have uncovered the sleeping lake, or while they and the heavens are lighting up with that glory of sunrise which no one ever enjoyed as he who met it alone and rising from no bed.   Or, again, rising at midnight to a moonlight clear, calm, glorious, etc., etc.   This is incoherent, nonsensical, anything you will, but I have had a week of it, varied with pleasure and disappointment, success and failure, great luck in fishing, no luck in shooting, but full of sport and life and health.

" To tread with a sensation of leg, to strike with a sensation of arm, to thrill with a quickness and buoyancy of life, is the boon of great worth which comes of such a trip To write without grammar or sequence is one of its fatal consequences.   Life in the woods, — the minimum of convenience and comfort, and, at the same time, the minimum of desire and need.   The few necessities more than supplied.   Every spring is your fountain, every brook holds your food, the whole forest for your fuel, the nearest bush gives you a pot-hook, a crane, and a spit. . . . .

" I need not say that I have enjoyed the sensation of perfect health and animal vigor, and the exhilaration of the life very much."

For several successive years he visited his chosen haunts in " the forest primeval " of the Adirondacks.

In one dwelling, at the foot of the Upper Saranac, where year after year he stopped to be fitted out for camp life, his memory is cherished as one would hardly expect it to be beyond his own home. " When I heard of his death," said the kind hostess, " it made me sick, and I think I have shed more tears for him than for any relation I ever lost.   I know it is wrong to mourn so for him ; but though two years have passed, every spot in the house seems to bring him to my mind, and I can't be reconciled to the thought that I shall never see him here again." Thus did he impress himself upon all with whom he had to do.

During his last expedition of the kind, in August, 1860, he wrote gayly : —

"CAMP CONTENT, FORKED LAKE, August 25, 1860.

"This letter comes from our pleasant camping-ground, and its date may indicate that the week here has flown on even wing. . . . . There is little enough to write you in the way of news. It is the glad tidings of ' no news ' to which I am listening with great tranquillity. A fly skipping lightly over the water, and anon a trout rising snappishly and spinning away with the hook. The same, subsequently fried, — *not* the hook. A buck leaping into the lake, and swimming wildly right into the muzzle of a rifle, — a subsequent honorable career of steaks and roasts. A morning sunrise and a glowing sunset, — to pass from the more material phenomena. John King for guide, who just suggests, — seeing me use fine salt for sand on my page, — ' I guess that letter won't spile before it gets there.' An occasional novel, and a great many vacant naps and reveries, are the positive enjoyments. The absence of everything else kindles a glow of negative delights. . . . . We have had no end of sport, in its technical sense ; — eight deer, and sixty trout in a week ! "

A year from that day, " Camp Content, Forked Lake," was exchanged for a soldier's tent in a military camp, on the soil of Maryland.

CHAPTER II.

Mr. Lincoln's Inauguration. — Fall of Sumter. — Efforts to raise a Regiment for the War. — Journey to Washington. — Approval of the proposed Regiment by the Secretary of War.

WILDER DWIGHT never entered so zealously into any political campaign as he did into that of the autumn of 1860, which preceded Mr. Lincoln's election to the Presidency, to which object he gave himself with his accustomed energy. Some weeks after the election he wrote as follows to the beloved brother, who was then a citizen of Tennessee : —

" Dear Howard, — A merry Christmas and a happy New Year. Liberty and Union. Any Session except Secession. If the order of things is not subverted, and if the United States mail has not become a reminiscence and a regret, this will bring you a token of the kind remembrance of your *foreign* relations. Whatever national flag floats over you, we wish you a better year than ever before. We drank to you (only with our eyes) on Christmas Day, and all empowered me to send you greeting. Acting under that informal power of attorney, — the power of an attorney is my constant strength, — I wish you a God speed on your journey, and pray that out of the present darkness there may come a light. Just now, I can't for the life of me see where it is to come from. But I have faith in the Constitution, not as a legend or a bargain, but as a great social and physical national condition. Those who kick against it will soon feel the pricks. But madness and folly often produce damnable consequences. I send you an anchor, and commend

you to the hope it symbolizes. I know no other wisdom.
God bless you."

After attending the inauguration of Mr. Lincoln,
he wrote, at the close of the day, the following hasty
sketch of the scene : —

"WASHINGTON, March 4, 1861.

" DEAR FATHER, — This morning broke badly, but at noon
the sky cleared.   I remained quietly at Willard's, and was
present when Mr. Buchanan came to receive the President
elect, and saw the interview, which was a formal one ; then
I saw Lincoln and Buchanan take their carriage, and the
whole procession pass.   I then took a carriage, and, by back
streets, reached the Capitol grounds, and got a good place.
Soon Lincoln and Judge Taney, followed by Buchanan and
the other judges, etc., appeared.   The band played Hail
Columbia.   The crowd was immense.   The Capitol steps
were covered with uniforms, etc.   Baker, of Oregon, of the
Committee of Arrangements, announced that Mr. Lincoln
would speak ; and when Abraham rose and came forward
and rang out the words, ' Fellow-citizens of the *United*
States,' he loomed and grew, and was ugly no longer.   I
was not very near, but heard him perfectly.   The address
you will read, and like, I hope.   Its effect was very good.
An immense concourse — thousands — stood uncovered and
silent, except occasional applause ; the voice clear and ringing ; the manner very good, often impressive, and even
solemn ; the words I think to the point, direct, and clear.
The scene itself was of its own kind.   And I must say its
effect upon me was far greater than I had supposed.   When
the address closed, and the cheering subsided, Taney rose,
and, almost as tall as Lincoln, he administered the oath,
Lincoln repeating it ; and as the words, ' preserve, protect,
and defend the Constitution ' came ringing out, he bent and
kissed the book ; and for one, I breathed freer and gladder

than for months. The man looked a man, and acted a man and a President. So much for inauguration."

A month later, on the 1st of April, 1861, he wrote : —

"DEAR HOWARD, — You will hear by mail of grandfather's death * through D.'s letter. It was worthy of a calm, wise, and benevolent life, and was full of every hope which belongs to the last hour."

Two weeks later he received his own call to "arise and depart." The first gun fired on Sumter was his summons. When the awful tidings came, he closed his law-books, never again to return to his beloved profession. Then he wrote hastily from Boston, where for some days he had been detained : —

"DEAR MOTHER, — I expect to bring out Mr. Blight, of Philadelphia, to tea to-morrow evening. I will send you word if it turns out he cannot come, to-morrow, by father. I am glad to hear that you are up to the part of the Spartan mother. I shall not come out to Brookline on my shield, but I am all ready to go."

Of his position and prospects at this time none are so competent to speak as those who were connected with him in his profession. At the meeting of the Bar,† upon the occasion of his death, his friend Francis E. Parker, Esq. said : —

"He had everything which a man of high ambition most desires. He had youth and health, fortune and friends, a profession in which he delighted, the practical talents

* The Honorable Daniel Appleton White died March 30, 1861, in the eighty-fifth year of his age.
† See Appendix III.

which smooth the way in it, and the confidence in himself which made labor light.   But when the trouble of our country came, he thought that all advantages and successes which did not aid her were to be trampled under foot.   He gave up to his country, without a moment's hesitation, all that he had gained and all that he was."

While a school-boy at West Point, as the term drew near its close, he had playfully written home : " I shall ' to the right about face ' and ' forward quick march,' when the term is over, and I shall never evince any desire hereafter to shoulder a musket or wear a sword."   Even now, his taste was unchanged.   Truly did Mr. Parker say of him : " He looked the dangers of his new profession in the face, not fascinated by its glitter, nor drawn from weightier thoughts by the sound of martial music ; but deliberately, for the defence of the law and the support of a cause which he solemnly considered to be just."

We cannot better present the efficient manner in which he responded to his country's call than by quoting the language used by Hon. Richard H. Dana concerning him, at the meeting of the Bar on the occasion already alluded to.*   Mr. Dana said : —

" He had that combination of qualities which led to success in whatever he undertook. . . . . His love was for that kind of intelligent labor which looks to specific results. . . . . He had an intuitive knowledge of himself, and an instinctive knowledge of other men.   He adapted his means to his ends.   He knew what he was suited to do, and he had a power of will, a faculty of concentration, and patience, perseverance, and confidence, which insured success.

* See Appendix III.

" He allowed no waste.   He was as far as possible from anything desultory.   When the war broke out, he determined to become a soldier.   His friends knew he would make himself one.   He determined to offer the first regiment of three years' men to the army, and he did so.   He went to Washington to obtain advantages and opportunities most difficult to secure, but we felt that he would succeed, and he did succeed.   I remember seeing him at the State-House seeking to accomplish certain things for his regiment then most difficult of attainment.   He had the cheerful and satisfied look of one who had succeeded, yet he had but begun.   A common friend whom I met, a member of the Governor's staff, said to me : ' It is hard to do, but it is Wilder Dwight, and he will carry it through,' and he did."

Every step he took towards the prosecution of his work illustrates the truth of Mr. Dana's words.   He began by associating himself with two gentlemen whose West Point education and military ability and experience secured the creation of such a regiment as should do honor to Massachusetts.   Under these teachers he was a faithful student in military tactics, and made rapid progress in his new profession.   He suffered not a day to pass, after the news from Sumter, before opening a subscription-paper to guarantee the expenses which would be incurred in the enterprise.   His cheerful presence met a warm welcome from all whom he approached, and he had but to present his claim to receive a cordial response.   The money thus raised enabled him and his associates to prosecute their enterprise without delay.

The practical difficulty in their way was, that there was no law at that time, either of the United States or the Commonwealth, under which it could be car-

ried into operation.   It was necessary to obtain from
the Secretary of War special authority for the enlistment and control of the proposed regiment.   For
this purpose, on the 25th of April, 1861, while the
excitement which followed the Baltimore riot was at
its height, and the usual communication with the
seat of government was cut off, he left Boston with
Mr. Andrews (the future lieutenant-colonel of the
regiment), and went by the way of Annapolis to
Washington.   Of this eventful journey he wrote the
following account, which was published at the time.

"To the Editor of the Transcript: —

   " A visit to Washington is not, now, a peaceful excursion
to the theatre of party politics.   It is a military expedition
to the seat of war.   The path is not crowded with hungry
or satisfied office-seekers, but it is lined with eager, devoted,
and patriotic soldiers.   There is much to learn by the way,
and I propose to give you a few of the incidents and reflections of my journey.

   " The ticket-master at the depot in Philadelphia, on Friday, April 26, at noon, said, as he gave me my ticket: ' This
will take you to Perryville, and there you must trust to
luck.'   When we reached Elkton, we found Sherman's Battery, which is there stationed, actively engaged in going
through a drill, loading palpable cannon with imaginary
grape, and discharging them without fire, making the mo-
tions of attack.   There were violent secession symptoms
there a few days before the arrival of these silent but eloquent monitors.   Now the American flag feels the breeze
without a shiver.   Long before we reached Perryville, the
armed sentinels along the road showed that we were within
the sphere of the rebellion.   At Perryville we reported to
Colonel Dare, who is in command of that post, and by him
we were put on our journey in a small steam-tug, crowded

with troops.   A tedious sail of six hours brought us to Annapolis at ten o'clock in the evening.   Here we reported to
General Butler at his head-quarters, and, delivering our
despatches, asked him to put us on our journey to Washington.   The General was the centre of action and influence.
His rapid and dashing executive ability had just opened the
path to the Capital.   Bringing with him, in his regiment,
every resource of Yankee ingenuity and courage, he rebuilt
a railroad, revived an exhausted engine, or renewed a telegraphic battery, with equal facility.   But we found him at
the more difficult duty of feeding troops without proper
food, and sheltering them almost without tent or blanket.
Luckily, however, the mild climate made exposure less
dangerous, and every day things were growing better.

" After tedious but inevitable delays, the special train
started on Saturday morning at nine o'clock.   We went on
our way, escorted by a detachment of Massachusetts troops.
At intervals of a quarter of a mile, we stopped to replace a
rail, drive a spike, and secure still further the many defects
of the hasty reconstruction.   Our train labored tediously
along.   We crept slowly and with careful watch through a
' secession village.'   One incident alone relieved the monotony of our journey to the Junction.   As we approached a
small settlement, two women appeared on the piazza of a
house standing on the hill overlooking the track, and waved
a welcome with the American flag.   On the fence by the
station were seated, or hanging, half a dozen boys.   One
of them wore on his cap a small flag.   A passenger called
to him, ' What have you got on your cap ? '   ' *The flag,*'
he answered briskly.   ' Are you true to it ? '   The little
fellow thought he was.   ' Take your cap off then, and hold
it up here.'   He did so, and from many hands in the car
there fell into the ready cap a small shower of *federal coin,*
which we had already found to be legal tender still, in
Maryland.   As the train moved off, the boys were gathering
around their new hero, and we caught the remark, ' By

Jove, see what Johnny got by wearing a flag.' Repentant
Baltimore seems now to be trimming her cap anew. How
long will it be before she is holding it out imploringly to the
Union treasury ?

"With a delay at the Junction to change from our short
train to a long one filled with Pennsylvania troops, and with
occasional stops to relieve the pickets along the road with
fresh men, we reached Washington in eight hours. Washington was just reviving under that Union blast which had
been bearing the echo of the guns of Sumter all over the
loyal North. For six days the city had been stifled by secession rumors ; now it was awaking to the fact that the
people were resolved to have a government, and their will
was absolute. Troops were pouring in, and the Capital was
safe. On the previous Sunday panic had seized the city,
and rumor had almost brought Jefferson Davis to the Potomac. Now it was known that the Rebels had no plan of
immediate attack, but the free and spontaneous North was
organizing for immediate defence. Mail communication,
however, was not yet open. On Sunday, the 28th, the news-
boys were crying in the street the Herald of Sunday, the
21st, as the ' Latest from New York ' ; and so it was, except
the few papers which came by private hands.

"But Washington was not only unprepared for its *defence*,
it was also unprepared for its *defenders*. In the Capital
itself our own troops had found the Balaklava experience
of want within reach of plenty, and spent a day without
food. It gladdens us to know that this cannot be so again.
Still, much remains to do for the comfort and health of the
troops. A sudden army is a most unmanageable organization. But Jefferson Davis will find it so too.

"At the Capitol we found, in the Senate Chamber, the
Sixth, the Bloody Sixth, as they are called. A young officer was writing a loyal letter on Senator Wigfall's desk. I
recollected that the last time I was in the Senate, Colonel
Wigfall was talking treason there, and I thought, what a

very honorable body had succeeded to the seats of the Senators. The gallant Seventh, of New York, quitting, at a moment's notice, their homes and business and pleasure, to 'defend the Capitol,' were rewarded, after their severe march, by becoming entitled to the 'privilege of the floor of the House.' The Seventh enlisted for a month only, and were taking their meals at Brown's and the National. Though not soldiers for the field, they have rendered great service in expressing the prompt resolve of New York. Between them and the Massachusetts Eighth there exists the most cordial good-will and attachment, kindled by mutual services on their march.

"There seemed to be a sudden infusion of life into all departments of the government, but as yet great want of plan, system, and order. This must come, or we must suffer. The Ordnance Department, whose duty it is to provide arms and munitions of war, exhibits every evidence of the new life which its new head brings to it. Colonel James W. Ripley, formerly of the Springfield Armory, where his organizing energy is still felt, as he was returning from Japan, heard, in the Red Sea, a few weeks ago, the first news of 'Secession.' He hurried impatiently home, to give himself to his country. 'Nothing but the *thirty-four stars* and thirteen stripes,' he says, 'will satisfy me ; I must have the *whole flag*.' In this temper he is arming the whole country. Of this temper must every man be who lifts a hand in this struggle.

"Though we came among the first who brought to Washington full proof of the temper of the North, there followed us, on Sunday and Monday, impatient and ardent men from the West, to give her warm impulses in support of the government. Never, in the history of the world, did opinion, or rather sentiment, take such sudden form. It has leaped, full-armed, into life. May the government have wisdom to organize it promptly, and direct it wisely and boldly. What we now need is, not so much men as soldiers.

An extempore army is an impossibility. Every State must give herself, with energy, to the organization of men, to their full equipment, and to immediate instruction in every duty and habit of the soldier. One practical suggestion may be given here. The soldier in the ranks has no need of a revolver. Let us stop that foolish expense and waste. The musket is the best weapon, and its bayonet is always loaded. The revolver is dangerous to its wearer and his companions. It cannot be used without abandoning the musket, and a divided man is inferior to one who has one will and one weapon. This view comes from the highest authority. To teach men the use of the bayonet is better than to give them a revolver.

" An observation of troops on the march and in the barracks shows plainly, also, that the deficiencies of outfit must be rapidly supplied, or the health of the troops will fail. Tents, above all, are imperatively called for to release the men from their crowded and unhealthy quarters in the public buildings. Vegetables,.too, must go forward to relieve them from the indigestible monotony of raw pork and hard bread. In these directions our State government has already acted. In such direction there remains much to do. But all honor to the Governor of Massachusetts. Her troops were first in the field ; her troops were the first to fire a gun ; her troops, on that Sunday of panic in Washington, were a main reliance and hope; and it was the vigorous and ardent patriotism of Governor Andrew that created this sudden army. ' What is that noise ? ' I asked, last Sunday, of an officer of our regular army, in whose quarters I was sitting. ' That ? ' said he ; ' O, that is the Massachusetts Sixth! You had better go and see 'em: every one of 'em is a soldier ! ' The willing patriotism of Massachusetts is a part of the history of our Great Rebellion.

" On Monday, April 29, at noon, with a military passport from Colonel Stone, we left Washington. Twenty thousand troops were within the city limits, and the Capital was safe.

At the Junction we found Colonel Corcoran, of the New York Sixty-Ninth, and his gallant Irishmen. They worship the Colonel, and, in a free fight, I should rather meet any other man. Annapolis, too, was full of troops. I ought not to forget Governor Sprague's Rhode Island regiment at Washington. A model, in its equipment and drill, and showing how much those incidents increase the efficiency of the men, how necessary they are to make the soldier.

"One suggestion, in closing. The immediate security of Washington is accomplished. Massachusetts was the pioneer in that enterprise. The creation of regiments, on a permanent basis for service, as long as there is a rebel in arms, is the next duty of patriotism. Soldiers for a campaign, — that is the pressing necessity of a struggle for the *whole flag*. Let Massachusetts also be the pioneer in this enterprise."

He reached Washington on the evening of the 27th, at which time he wrote to his father a brief account of his journey through " the enemy's country," saying : "At the hotel I found Colonel Ripley. He will help me in my object, and, I think, enters into the project very favorably. I go with him to see the Secretary of War this evening."

After submitting his plan to the Secretary in conversation, he addressed to him a written statement of the same. On the next day, the following letter was received from the War Department : —

"WASHINGTON CITY, April 28, 1861.
"TO MESSRS. WILDER DWIGHT AND GEORGE L. ANDREWS : —

"The plan which you communicated for raising a regiment in Massachusetts for service during the war meets my approval. Such a regiment shall be immediately enlisted in the service of the government, as one of those which are to be called for immediately. The regiment shall be ordered to Fort Independence, or some other station in Boston Harbor, for purposes of training, equipment, and drill, and shall be kept there two months, unless an emergency compels their presence elsewhere.

"I am, gentlemen, very respectfully,

"SIMON CAMERON,
Secretary of War."

CHAPTER III.

FROM this time Wilder Dwight seemed to have
but one interest in life. To see the Massachusetts Second become, in organization and in discipline, a perfect regiment, and to do, in connection
with it, all that such a power could do towards sup-
pressing the Rebellion, — this was the aim which
bounded his horizon.

He was appointed, by Colonel Gordon's recommendation, Major of the regiment, which position he
held until June, 1862, when he was promoted by
Governor Andrew to be its Lieutenant-Colonel.

During what remained to him of life the history of
the regiment is his history. " All I want," he once
wrote, " is the success of the regiment itself, — nothing more or less ; and there is room enough for distinction, for any one who does his share, in any
regiment, to make it a good one."

To the duties of his new position, however petty
in detail, he was content to give all his energies. To
no service assigned him by his superior officers was
he ever found unequal. And as at the very entrance
upon the practice of the law he had the confidence
of one who had spent his life in courts, so now, a beginner in military duty, he was relied upon by his
superiors in command.

The months given to the training, equipment, and drill of the regiment, at their pleasant camp on Brook Farm, West Roxbury, were full of interest to him. On the 8th of July, 1861, the regiment left "Camp Andrew," and entered Boston, to take its departure for the seat of war. The day was one of intense heat, to which circumstance he refers in the following lines written from New York the next morning : —

"TUESDAY MORNING, July 9.

"DEAR MOTHER, — I suppose you will be glad to hear that we came out of the furnace like gold. Everything has gone well. I feel better than before starting, and the regiment, as soon as it got on board ship, found itself cool and well. We are off this afternoon. Good by. God bless you."

Surprise has been often expressed that he found time to write so many letters while he was in the army. This is explained by the rapidity with which he wrote, and the fact that he kept no other journal of events, some record of which he felt would be invaluable to him, should he survive the war.

The haste in which these letters were necessarily written, while it should be remembered in judging of their literary merit, makes them none the less valuable as a graphic picture of the scenes through which he passed.

He again writes : —

"HAGERSTOWN, MARYLAND, July 11, 1861.

"If any one supposes that an advance under pressure to join General Patterson's column is fun, let him try it. From Boston, as soon as we got the train, all went well. At New York, on the whole, everything was *warm*, but cheerful. We gave them a show in the Park, and made our speeches. But best of all was our prompt and orderly embarkation at the wharf, and our start for Harrisburg and Hagerstown. Luck, however, did not follow us beyond New York. We spent in the cars, on our way to Hagerstown, nearly thirty-six hours, — more than twice too long. But, *per contra*, discipline was maintained, and every man found himself fed, and in as good shape as possible. Here we are. Our band filled the town with its music at five o'clock this morning. The advance train, in which I was, arrived at one o'clock. We are in the midst of preparation to commence our march upon Martinsburg, where we join General Patterson. I do not think there will be any fighting immediately, — others think otherwise ; but to-day's rumors show Johnson falling back to Winchester. Unless he does voluntarily, he must per force. We ford the Potomac, and I am impatient to feel, with my horses' hoofs, the sacred soil of Virginia. I have been very well, notwithstanding the intense heat. Saw William in New York, and he helped me a good deal. You would laugh to see how our pretty things are getting spoiled with the *service*.

"Our present position and duty cannot be regarded otherwise than as a high compliment. With other regiments almost on the spot, we are called to the post most threatened, and we are called from a distance, too. It shows that, somehow or other, we have got a reputation. Excuse haste and all incoherency.

"I was sorry not to see you more on the Common, but it was best to cut short the parting. Give warm love to father and all the boys, and every one else. God bless you all."

Some hours later he writes : —

"I wrote a note this morning, just before breakfast, expecting an immediate start for Martinsburg ; but, owing to the necessary delays of our movements, we shall not start until four o'clock this afternoon. To-night we camp on this side the Potomac. Everything is as well with us as it can be. I think the organization shows, by its practical working on the way, that it is a success. The men are quiet, orderly, and disciplined. Their rations have held out well, and their health and spirits are remarkably good. I see very clearly that there is to be no limit of work, but much of it will be work that I can do, which is all I want. As to fatigue, I expect to bear it well. Since Sunday morning I have not had three successive hours of sleep, but I feel well and vigorous, notwithstanding. We start from here very soon, and, as the regiment moves out on its first march, we expect to make a fine appearance. I shall write as often as I can, and hope to hear."

Two days later he writes : —

"IN CAMP, MARTINSBURG, Saturday, July 13, 1861.

" *Voici que nous sommes arrivés.* I am in my tent, on the high ground, south of the town of Martinsburg. Our regiment is a part of what is called General Patterson's column, and we are on the advance post. It would have done your pride good to have seen us form the regiment, and start on our march from Hagerstown. My own responsible position, in rear of the column, led me to watch its progress, to return to give orders to the rear-guard and wagons, and, in general, to be lively. I am very well, and, though living under high pressure, getting my load along. At about half past six on Thursday afternoon we reached the bank of the Potomac, passing down from the high ground on which Doubleday's battery stood two weeks ago. We camped on the bank, without crossing the river. It was a long job getting the men into camp, and getting their supper into the men. At four the next (yesterday) morning we were up striking tents and getting breakfast. Then the battalion formed, and then came our first regular *undress* parade. At the command, the men prepared to ford the Potomac. In a few moments, the regiment was without its *pantaloons.* The vulgar prejudices of society, I am aware, are on the side of these appendages, but society does not cross the Potomac on foot in the freshness of the morning. The column moved forward in regular order. The band advanced into the stream playing a confident march, and so we passed the river gayly. Then came a long march, — thirteen miles. We were told that the enemy's cavalry were on the hills on the Virginia bank of the river, but we saw nothing of them, though the regiment marched with loaded muskets. The march was a new experience, — it was an interesting one. The morning was fresh and cool ; the horses and wagons were our chief source of delay. One balky horse jumped up, leaped over the wheel-horses, fell, and hooked himself to the pole. He was left behind. One team spent a long time in the river. Still, at last, the train moved on. With frequent halts, we reached Martinsburg at three in the afternoon. We marched with music playing, and amid some attention of thousands of troops, to our camping-ground. Then we pitched our tents, and, in the midst of a violent thunder-storm, mounted our guns, got supper, and then I suppose you expect me to say went to bed. Not so, however, the Major. Instead of bed, which I desired, I went about in the pouring rain to visit sentinels, see that the men had supper, &c., &c. At twelve o'clock I crept under cover. At five this morning, got up, put on wet boots, and went on duty again. To-day I have been attending drills, &c. I see clearly that there is no rest in this life. With care, I can keep well, I think, and I hope can do well for the men. But the care is a very great one. I have written this note in the midst of interruptions of every kind, and I have no more time now. We are under orders to move on Monday somewhither. We are in a beautiful country ; everything here is new under the sun, or rather under the clouds. That, in itself, is spicy and cheering. In great haste . . . . with much love to all."

Again he writes : —

"IN BIVOUAC AT BUNKER HILL, July 16, 1861.

" We paused last evening, on our march toward Winchester, and lay down on the side of a hill in a pine grove. Late Sunday evening, at Martinsburg, the order came to be in readiness to march at five o'clock the next morning. No intimation whither. We had reveillé at three o'clock, packed wagons, breakfasted, formed the battalion, and then came our marching orders. The whole command of General Patterson commenced its movement at five. The march was without incident. We found our place in column at about eight o'clock, and moved on till three, when we reached Bunker Hill. There was firing by our advanced guard, who drove fifteen hundred of the enemy's cavalry before them. We came upon their deserted camp. The movement was steady but slow. From the high ground, and in turnings of the road, the sight was a fine one. Our regiment excited universal admiration. It is already considered *the* regiment of the whole command. My horse works beautifully, and keeps perfectly well. I have great comfort in him. When one is twelve hours in saddle, it makes a difference what the saddle is on. The camp-ground assigned us was the one we now occupy. It is very much exposed, and in advance of the main body. On taking possession of it, we found every indication of recent occupation, and find that the Rebels occupied it night before last. The men lay right down to rest. I continued upon duty, under direction of the Colonel, till five o'clock in the afternoon. Then, a man who lived near by invited us to tea with him. Our wagons were back in the interminable train, and we had given up all hope of them till late. The man spoke strongly of Union, &c. We accepted his offer, and went down to his farm-house and ate our bacon and eggs in the midst of his pickaninnies and slaves. The poor man could not speak of the American flag without choking. He said the other army had pressed their horses and food, &c., and given them nothing in return but receipts of the South-

4

ern Confederacy, and ' there ain't any Southern Confederacy,' said he.   Still the prevailing tone here is secession. We lay down at night under the trees.   I posted a picket-guard outside the lines, and, after attending to other duties, was right glad to go to sleep.

"Our men are toughening to it slowly, but their knapsacks still pull heavily at them.

"To-day we have been resting the men, and having skirmish-drill in the wheat-fields.   One of our companies is off on picket duty, three miles down the road towards Winchester.   We had a call this morning from Major Doubleday. His battery is the terror of the enemy.   He got out his map, and we studied the localities.   He talked very agreeably about Sumter, &c.   We have just received (four P. M., Tuesday) our orders for the advance upon Winchester.   A very good place is assigned us.   The impression is that the advance forms part of a grand concerted movement, and that to-morrow will be a decisive day in the history of the campaign.   I hope for a big, worthy battle, one that means something and decides something.   And I hope to have strength, courage, and wisdom to do my duty in it.   I never felt happier or more earnest than for the last few days, and I never realized more fully the best significance of life.   I have always had a dream and theory about the virtues that are called out by war.   I have nothing to say of the *supply* which I can furnish, but I am vividly impressed with the *demand*.   The calling needs a whole man ; and it exacts very much from him.   Self gets thrown into the background.   It straggles out of the column, and is picked up, if at all, very late, by the rear-guard.   I am writing this letter upon an empty case of cartridges, which were distributed this morning, sitting under an oak-tree back of the lines by the side of the Colonel, who has just returned from a conference with Colonel Abercrombie, and who is full of the duties of to-morrow.   Good by, and God bless you.   Love to all.

"If anything should happen to me, remember that I meant to do my duty."

"*Wednesday morning*, 17th. — The battalion is in marching order since four o'clock. Day, bright and clear. It is half past six, and no advance yet."

"CHARLESTOWN, VA., July 18, 1861.

"From Bunker Hill to Charlestown may not seem a long way to a Massachusetts man, but in Virginia it is a hard day's work. Our regiment slept on its arms at Bunker Hill Tuesday night. We thought the forward movement was to be on Winchester. A feint was made that way. The enemy had obstructed the main road. We held Johnston's men, expecting attack. By our sudden flank movement we have got him. If McDowell has done rightly by Manassas, we will put Johnston in a tight place. Yesterday we were ready to start at three, A. M. Twenty thousand men move slowly. It took till nine in the evening to get the regiment into position at Charlestown, twelve miles off. We were in the reserve, fifteen hours in the saddle. When the men were drawn up, and had stacked their arms, they fell right down to sleep as they stood. The day was bitterly hot; the march terribly tedious, but glorious. Twenty-five thousand men occupy the town where John Brown was hung. We are the first Massachusetts regiment which has defiantly, and without interruption, stalked through Virginia. In the afternoon we entered a small village on our route. The band played first the Star Spangled Banner, then Hail Columbia, then Yankee Doodle. Our horses arched their necks and moved to the music. The men moved with fresh life and spirit. Our splendid banner, not a star dimmed, flaunted in the faces of the sulky Virginians.

"The country is splendid; but, as the hymn-book says, 'Only man is vile!' My cook came to me on the route, after vainly endeavoring to forage for our dinner, and said, 'I *tout* Virginny was a *perducing* country, but I don't see nothin' growin' fit to eat nohow.' The negroes sat on the fences along the route, and wondered. Our march means freedom to them. It means, too, the restoration of the Union line wherever we move. The American flag sprouts in the furrow of our ploughshare. It is hard work, slow work, new work ; but it has its compensations, this military occupation of a country. ' Southern blood has been boiling all day,' said a woman standing on the door of a farm-house on our line of march. Just at dusk, as we neared Charles-town, there was a cannonading in front. We threw out skirmishers and drew up the battalion, but have not yet learned the cause of the alarm. This is not a very coherent epistle. It exhibits only an echo of the tone of feeling which animates one on an expedition like ours. You would have wondered to see our jaded men prick up their ears, and stand alive again, when they thought a brush was at hand. The Indiana regiment in our rear yelled like wild Indians. I think Johnston will retire without much of a fight. But here we know nothing except the movements of our own brigade. Half of our force goes out of service to-morrow. This will hamper our movements."

"HEAD-QUARTERS SECOND REGIMENT M. V., HARPER'S FERRY,
Friday Morning, July 19, 1861.

" A soldier's life is always gay ! Here we are ! Yester-day morning, just as I had finished my letter to you from Charlestown, from our camp, an order came from General Patterson for our brigade to prepare itself with two days' rations in haversacks, to march without baggage. This made us lively under the hot sun. The Colonel and I went and reported to General Patterson, whose head-quarters were in the house of Senator Hunter, the traitor, who had fled to Richmond. There we saw the General and Major Porter. It was evident that no vigorous move was to be attempted, and that this column awaited the news from Manassas. We returned to camp. I had just got to sleep, to make up for the fatigues of the day before (our march from Bunker Hill to Charlestown, Colonel Abercrombie says, was as hard a one as he ever knew), when the Colonel came to my tent and said, ' No sleep for you ; I 've got orders.' A new order had come, directing our regiment to get ready for detached service. No indication had come of our destination, but we were to report to General Patterson as soon as ready. At three, we got under way with all our train. We were sent to Harper's Ferry. After a march of three hours we reached Harper's Ferry. The people received us with perfect enthusiasm, cheering and shouting after our flag. We are sent here to hold Harper's Ferry. Our head-quarters are in the house of the Superintendent of the Arsenal. We succeed in its occupation to Johnston, the rebel. There are a good many of the secession horsemen home-guard, who are a terror to the country, and whom we are to quell. We shall establish our pickets in various directions, and hold the place, unless, indeed, we get orders to go elsewhere, which we are prepared to expect at any time. So, after all our expectation, there is no battle yet. The rumor is that Johnston is withdrawing from Winchester, and does not mean to fight. We know nothing here except by rumor. The country here is magnificent ; the scenery glorious. Our camp is on the high ground, and faces the gorge through which the Potomac flows. The service on which our regiment is detached, though not a dangerous, is a very responsible and honorable one. The climate here is delightful, and I hope that all our men and officers will entirely recover from the fatigues of their sudden and recent duty. It is an odd life, and full of variety. Just now we seem to be about to see a little comfort. Our post here is due to the reputation the regiment has already acquired for discipline and promptness. It stirs one's blood to see the reign of terror under which these people have been living. Men come in and claim protection. Wives come and ask that their husbands may be assured of safety in returning to their homes. The most villanous system of oppression

has been practised here in Virginia. The house in which
we are now quartered is a fine house, and has a view which
you would like, I think."

" HARPER'S FERRY, Monday Morning, July 22, 1861.

" War is a game, but you must hold a few cards to play
it !   Our column, which marched so proudly out of Martinsburg, is now melting away.   The time of the regiments
expires, and they go.   This cripples our movement.   Since
I wrote you, Colonel Gordon has been in command here.
The order under which he came stated, ' You will organize
the department for a military depot.   Your regiment is
selected because the general commanding wishes the town
" placed, from the commencement, in a proper condition of
military order and discipline."   Once so, it can be easily
retained.'

" I have been very busy organizing the thing, under
the Colonel.   Just after I last wrote you, I established and
posted the town guard, selecting for the guard-house the
engine-house within the Arsenal enclosure, which was held
by John Brown, and which is one of the few buildings left
amid the general wreck.   Then arrests were to be made of
suspected men, pickets and outposts to be established, &c.

" We started a regular post-office, selecting as postmaster
a sergeant of Captain Savage's company, who was formerly
postmaster of his native town.

" Treason and conspiracy are all about us. . . . . We
had quite a scene at our flag-raising the day after our arrival.   The tall flagstaff on the Arsenal grounds had borne
the secession rag for weeks.   We wished to put our banner
there.   After several attempts to adjust the halliards, which
failed, Sergeant Hill, of Company B, volunteered to climb
the tree pole to its top and fasten the rope.   This he did,
amid the cheers, &c., of the people and soldiers. I
hope to hear to-day of the fall of Manassas, and then all will
be well. . . . . I am very well and very happy.   To be well

is a great blessing, for the water and fatigue combined take down a great many stronger men."

" The news from Manassas has filled us with gloom and bitterness. We can only rejoice that we were not *misled* into such a rout and panic. I cannot tell whose fault it is, or how the explanation may alleviate the disgrace, but it seems to me that the disaster is a most terrible one. . . . . O that we had force and energy to strike again immediately! But we cannot judge here. Yesterday a lot of negro fugitives came in. We are obliged to stop them, though it went against my grain to throw any obstacles in their way. One of them, a fine-looking fellow called Bob, we took as a waiter. He was the slave of Colonel Baylor of the secession army, and I think Colonel Gordon will retain his services until Colonel Baylor returns to his allegiance. A moment ago a man was brought up under guard, and Colonel Gordon ordered him into the office. ' Where do you come from ? ' asked he. ' From Charlestown,' said the man, a rather dark-complexioned fellow, with curly hair. ' I ran away,' said he, ' last night.' ' Ran away ! from whom ? ' ' From my mistress.' ' Are you a slave ? ' ' Yes.' Nothing could have been more unexpected than this reply. The fellow says he has brothers and sisters as white as himself, and all slaves. His father a white man, his mother a yellow woman. The man's features and accent were European. O, this is a beautiful system, in its practical details, — a firm basis for a Christian commonwealth ! It is an order of things worth fighting for ! Bah !

" By our maintenance of good order and discipline, by our protection of the inhabitants of the town against the undisciplined of our own army and against lawless oppression from the Rebels, and by the fact of our being the first regiment to bring back the flag to this town, we have so far won the affection of the townspeople that they propose, this

evening, to present us with a flag.   We shall accept it, and
add it to our bundle of banners.   Yesterday afternoon
(Tuesday) we had quite a flurry.   Orders came to be ready
to march at a moment's notice.   We packed up speedily,
and were just ready to move when an order came that a
telegram was received from General Scott telling us to stay
where we are.   Such is camp life.   We do not know what a
day will bring forth, literally.   I see no immediate prospect
of our getting into active military duty ; but one cannot tell
how the aspect will change before night.

" One thing is clear, our column would have met the fate
of McDowell's, had it made an attack upon Johnston in
position at Winchester.   But, on the other hand, had
McDowell made his attack when we threatened Johnston at
Bunker Hill, perhaps the result would have been different.

" One thing is certain, there has been no concert, no union
in the movement of the two columns.   But what good is
there in speculating upon what might have been !   I do hope
that the government will wake up and put out its power.
These rebels mean fight.   We must have an army, an armament, — *generals* and *soldiers*, if we mean to whip them.
. . . . Here's hoping the good time is coming."

" HEAD-QUARTERS, HARPER'S FERRY,
Wednesday, July 24, 1861.

" If you knew the pleasure I have had to-day in receiving
my first letter from you, you would write — write — write.
A letter written on Sunday with C.'s charming postscript.
Its arrival is the incident of our bloodless campaign.   Yet
our progress is not without its triumphs.   To-day, for instance, we have had another flag presented.   The ladies of
Harper's Ferry, this evening, assembled on the Square, and
our officers, with the band and color-bearer, went out to
receive the national color.   The flag, during the occupation
of the town by Johnston, had been sent off to Frederick City,
in Maryland.   It was brought back last Saturday, to be

given to the first regiment of Federal troops which brought its protection to the people. The scene and the occasion were striking. One of the ladies made a short speech. The Colonel responded, and the band rang out, ' Long may it wave ! '

" Virginia gives an American flag to Massachusetts, and Massachusetts restores the blessings of that flag to Virginia. I cannot help attaching a good deal of significance to the occasion. I fancy, too, that there are Virginians whose blood will boil with the desire to tear down that flag, which we will certainly carry into action when the time comes.

" Since I began to write news has come that General Banks has arrived to take command of this division. . . . . We hear from Winchester that there is great mourning and no joy over the battle at Manassas. Their dead are coming home to them in great numbers. If I am not mistaken, it will turn out that, if that senseless panic had not overtaken our troops, a half-hour more would have given them a decided success. These speculations and discussions fill our minds here, for want of something more practical and direct."

" HARPER'S FERRY, July 26, 1861.

" We are here waiting on Providence, and holding on to this corner of Virginia by the skin of our teeth. I am not uneasy, for I do not care whether it comes or not ; but why Beauregard with his large force should not kick our broken column into Maryland I do not see. This is not a cheerful view, but it is reasonable at least. You conclude, do you not ? that the South has still got the start of us in preparation and in energy. Hope now hangs on McClellan, who has a prestige that will enable him to revive the spirit that belongs to our army. Manassas shows three things : First, our infantry, even in its present loosely organized condition, is better than theirs ; our foot-soldiers will face and drive theirs. Second, our artillery outweighs theirs; and batteries are to be silenced, not stormed. Third, cavalry gives them great advantage. We must have more cavalry. In fact, we must create and organize a well-appointed army and armament: our ' rash levied numbers ' are mere numbers, not *forces*.

" I seem to myself, here on the spot, to realize afresh the immensity of our task. I pity the statesman who is to recreate liberty and order upon the ashes of this *civil war*. You cannot form any idea of the real significance of civil war, without being in the midst of its experience, as we have been. I do hope that the Union will have power to shorten it, and I regard the disaster of last Sunday chiefly important because it checks the reaction which was restoring men in these Border States to their courage and allegiance. Panic and terrorism are doing their worst here, and they are terrible agencies in such times as these."

" HEAD-QUARTERS, HARPER'S FERRY, Sunday, July 28, 1861.

" There is so much of drag and so little of incident in my present life that a letter seems hardly worth while. The sunlight, as it breaks the fog this Sunday morning, discloses some of our batteries on the hills commanding our somewhat defenceless position. On Friday General Banks ordered all the wagons to be sent across the river, and all stores of every kind to be removed from our temporary storehouses. We have been in bivouac ever since, sleeping on hay, and indulging in every variety of soldierly discomfort. General Banks is unwilling to signalize his first military service by ordering a retreat; yet, unless we are promptly reinforced, there is no other way. I feel very sorry to desert the Union-loving men of this country. Our army *never* should retreat, because no sooner do loyal men under its protection avow themselves, than they are marked for the first prey by the rebels which our retreat allows. O for a strong will and a large energy and patience, till every preparation is made! Then we can walk to the Gulf and wipe out these villains. Yesterday we had scouting-parties out, and as our spies came in at night, they reported the enemy's pickets near our lines, and a movement of a large body making in our direction. So at eleven o'clock I took through the drowsy camp, rousing sleeping piles of humanity and blankets, an order for their action, in case of alarm during the night. No such alarm came. Yesterday the Massachusetts Twelfth, Colonel Webster, arrived on the other side of the river, and is now in camp there; so we are stronger by one regiment. I do not know how long we shall stay here, but suppose that either our wagons will come back or we shall join them soon. Indeed, a mere nominal holding of Harper's Ferry like the present one does not seem to indicate great strength. I am right in my conjecture. At this moment an order comes in from the commanding general directing the passage of the troops across the river to-day, and indicating the order of march. The order concluded, however, with the direction : ' The Second Massachusetts Regiment will remain as a garrison to this place. The colonel of this regiment will so establish his pickets as to give him timely warning of the enemy's approach. For this object, twenty men of the cavalry and one non-commissioned officer will be left with the garrison of the place.' So we are to have the honor to be the first to occupy and the last to quit the sacred soil of Harper's Ferry. Well, we marched into Virginia full of hope and fight and purpose. We dinned the Star Spangled Banner into the unwilling ears of the startled villagers. We had doleful marches but delightful measures. ' Grim-visaged war ' had her front smoothed of its wrinkles, to be sure, but we thought to meet the front of fearful adversaries.

" Now, however, instead of all this ecstasy of advance, we are employed in the anxious endeavor to retreat as little as possible. No matter, the fulness of time will bring only one result, and we can wait for it. Military glory, however, will not turn out to be so cheap an article as some of our

holiday soldiers thought it.   The price of it is rising every
day. . . . . Doubleday's battery just went by with the long
rifled cannon which throws a ball five miles, and now the
air is full of the dust and music of the New York Twelfth,
which is also on the march.   They will soon leave us alone
in our glory.   We shall occupy the lower part of the town,
near the ford, and shall only hold the place till some
stronger force comes to claim it.   This duty will exact a
lively vigilance, but it is free from danger, I think, and my
own strong belief is, that, with our cannon frowning from
the hills, the Rebels will not think it worth while to claim
the town, especially as it is utterly worthless for any military
purpose.

" I think of you all enjoying a quiet Sunday morning at
home, and should like to join you for a time ; but I am
getting, in the presence of these outrages, to desire only the
results of war.   Cavalry and artillery, — we must have
these before we can be completely effective."

CHAPTER IV.

LETTERS FROM MARYLAND HEIGHTS.

" MARYLAND HEIGHTS, ADVANCED POST, July 30, 1861,
Tuesday Afternoon, in Camp.

" WITH your passion for fine prospects and high hills,
you would like to climb with me from the dripping
ford of the Potomac up the abrupt steep that overhangs it
to the thick wooded side of the Heights on the Maryland
shore.   You might enjoy the tangled pathway through the
woods ; you would certainly find a thirsty pleasure at the
spring of pure water which pulses from the heart of the
mountain ; and when you came out of the silent wood-path
upon a broad table-flat, and found it white with tents and
alive with armed men and vocal with martial music, you
would wonder, as King George before the dumpling, how
the d——l we got there.   This is precisely what I am going
to tell you.   Giving you first, however, a moment to cast
your delighted eyes up the Potomac Valley to the blue hills
beyond, and across Harper's Ferry town to the gorge of the
Shenandoah, which gives the name to the lazy military department which waits a new life from the energy of General
Banks.   And, interrupting you again, to say that I have all
your letters safe, and have every pleasure in reading them
and in rereading them.   Now for the story.   In this melting heat of the sultriest afternoon my memory is relaxed,
and I cannot recollect when I wrote.   On Sunday, however,
the army moved across the Potomac and occupied Maryland Heights below Sandy Hook, leaving the Massachusetts
Second in full possession of Harper's Ferry.   The Colonel
leaving the upper part of the town where we had been, I

spent Sunday evening in posting our pickets and outposts, and in taking what military precautions were possible against a night surprise and attack. Of course we spent a wakeful night, though I could not think there was any chance of attack. The next morning I was off again on the road towards Charlestown to fix a point for a strong picket, and generally to cruise about the country. Colonel Andrews and myself spent three hours in sunny riding (you don't quite appreciate the meaning of the sunny South). When we got back we found that Colonel Gordon had got an order changing the disposition of our forces thus : Colonel Andrews to remain in Harper's Ferry with three companies (Captains Cary's, Abbott's, and Cogswell's), a battery of three guns to be mounted on the table-land above the ford on the Maryland shore, and the rest of the regiment to cross and encamp near it, to support the battery and protect the ford. This sounds plain and easy, but it gave us a lively afternoon. I will tell you the story by and by. Now the call is sounding for dress-parade. The heat is ridiculous. I have philosophized myself, however, into great good spirits, and I do not wilt. With humility I hope to get through. Now for parade. . . . .

" If you had happened in on our parade you would have had the pleasure to see me preside. We do not look as gay as we did at Camp Andrew, but we also do not have so many friends to see us. I have got my tent finely pitched, with a rich carpet of oak-leaves, and have extemporized a writing-desk. Tattoo is just beating, and I will go on with my story.

" After the order to divide our forces came, the regiment was soon paddling and splashing through the water. We left Colonel Andrews making everything secure. The regiment mounted the steep ascent on this side, and at last made the plateau. But our wagons, which had to take a longer and more circuitous ascent, were not so lucky ; and tentless, almost supperless, the men bivouacked for the night.   The officers found a friendly supper in the house of a man on whose farm we are, — the only inhabitant of the neighborhood, if that can be called a neighborhood where neighbors there are none.   This farmer * knew John Brown ; and, indeed, John Brown's school-house, where he hid his arms, is down just below our camp, in the woods.   I may exaggerate the effect of John Brown, but certain it is that the whole military organization in Virginia dates from his raid.   And the other day a woman said, ' We have not dared to command our slaves since John Brown came.' The man's name is a terror and a bitterness to them.   To day we have been getting our wagons up, pitching tents, organizing an encampment.   In Colonel Andrews's absence this falls a good deal on me.   New work is hard work, but the aptitude, I suppose, will come.   I suppose when an old dog is going to learn new tricks he does not do it in *dog-days*.   I certainly should like to take my lessons in cooler weather.   I have been riding about the hills a good deal, and have been to head-quarters to see General Banks.   Old Mr. Weller generalized quite broadly when he said, ' Sammy, a man as can form a ackerate judgment of a horse can form a ackerate judgment of anything.'   Perhaps we *generalize* a little rapidly in making Governor Banks the commander of a division and a department.   We shall see. Just now military civilians must look sharp lest they fall. I am making a long story of very little, but if I could have brought you up to our sunset view, you would have easily understood the new pleasure of our fine camp life after the dull work of garrisoning Harper's Ferry.   It does no good to write of scenery, you want to hear of achievement.   We must wait for that.   Think of us, now in perfect safety, getting ready for better things, I hope.   The events of the past week show that every man who is fit for it must do his part to fight now."

* See Appendix VIII.

"Three letters?! Yes, one from you, one from father, one from C. Blake, — all at once. The sun shines less fiercely, and the glaring afternoon has lost its power, or is forgotten. I write in the memory of yesterday. This morning the rattle of the rain-drops on my tent roused me before the regular reveillé of the drum, and I am writing now, after breakfast, to the same cool music. If you really like to listen to the monotony of our eventless experience, I cannot do less than to write it for you. Yesterday was a busy day. Battalion drill after breakfast, and then a ride with Colonel Gordon over the mountain to head-quarters. We climbed, by a rough path cut two months ago by the Rebels, to the very top of the mountain. There we found a picket from the Twelfth Massachusetts Regiment (Colonel Webster), and upon the lookout floated the American flag. After a wide survey and a view most glorious, we descended the other side of the mountain to head-quarters. There, business and a short chat with Major Doubleday, whose battery is there in position. By the new organization of brigades, Doubleday is in ours. He is of Fort Sumter fame, as you know, and is a fine fellow with a grand battery.

"I wrote thus far yesterday evening, and was expecting a quiet rainy day, when out blazed the sun and kindled our work again. Rations were to be issued, &c., then, at noon, came the sudden order : ' Pack wagons with everything, and prepare to bivouac for several days.' It seems head-quarters got frightened about our wagons. The road is so exposed that, in case of attack, they would certainly be lost. Our pretty encampment had to yield, therefore, to the necessities of war. It made a long afternoon, and when the tents were struck, the wagons loaded, and the balking and unwilling teams made to draw, we were enjoying another sunset. The men were sent into the woods to cut brush for huts, and there sprang up a camp of green leaves, as if by magic. I am now writing under a bower of chestnut leaves, and am quite fascinated by my new quarters. The inconvenience of sending off all your luggage, most of your bedding and camp furniture, is not a slight one. In the absence of other hardships and perils, one can make a hardship of that. Last night we had an animated time. Just after taps one of our pickets fired, and it turned out that a man was prowling through the bushes. Soon after an excited Indiana picket fired on our men in a small picket down the hill, and that kicked up a small bobbery. But the morning makes all quiet again. The mists are lifting from the river and hillsides, and the day is already started on its uncertain course again. The kitchen fires are smoking, the axes are ringing in the wood. ' Jim along Josey,' or sick-call, has just sounded. The thoughts turn fondly on breakfast. Good by. Love to all."

"MARYLAND HEIGHTS, August 3, 1861, in Bivouac.

" Our new leafy camp presents an odd appearance. Two or three ingenious men belonging to the band have fitted me up a bedstead of branches and boughs, and have thatched my tent with leaves, so that the breeze rustles cool through it as I write. But we have few incidents. The bugler is teaching the skirmish calls, which makes a confused variety of very bad music ; but except that, we are in the sultry stillness of high noon. . . . .

" I think we are doomed to a life of warm inaction for many weeks, while the awakened North will, I trust, give itself cordially to the task of organization. We must have an immense army. We must feed it, teach it, equip it, and all this must be done without delay. We must pay it promptly too. Our men all suffer now for want of the few comforts their pay would bring. Again, we must feed them well, *honestly*, not with bad meat or mouldy bread. I believe a little attention to these two matters will shorten the war six months. We demand a great deal of the men, we

5

must give them all they are entitled to, and we must do this a great deal better than it has been done. I could write much on this score, but I am not inspector-general, my report will not go to head-quarters, so I will try to give you something more lively. Yet these are the pressing thoughts of one in the system who feels its pressure. Men willing and devoted you can have ; but one central, organizing will you cannot have, I fear. Never mind, we have got to accomplish the result sooner or later. Only I think I can see most clearly how it ought to be done. Health is a condition of courage, and without it you cannot have an army Yet there are colonels, within three miles of us, who have not had their men in bathing within a month, though the rivers flow close by. Discipline is another condition of concerted and organized movement ; yet, in several regiments, obedience is the exception, and orders take the shape of diffident requests. This has been unavoidable in the three months' militia. It must be corrected in the three years' army that is to fight the war. Here I am preaching away on the same text. I will stop and try again tomorrow.

" Sunday has come, and brought with it the usual inspection of the regiment. Under the glaring sun, it was a severer work than common. The Colonel was bent upon having it thoroughly done, however, and so we made a long story of it. On our outpost, special duty, the regiment must be kept efficiently ready for sudden emergencies ; and all matters which at Camp Andrew might have seemed merely formal, here assume practical and obvious importance. The hard work, hot weather, and soldier's fare begin to tell upon the men, and they are not as well satisfied as they were. They see the undertaking in a new form, and they are in the worst stages of homesickness too. The contagious disorderliness of other regiments, with lower standards of discipline and drill, also has its bad effect on them. Again, the inaction is depressing to the men, and they long for an occasion to fight. Still further, the want of vigorous health is a predisposing cause of discontent. The result is, that the regiment seems to lack willingness, obedience, enthusiasm, and vigor. It wants what is called *tone morale.* How to get it ? There is the problem. Colonel Andrews has been over to see me to-day, and we have been talking regiment for a couple of hours. Vexing our minds with problems, and inquiring eagerly for solutions. I do not mean to intimate that we are not better off than others. I trust we are, much. In all military and material advantages, we certainly have got the start of them. And in these respects we are making every effort to hold our own. But there are and will be new problems before us at every step. Several of our officers are sick or disabled, and we are working with a short allowance. This adds to the bother. There you have the lees of a conversation with the Lieutenant-Colonel, which I have just finished. It indicates a few of the perplexities that belong to my position, but you need not let them discourage you. Nor do I allow them to halt me on my way. The march is to be kept up, and the obstacles are to be overcome or removed. Still, let no one think that because we are not fighting battles, therefore we are not serving our country. With all diffidence, and awaiting the correction of experience, I think we are now doing our hardest work. I should not write so much on this subject if it were not filling my mind completely. The same languor, undoubtedly, is creeping over the army everywhere. The only remedy for the trouble is to bring the men to their duty with a strong hand. The romance is gone. The *voluntariness* has died out in the volunteer. He finds himself devoted to *regular* service. A *regular* he must be made, and the rules and articles of war, in all their arbitrary severity, will not sit lightly upon him. So much for my Sunday sermon. I got your pleasant note of Thursday yesterday afternoon. I hope the boys will enjoy the Adirondacks. I am having my camp-life, this summer, on other terms. Everything goes well with me. I never was happier in my life."

"MONDAY MORNING, August 5, 5 A.M.

"I am just going to battalion drill. All is well, and the sun is not yet over the mountain, though we see its glow on the clouds. Good by."

"DEPARTMENT SHENANDOAH, MARYLAND HEIGHTS, August 8, 1861.

"I am in the midst of pay rolls and pay accounts, trying to get the regiment paid. Two days ago I went to Washington, made a flying visit to the Department, and, I think, got our pay business in shape. Spent several hours with William at his camp, found everything in good order there. I should think he would make a capital colonel. Wish I felt sure of making as good a major. Find no end of bother in this whole business. Keep up good courage, and, I believe, good nature. Am driven to death, as one might say, and yet it seems to me as if I was only driven to a livelier life. Can't help feeling very thankful for health and strength, which I pray for. The hill is steep, the way is long; I must be climbing: would much rather write to you, — shall get leisure soon. . . . . Those men who sit at home indulging their spleen had better come out here and work it off. Let us shorten this war, or it will shorten us. Washington is in the dumps. All *will* yet be well. Your letter, yesterday, was a god-send."

"DEPARTMENT SHENANDOAH, MARYLAND HEIGHTS, August 10, 1861.

"'How pleasant of Saturday night, when you 've tried all the week to be good,' &c. Pleasant, indeed, of a Saturday night to note the gathering clouds, and to look up through the withered and twinkling thatch of your rude boughs, and to think of the 'drop too much' you will be taking all

night. The muttering thunder will be the ' sound of rev-
elry,' and the pattering rain will soon be falling. Yet it
is pleasant of Saturday night to have the *retrospect* of busiest
occupation, — the prospect of a quiet Sunday. There is the
uncertainty, too, which spices every joy. Let me just sched-
ule my day for you, and you will see that life is not exactly
a dream, and if a shadow, a most substantial one. Half
past four, A. M. The Major wakes and wonders where ' that
first call is.' Quarter before five, A. M., he is getting up
to the intrusive melody of that sleepless reveillé. Five,
A. M., he is walking about camp to see that ' things is
workin'.' Half past five, A. M., he is strapping on his
sword, and, with the bugler, going out on to the broad
field with six companies to skirmish-drill. Soon the men
are scattered over the plain, rallying, deploying, advancing,
retreating, firing, ceasing to fire, lying down, getting up,
swarming in masses, and scattering again singly, double-
quicking upon their reserves, forming squares to resist imaginary cavalry, forming column again, &c., &c. This, in
the cool of the morning, in obedience to the bugle-note
which obeys him. Then, again, at a quarter to seven, the
companies return. The Major goes to the kitchens and
sees what each company is going to have for breakfast.
Then, at eight o'clock, comes first mail. The Major franks
the soldier's letters, attends to requisitions, &c., looks up
the Tactics. At half past nine he goes out to battalion drill.
The sun blazes, the regiment manœuvres. It breaks into
column ; it forms into line ; it closes into a square ; it again
shapes itself into column and line ; and the sunshine glows
with satisfaction over all. The impatient Colonel urges on
the movements. The Major flies round and means well.
Two hours have passed and he returns ; O, how hot ! His
horse is ordered, and, at twelve, he is in the saddle, on his
way to head-quarters. There is always business enough to
make him late to dinner, at two, P. M. At three the mail
comes, and brings the refreshment of a letter or the disap-

pointment of none. Perhaps the saddle again in the afternoon ; perhaps other work ; perhaps a nap.' At half past
five, drill again ; at half past six, parade. In the evening,
tactics, picket posting, discussion, reflection, schemes, bick-
erings, &c., &c. And bed soon after taps at half past nine.
Bed in the open field. Rest conditional and precarious, —
broken by the frown of the sky, or by the false alarms of
trepid sentinels. But rest which, scorning all these accidental obstacles, these chances and mischances, comes willingly and wooingly to eyelids that have gazed their fill of
wakeful activity. So, *da capo*, one day treads closely on
another, and variety is always at hand. Here I give you
the *prose* of it, — the treadmill without the song. But there
is poetry in it, too. There is a sentiment which gives the
impulse to this duty, and which rewards and *halos* the effort.
I have been to Washington, and returned with a sort of
desperate, teeth-set determination to do all that I can within
the sphere of my duty. It seems to me that the country
wants active, busy, self-forgetting endeavor. More than
that, it needs guidance from a wisdom that has not guided
it yet. It makes me chafe with indignation to see the helplessness of the administration. Misconceiving the emergency, mismeasuring their foe ; dallying with a rabble of
volunteers when they should be disciplining soldiers. Thinking, forsooth, that bold conspirators, with the halter at the
end of one path and wealth and honors looming in the other
vista, do not mean to fight for their very existence. Where
is the evidence, either of civil or military administrative
faculty, in anything they (the administration) have done ?
Where is the will ? Who is the leader ? McClellan, they
hope. It is a hope so young and tender, yet so fair in its
promise, that I will indulge it ; yet it is only a hope. Are
we to drift into another Bull Run ? If not, we must all
wake up. Those unappreciative politicians had not the tact
or energy to utilize the first noble impulse of the country
when it leapt to arms. Now they will find the drooping

influence of mismanagement and defeat a fearful obstacle, as I forebode. But out of this nettle I pluck one flower, namely, that I can be of service ; and it cheers me to hope that, by active and constant endeavor, I may, perhaps, do my small mite towards organization and efficiency. I wish I could do more. To will is present with me. At all events, let men awake to it. The opportunity to save the country will not wait much longer. A leader, however, we must have. . . . . But too much of this. The darker the sky, the warmer my purpose.

"But I cannot help writing a little of the atmosphere that is about us. They say that when some prating talker in Washington told McClellan, ' You have undertaken a fearful task,' he quietly replied, ' I know it, and *I can do it.*' Whether *vero* or *bentrovato*, I hail the omen. The rain drops now and then upon my paper. The camp is quieting itself to sleep. The other morning General Banks came over to our camp and happened in on a battalion drill. The Colonel rattled things, and General Banks was delighted. It was a clever drill, and General Banks thought it better than it was, so we are the pet of head-quarters. I wrote you a line after my return from Washington. Colonel William reigns at his camp, as of course he would. I think his military career will credit him. He has the energy and purpose for achievement. He gives spirit to his men. Barring accident or impatience, he will do well. If every man will be content to fill his place in this war, without pushing for the next *higher*, all will go well.

"I broke off, last night, at this point, and now it is Sunday morning, before breakfast. A bright, glowing morning, with mists rising from the river and hills, promising a hot day. The Doctor is at the door of my bower, as he calls it, beckoning me away to breakfast. The Doctor's servant got hold of some whiskey, the other night, which had been seized from a secessionist, and got crazy drunk with it. He roused the whole camp. He had gone off in the woods, and suddenly fancied himself commanding an army, and made the woods resound with ' forward,' ' charge bayonets,' &c., &c. He had to be tied and gagged, which made an incident for the late evening. The Doctor * is now reproving him with copious satire. ' Peas on the trencher,' or breakfast-call, is beating. I will go to breakfast, and later, will wind up my story. . . . .

" You say that the three months' men ought not to come back. Yes they ought, unless in the presence of immediate duty. You cannot expect anything else. But it was a big blunder having three months' men. The law is at fault, not the men. Human nature is not such an exalted thing that you can expect men to move by regiments, and at a double-quick, in the path of duty and self-sacrifice. Here and there one, but not armies, move *voluntarily* in that direction. Impulse is transitory. Continued and sustained hard work, hunger and discomfort are not palatable. . . . .

" Monday Morning.

" Rain ! rain ! rain ! since yesterday noon. And such a night ! Pouring water, India-rubber blankets ! Dripping from the branches and leaves of my bower like a damp cave with its dropping stalactites. A leak here and a wet place there on the bed. A sudden, more violent shower. The Doctor wakes in his bower, and says, ' By Jove, I might as well try to sleep on lily-pads in a pond.' The Major cachinates. The Colonel rouses himself and laughs in his dribbling bower. Doctor, again : ' There, my pistol is wet to the skin.' At last, morning, and still rain. So we go. To-morrow, sun again. I wish you all health and happiness. Let us pray for a strong government, bent on immediate *war*."

* Lucius Manlius Sargent, Jr ; then Surgeon of the Second Massachusetts Infantry, afterwards Lieutenant-Colonel of the Second Massachusetts Cavalry. In a " most gallant charge " upon the enemy, near Bellefield, Virginia, he fell mortally wounded on the 9th of December, 1864.

"DEPARTMENT SHENANDOAH, MARYLAND HEIGHTS,
August 15, 1861.

"I have, probably, just time, this morning, to report to you our progress. The cold and wet made our tents an absolute necessity to us, and so yesterday General Banks ordered them brought on to the hill. The bushes were swept away, and again the plain whitened with our tents; and, as if to celebrate the occasion, the dull sky broke, the sun came out, and at evening the band was playing in the moonlight, and we were in camp again. Only our tents were left by the wagons. The rest of the baggage prudently retired behind the hill before sunset.

"Yesterday the accounts from down the river of skirmishings and of a movement of the enemy kept up a flight of lively rumors through the camps. Two of the pieces of our battery were taken down the hill, and there was a preparation for movement, if necessary. We heard nothing during the night, however, and this morning, as the mist rises, it does not disclose the rapid advance of cavalry or the frowning presence of angry batteries. It is odd, however, to notice how imaginative are the optics of some men in camp. They are always seeing the enemy. A wagon-load of rails seems a squadron of cavalry. A large Monday's wash near the horizon is an encampment. A clump of firs with two cows and a flock of sheep are as many as a thousand infantry. Their heated fancy detects a heavy cannonading or the rattle of musketry in every sound. All these thick-coming fancies are dissipated by a correct ear, or resolved by a good glass. It is a part of our life. . . . . I am giving personal attention to every detail of feeding and clothing, and expect to get the system so organized that it must always work right. It does work so now, but, in the exigencies of service, there are hitches and rubs inevitable. To allow for friction in human affairs, and to overcome it, is a problem that, in all new enterprises, has to be learned out of practical, experimental teachings.

What an outrage it is that the newspaper reporters cannot be checked! Yesterday's New York Times contains a full statement of number and strength of the regiments with this Division. These papers go South freely. Think what it would be to us if we could have daily papers from the South with statements of their forces, positions, and movements. It would give certainty to what is now the chief element of uncertainty. But the South does not allow the printing of such information, and would not let it come North if it did. I do not see how we can succeed, if we do not take the obvious precaution of military affairs. . . . . I must go and see about a survey of condemned bread, about an issue of new shoes, about drill, &c., &c. . . . . We are building a road over the mountain fit for the passage of artillery and wagons. That keeps two companies busy every day.

"Wednesday Evening.

"Yesterday was made famous and busy by the arrival of the paymaster, laden with gold. I was active all the afternoon, getting the men to the pay-table with order and system. Harper's Ferry was quiet, showing no sign. Orders came to go over there with a small force and destroy the mill and remaining wheat of Mr. Herr. Colonel Andrews was despatched with two companies. Delays in crossing brought their work into the night. The artillery was no longer a protection. Colonel Gordon determined to recall the party. I went to do it. The Doctor and I crossed at about eight o'clock. Found the town deserted. The panic-stricken had left. Blinds were closed. Deadness everywhere. Went up to the mill, ordered in the companies. At half past nine o'clock we were returning, in the moonlight, over the river, — companies in flat-boats, — a magnificent night. But the uncertainty of moonlight did not favor the nature of our enterprise, and would aid them. There is no appearance of any force near Harper's Ferry. I do not believe the enemy are in any strength near us. Their cavalry comes in cautiously every day, and presses teams, &c. The town has run away from itself, and it is sad to see the change since our entry. Sad to hear the accounts of oppression and ruin which come to us from the Union people who are running from the sinking ship.

" This morning, Colonel Andrews has just gone off with a company to complete the destruction of the mill. We have orders to leave Harper's Ferry, and go to Buckeyestown, or some such euphonious place. I suppose that before night we shall have our tents struck, and be on the march again."

CHAPTER V.

"CAMP BELOW SANDY HOOK, August 18, 1861.

"PROGRESS is the law of life. Therefore retreat is abnormal and depressing. When I looked at Harper's Ferry drifting again under *bare poles* into secessionism, I felt low. There was the flagstaff in the silent town, — the flag had just been hauled down. The last flat-boat, with its last company, was coming across the river. On Friday evening the orders came to strike tents, leave a force on the Heights, and for the regiment to be ready to move. Colonel Gordon left me, with three companies, on our old ground. He took the rest below and waited the crossing of the river by Colonel Andrews.

"It was just at dusk when the regiment moved off. The mists were drifting thickly down the mountain sides as the men wound off into the woods. I posted a new guard, got the men under cover as well as I could, and awaited the inevitable rain. We were without tents and without huts. The night passed wearily in a driving rain. The bands were playing confusedly on the other side of the mountain, as the forces were moving down the river. At last came light enough to call it Saturday morning. I was up and out agitating the breakfast question. By good luck I got hold of some stores accidentally left by the Quartermaster, and distributing them, succeeded in getting a hot breakfast into my three wet companies. Then I waited orders. At last Colonel Andrews brought them. I got the men in march- ing order, and in the *blue* rain we started. I got my command safely down to the river, and rejoined the regiment in Sandy Hook, where I found it just ready to march. Then again came orders to remain to hold Sandy Hook, and to send a force over to Harper's Ferry to seize all the flour in Herr's mill. Colonel Andrews returned to the Ferry with five companies. All last night the flour was coming across the river in boats. Our friend Mr. Herr was treated very unceremoniously, but he liked it. He seemed to think it a choice between secession bonds and Union gold ; and if he could get the latter for his flour, he would be content. So the troops seized his premises and took his flour, and he acquiesced with a good grace. The rest of the regiment came down two miles below Harper's Ferry, and here we are, this Sunday morning, waiting to be joined by Colonel Andrews's companies, who have recrossed the river this morning, with all their flour safe on this side. I am scribbling this letter in the Doctor's tent, interrupted by questions, and bothered by difficulties of commissariat. These sudden moves and this detached service are hard tests of ingenuity. You see all the army conveniences move with the army. The regiment that is left behind is ill provided. We have been using the telegraph, and killing fresh beef, and seizing flour, and I think we shall not go hungry. The impression seems to be, that an attempt will be made by the Rebels to reach Baltimore, or get round Washington. That is thought to be the cause of our movement. If such an attempt is made, *it will fail.* . . . . My baggage is all gone. I have nothing but a tent and a blanket, and so am free from care. Colonel Gordon is just galloping into camp. Orders are out for striking tents. We shall soon be in the midst of the work of getting into shape in a new camp nearer Harper's Ferry."

"CAMP BELOW SANDY HOOK, August 18, 1861.

" Well, not so quiet and slow a Sunday, after all. When I closed and mailed my letter this morning, on the abrupt order to 'strike tents and pack wagons,' I did not foresee the briskness of the day. The whole regiment, with much expedition, got upon its new camping-ground nearer the hills and nearer Harper's Ferry. At one o'clock the field of our new encampment was already white. At about three I started on my horse to ride down to the canal and hurry off the boat-load of flour that had been seized. Before I got there I met the report that the Rebel cavalry had entered Harper's Ferry, and that our men were firing on them from the opposite bank of the Potomac. I hurried on and galloped into Sandy Hook. The citizens had gathered under the protection of some buildings. When I got to the Ferry, just above where the old bridge was burnt, I found Captain Cogswell's company, which was there stationed, watching its chances to fire on the enemy who might show themselves in the town opposite. Colonel Andrews, who was there superintending the exit of the flour, was watching to direct their fire. They had succeeded in *dismounting* one or two horsemen, and in scattering the whole body round the point beyond the hill. Lieutenant Brown, who was loading the ferry-boat, saw the cavalry coming down the Shenandoah road. His citizen workmen fled incontinently. His soldiers put the few remaining barrels on board, including that portion of flour which was the promised pay of the citizen workmen, Brown telling them afterwards they had lost it *by running*. Colonel Andrews immediately ordered some of Captain Cogswell's men to climb the hill so as to bring the Rebel horse within range. Their shots scattered the cavalry who had formed in the square by the Armory. A brisk interchange of shots ensued. Captain Cary's company was stationed above, on the Potomac, to guard the ford. A fatigue party from his company were down at the river-bank obstructing the passage-way from the ford. The Rebels opened fire on them.

" Captain Cary deployed his company as skirmishers, and they returned the whistling bullets. I arrived just as the fire was ceasing. After starting the boat, which, as good luck would have it, had on board every barrel of flour seized except thirty kept for our own use, I went on to give some orders to Captain Cary. I found him and his company in cheerful temper, and watching for ' good shots.' Then I went up the hill to our lookout. Lieutenant Horton was there with a picket. He pointed out where the troops had been, and I also saw a retreating body of horse on the Charlestown road. Leaving him, I returned to Colonel Andrews, below, at the ford, found everything quiet, and then came back to camp to report. This evening I have been again to Sandy Hook, and all is quiet. We think it is only a sudden dash to prevent our seizure of the flour which they coveted. By working all night we had got our prey the right side of the swift river, and the boat went out of range of them on the canal just as they got to the ferry. Our position, too, on the side of the mountain in shelter of the trees, enabled us to sprinkle our shots freely through the town. So their scheme failed. Still we may from time to time exchange shots with them. We are well posted. They cannot cross the river easily, and we are not in force to attempt it, so there is no danger, and much amusement and liveliness in possible store for us. Our flour and some other stores taken have given us a fine commissariat. We have plenty to eat, and are in good spirits.

" A scout from Harper's Ferry reports a company of infantry in one of their churches. So our successors followed close upon our heels."

" CAMP STAMPEDE, MARYLAND HEIGHTS,
Tuesday Evening, August 20, 1861.

" A soldier's life is always gay! Yesterday, Colonel Andrews and I went out *prospecting*, as they say in this country, — reconnoitring, I prefer to call it.

" At the Ferry we found a slight panic caused by the reported advent of a few cavalry in the town. Colonel A. and I went on up the mountain and spent the afternoon in looking about, &c. We wound down the new mountain road, built by the immortal Massachusetts Second, just at sunset, after enjoying the glorious views up the two valleys. Then we had a quiet dress-parade, and composed ourselves for the night. Composed ourselves for the night! Here comes the incident of my letter. Now for the catastrophe of my story. The Doctor appeared at the door of my tent, breaking the first sleep, to say the Colonel had just received a special message, and ridden off on horse. I refused to be disturbed or excited, and got asleep again. At half past one the Colonel appeared. ' Major, get the tents struck, and set the men cooking rations. I have information that the Rebels are advancing on Harper's Ferry.' Up I went. Captains were awakened. Soon the camp was silently busy on its work for starting. Then I was ordered to saddle my horse and get a messenger to call the Massachusetts Thirteenth, Colonel Leonard, from Sharpsburg. I went galloping off in the night through the fields to a house where a Union man lives, who gave me the direction of a safe messenger, then back to camp. Then Dr. Sargent was despatched to Berlin, down the river, to get two pieces of artillery which General Banks had ordered up to protect the ford. Then the camp-fires were glowing, and I spent an hour among the cooks, urging on the rations. Then the dawn began to peep. Colonel Andrews went up the hill to gaze, through the first light, at Harper's Ferry and its surroundings. Light· brought the conviction that our haste was premature.

" The packed wagons were ready to move. The regiment was ready to hold ford and ferry as long as possible, and we were all *agog*. The morning came, and no enemy were in position. We had our stampede. The reports of the enemy were circumstantial and probable, but the appearance failed to confirm them. This morning the camp is composed again. But life has been lively and brisk, though fruitless, for the last twelve hours. . . . .

"Here comes the Colonel, who has been down to Sandy
Hook. He brings news that the paymaster is coming.
Hurrah! Also that three hundred car-loads of troops went
into Washington on Monday. Good!

"We are awaking, I hope, to the size of the work. A
short war is the policy, but a *war*. I am glad you are getting awake to it. No one who can come, effectively, has a
right to stay at home."

"BUCKEYESTOWN, August 23, 1861, Friday, in Camp.

"I began a letter before breakfast this morning, but my
pen dragged so that I tore it up. Now I have a short time,
and perhaps not a long story, but certainly a good breakfast
to tell it on. And this same matter of a good breakfast is
not a small one. The foraging on a march is not easy.
Chickens and eggs and bread and butter and milk, &c., all
have to be extemporized by our darkies, as we go along.
Sometimes we do well ; sometimes, badly. This morning,
being bent on eggs, I sent my little English groom off on
horseback. He went to a farm-house, into a hen-yard, and
waited for cackling. Presently he returned, and said : 'I 've
an egg for ye, sir. I waited till the hen laid it, and then
brought the hen and the egg.' That is close work, I think.

"I sent you a letter Wednesday morning. Immediately
after came marching orders. I hurried off on horseback to
call in our scattered forces. First, I went to Harper's Ferry,
and found Colonel Andrews destroying our friend Herr's
mill. Herr was very sombre. His little boy, with whom
I have a friendship, rushed up to me, and said chokingly :
'It is too bad to destroy the mill ; but it 's the secessionists
that 's the cause of it, is n't it, Major ? ' I told him, Yes.
Andrews was breaking the buckets of the turbine wheel,
and smashing the gearing of the mill. He had Company
A, from Lowell, who are the mechanics of our regiment.
He was sorry to be interrupted, but there was no remedy,
and so off he came.

6

" Then I went back and off on to Battery Hill to get the
artillery off ; then again to recall an outlying picket on
top of the mountain ; then galloped back to camp to see
about rations ; then, at last, the regiment got in marching
array.   The day was bright and cool, — the regiment moved
off at twelve o'clock.   Hard bread in haversacks, and hoping for something better.   Money in pocket, and, I am sorry
to say, an occasional excess of whiskey in a guilty canteen.
Pay-day has its evils, as I thought when directing two
drunken men to be tied and put in a wagon.

" We made a brisk march of twelve miles to Jefferson.
There we spent the night.   The next morning, after a tedious delay in a depressing rain to get our wagons mended,
we again moved on up, up, up a long hill in a close, muggy
dog-day.   The men's knapsacks pulled on them, and when
we came on to our present camping-ground, at four o'clock,
there was a long trail of lame ducks behind.   They soon
came in, and now are looking forward to another tramp.

" The panic-stricken women and children pursued us, as
we came away from Harper's Ferry, not daring to remain
without our protection.   The Rebels are foraging all through
the country there ; but nothing more than that appears to
be done anywhere, though rumor is trumpet-tongued with
reports of armies large enough to conquer the hemisphere.
Mark my prophecy.   Beauregard lacks transportation.   He
cannot move one hundred thousand men across the Potomac.   This has prevented and will prevent his active operations.   But it is not improbable that there will be skirmishes
along the river."

                    " ROCKVILLE, MARYLAND, August 24, 1861.

" Here I turn up this evening, as much to my own surprise as yours.   I got a short note on its way to you from
Buckeyestown, just before we were off.   Friday morning at
twelve ' the general ' was beaten, and at the signal every
tent fell as by a single will.   Then the ' assembly ' sounded,
and the regiment formed into line.   The ceremony of start-

ing was for the first time performed with promptness and accuracy. We marched without knapsacks. The men were all paid, and we rattled along briskly. Our wagons were hardly as lucky, and, though the regiment got on to its camping-ground soon after four, the wagons dragged slowly in until nine. This made us late in camping, and late in supper. We were camped by the river-side, and the evening had an autumn chill and a heavy dew. I know of nothing more cheerless than the getting late into camp after a march. Every one is tired ; every one is hungry ; every one is cross. Everything seems to be going wrong. Yet at last all the men get their supper, or go without their supper. The last camp-fire falls down into sullen coals. The last tent-light fades out, and the chilly whiteness of the camp throws back the paleness of the moon. As the dawn reddens, reveillé comes fresh as the lark, and soon the sunshine lights up a busy scene. The men are rested, and have forgotten their hunger in a good breakfast. The band plays gayly at guard-mounting, and a fresh life begins for the day again. Such was our experience of camp last night and this morning. I was just composing myself to camp-life. We were encamped with our brigade. The New York Ninth was on our left. The two Wisconsin regiments were on the hill above us. Webster's regiment was just beyond them. I had listened to four reveillés in the morning, and soon after breakfast the hills were alive with skirmishers at drill. I was sitting in my tent when the Colonel called out, ' Major, you must go to Washington.' ' What ! ' said I, ' to Washington ? ' ' Yes.' You are ordered to go in command of an escort of a large wagon-train, and are to report for instructions immediately at head-quarters.'

"I found that two parts of the train, consisting of one hundred wagons each, had already gone on. The third was expected from Frederick to-day. Captain Mudge's company were ordered to escort that train when it arrived, and I was directed to choose my own time, but to proceed to

Washington, and see the wagons turned over to the Quarter-master, and take care of the battalion of three companies while it remained in Washington, and march it back to Hyattstown. The wagons to remain in Washington. ' The train may be interrupted by Rebel cavalry,' said Colonel Cromman, the Quartermaster, ' so it needs an escort.' I got everything in readiness, gave Captain Mudge his instructions, and directed him to 'wait for the wagons.' And at three o'clock this afternoon was in the saddle on my way in pursuit of the other companies and trains. I had a charming ride, — a little warm at first, — through a beautiful country, and animated by just the least uncertainty as to the path. But I met nothing but respect for my uniform. After a ride of eighteen miles I stopped at this town of Rockville, the ' county seat,' as they say in this country. I selected a tavern that had a Union flag flying, and rejoiced in the safe name of ' the Washington House.' This is a secession town of the worst kind, but they have not confidence enough yet to do anything more than *look cross*. At the tea-table we were protected from the flies by a series of fans worked by a rope and pulleys, and at the end of the rope was a little negro girl who swung back and forth and kept the fans moving indefatigably. It was an odd picture, worthy of Eastman Johnson's pencil. I shall be in the saddle again at five to-morrow morning, and in Washington before eight."

" WASHINGTON, Sunday Morning, Quartermaster's Office.

" I had a fine ride this morning, and got to the War Department at eight o'clock. Now I am waiting to find out where to camp, and how to turn over the wagons, &c. A maze without a plan does Washington seem to one who comes into it as I have. Camps met my eye within six miles of the city. I noticed, too, some fortifications of a rude kind ; but of course from one glance I know only a mass of things, *nothing distinctly*. . . . . Washington is evidently safe enough, just as I knew it was."

"WASHINGTON, August 26th, 1861.

" I am probably to leave for home, i. e. camp, to-morrow. Everything has gone quite well with me. I put up with my classmate, A. S. Hill, who is the correspondent of the Tribune. I slept as well as one can in a bed. To-day I have been in the saddle pursuing quartermasters, providing rations, arranging for a departure to-morrow if possible. I dined with William, and this evening we have been out together to see General Couch's camp. William is in fine spirits, full of energy and go. He is making his regiment as perfect as the material will allow, and is full of his work. I should be glad to feel in trim for a letter, but I am too tired for it now ; besides, General Heintzelman, who had a brigade, and was wounded at Bull Run, is in the room where I write, and is talking of the fight with one or two newspaper men who are in Hill's room, which is the Tribune head-quarters. The General is an unpretending man, and his conversation is interesting, my letter not. He says that ' a sufficient cause for the loss of the battle of Bull Run is, that a regiment appeared in front of Griffin's battery, within one hundred yards. The cannon were loaded with canister, just ready to fire. An officer of our army came up and begged Griffin not to fire, as the troops were our own. They carried no flag ; the cannon were turned, and fired to another point, then the regiment opened fire, killed all the cannoneers, and took the battery. The discharge of that canister would have cut that regiment to pieces, and changed the result in that part of the field.' These words are just from his lips. It shows the importance of a *uniform* uniform, and it shows the folly of States' rights in every shape. But it is not very profitable to speculate upon the various explanations of defeat. I think we are drawing lessons from that battle. I think, too, that McClellan's spirit is a fine one. Certainly there is more vigor, military ardor, and glow here than with our column. Another influence and a stronger spirit is at work here, and I want to get within its range."

"CAMP NEAR DARNESTOWN, August 30, 1861.

" It is broad, bright noon ; the men are cooking their breakfasts, the sun is drying out their clothes, the tents are ready to pitch, the Brigade Quartermaster is sitting in our tent rehearsing his exploits on the road, — how one teamster beat a horse's eye out ; how, if another had *hawed* instead of *geeing*, all would have been well ; how the one-line Pennsylvania saddle team-driving is better than our four-rein driving of our wagons ; how this and how that would have made the march easier, and a day march instead of a night one. And such a march ! But I must go back and bring myself from Washington. I wrote a hurried scratch one evening while listening to General Heintzelman's account of Bull Run. My next day was busy with the providing for my companies, and getting a delivery of the wagons to government. I was quartermaster, commissary, colonel, major, and all in one. At last, however, I succeeded in arranging things to my mind, and went out of town to my camp at Georgetown. Here I had collected the three companies which had come as escort of three separate trains. Here, too, I had packed two of the trains.

" On Wednesday morning we made a good start from camp, and Captain Handy, of the Webster regiment, led the column briskly. We marched nineteen miles, a strong day's work. It was a cloudy, drizzly day. The companies came into camp at four o'clock. Tents were pitched, supper got briskly. Captain Mudge, Lieutenants Shaw and Robeson were the officers of the company from our regiment.

" Mr. Desellum,* who lived near our camping-ground, invited us to supper with him, and gave us what we all prized, — a good one. Appetite and digestion wait on one another on a march. Mr. Desellum was a character. He had lived on his place all his life, and never gone beyond the limits of the two adjoining counties ; his father and grandfather were

* See Appendix VII.

rooted in the same soil. He gave me a full account of the surrounding country, and also a capital map. Both he and his maiden sister were ardent Union lovers, and bitter in their hatred of Jeff Davis. He was very calm and intelligent, formal and precise, full of talk of the war, of the battles of Napoleon, &c. He lives with his sister in their faultlessly clean home, with twenty-five negroes. When asked if he owned slaves, ' No, the slaves own me,' which, I think, expresses his conscientious performance of his duties. I gave orders to have reveillé at four o'clock in the morning and to have a brisk start. I took pleasure in attempting to realize some of my theories about the march, and had great satisfaction in accomplishing a good breakfast and an early start ; and before eight o'clock in the morning my men had marched from their camp on Muddy Creek to Nealsville, eight miles. There we met the report that the regiment had left Hyattstown, and was on the march with the whole column. I halted my detachment, and galloping on, met General Banks at the head of his division. I reported to him, and got his order to direct my companies to join their regiments when they came up. Then I went on myself, back to see our regiment ; I found them halted in a wood in the driving rain. After a greeting with the Colonel, whom I found acting as brigadier of our brigade in the absence of Colonel Abercrombie, I went back again to wait with my companies the slow progress of the column. It rained hard. The wagons made slow work. At about one o'clock our regiment, the first of the Second Brigade, reached us at Nealsville. There we turned off down towards Darnestown, — a charming name !

" At last we were pointed to a camping-ground at a place called Pleasant Mountain, — a valley or hill, I can't say which. But where were our wagons ? Far back on the heavy, wet, and swampy road. Just at dusk the regiment fell down, tired, into the wet stubble, and the fog settled chill upon it. The evening star looked mildly down, but it gave no cheer. Colonel Andrews was sick, Colonel Gordon in charge of the brigade. I did what I could, — got the guard posted, good fires built of the neighboring rail-fences, in the absence of other wood, and then, wet and tired, lay down myself. The march was mismanaged by the higher powers. It was wretched to see our cold and hungry men lying down dripping and supperless in the cold fog to sleep. The start was a late one. The rain ruined the road, and the delays were so many that the large column made a poor business of its day's work. This morning at five I hurried off to get up the wagons. The sun rose clear. By dint of activity, getting a party to mend road, &c., the wagons came in about ten o'clock, and hope revived. I also got a cup of tea and a breakfast, and I revived. Such is our life. I have certainly been active for a week, and now, to-day, comes shoe distributions and muster-rolls, &c. I quite envy those regiments that are quiet and in position near Washington, with every facility for order, discipline, drill, food, &c.; but, as Birdofredum Sawin says, ' I 'm *safe enlisted for the war*,' and come what will, I will be content. Though last evening, in the fog and dark and cold, I felt, as I lay down with wet feet and wet clothes, a little like grumbling at the stupidity of our Adjutant-General, who planned and executed our uncomfortable march, which hit me just as I wanted a little rest. I was happy to wake up this morning with only a little sensation of stiffness, which wore off in my early ride of six miles. During my ride I snatched a breakfast at a farm-house, and enjoyed the sensation of health and sunshine. Though I began this letter at noon, I am finishing it by candle-light. It has been interrupted variously; at this moment the Colonel comes to my tent, and says, ' That is a beautiful sight,' pointing to the camp-fires and lights on the hills about us. The Webster regiment is just opposite us, and their band is now playing. We are within six miles of the Potomac. Everything here looks every day more like business; but we have not the presence of McClellan, and one who has just come from that present influence misses it as he would the quick pulse of health. The coming man is not a mere phrase. There is no cant, either, in the phrase. How we have waited for him ! And has he come ? I hope. Discredit all rumor. That is my advice. . . . .

"I do not seem to myself to have given anything like a picture of the active life of the past week, but Colonel Andrews wants my help about rations, the Chaplain wants my letter for the mail, I want time for various things, and so good night."

CHAPTER VI.

LETTERS FROM PLEASANT HILL CAMP, NEAR DARNESTOWN.

"CAMP NEAR DARNESTOWN, August 31, 1861.

" IF you have a good map, you can see our present position just on Seneca Creek, two miles from Darnestown. We were ordered to Darnestown, but there is no water nearer than this point.   We are within striking distance of Washington, and also *vis-à-vis* of Leesburg, *about*.

" I wish you to buy, and forward by express, a large *coffee-roaster*, which will roast thirty or forty pounds at a time.   There is a kind, I am told.   It would be of immense advantage to us."

"CAMP NEAR DARNESTOWN, Monday, September 2, 1861,
Supply Train Camp.

" I have got a chance at pen and paper in the Commissary's office, and improve the chance for a letter.   I am here in charge of two companies guarding our Division Supply Train, but shall be relieved to-day.   The duty is a tedious one.   The event of yesterday was the arrival of the coffee-mills.   Colonel Gordon reports that the men are in ecstasies with them.   I am only a witness by his report, for I was ordered off on this duty just as the coffee-mills arrived.   I know how badly they were needed, and I hear how admirably they work.   Since our arrival here at this new camp we have undergone the invariable inconveniences attending the moving of a division, and for the past two days my mind and time have been absorbed with the problem of how to overcome them.   Night before last, having accumulated the evidence from reports of captains, and from our own quartermaster, about the want of tea, hard bread, salt pork, &c., I went up to General Banks's head-quarters, and had a long talk with him, urging the remedies which have occurred to me. The General *promises* to change all this, and to accomplish the regular and constant issue of the ration to the soldier in the form and at the moment required by law. I was so much struck with the difference between our condition and that of the grand army about Washington, that I have been the more exercised since my return. One consolation I have, that we are learning lessons and acquiring habits which will have to be learned, perhaps, under less favorable circumstances by others ; and I have hopes that something may be done to make feeding easier. We have had a grand reduction of baggage going on, in order to get us into easier moving train. I am persuaded that the true equipment for the soldier is the combination tent and knapsack, which enables him to carry his shelter on his back, and which dispenses with more than one half of the wagons of a regiment. By that arrangement every four men would carry their tent. It is put up in a moment, and they are never separated from it. In the future, if the war lasts, I hope to get our regiment equipped with it. The autumn campaign, however, must be made in our present trim, and we must prepare, as best we can, to make it. Where are the enemy ? In our isolated position we hear nothing of them. I confess that this quietness puzzles me. If they only knew their opportunities, what fine fun they might have had.

" My head-quarters in my present guard duty are on a pine hill, under a bower built of pine-boughs. We had a good camp-fire last night, and I enjoyed it very much. This morning I visited all my pickets and outposts very early, and had a fine ride through the woods. I am writing in the midst of a Babel of mule-teams, and am surrounded by huge piles of barrels of flour and hard bread, boxes of soap, bags of oats and corn, and other stores. The wagons are packed in two fields, and the work of distribution is going on all the time. The portable forges are just back of the

tent where I write, and a dozen busy blacksmiths are ringing their anvils. It is a lively scene. I do not know that
there is anything of narrative or prophecy that I can send
you entertaining. I hope father will send the coffee-roaster,
and have it as portable as the required result will allow.
It will complete my effort in that direction. I have been
some time without a letter, because our mail has not yet
found us out in our new position. I hope it will do so to-
morrow. I must get on my horse and go about to visit my
guard. We sent our pay-rolls to Washington to-day, which
is prompt work. Our pay will come again next week. The
men of our regiment are now contented and efficient, illustrating my statement, that the only trouble was the want
of pay. All those questions of enlistment, &c., have died
out. They never had any real hold on the men, but were
a form of grumbling. The change was abrupt and sudden. The paymaster came like a sunbeam. Good by.
Love to all."

" PLEASANT HILL, CAMP NEAR DARNESTOWN,
September 4, 1861.

" A picture ! Life is but a series of them. Stand on a
hill just above the creek. Let Major-General Banks, with
all his *un*won, *un*tried, not to say *un*comfortable or *un*fit,
glories, be by your side. It is evening ; you are at head-
quarters. The General will say, in full, deep tones, ' A fine
sight, Madam.' You will have anticipated his platitude ;
for you will find your eye filled with blazing camp-fires and
bright-lighted tents, on every hillside within the circle of
which you are a centre. Your ear will listen to the bands
playing in every camp. The distance softens and harmonizes
their discords. You have seen the camps at evening.

" A night's rest under the tent, with two blankets and a
bundle of straw extemporized into a bed, is a second picture.
Your dream is interrupted by a clang of kettle and bass
drums. It is the *infernal* reveillé of the Indiana Twelfth.
Presently you hear a clear rattle and shrill fife, and recog-

nize the reveillé of the drum-major of the Massachusetts Second. Follow it with your ear. You will see how it is measured. A little practice teaches the soldier at what point to open his eyes, when to throw back his blanket, and, at the moment, he is in ranks at the last ruffle of the drum. Regiments are known by their reveillés, you may say. But if you have obeyed the call, you will be looking upon the camps in the first glimmering of sunrise. You will glance at the old moon, in its second childhood almost as graceful as its first. You will see the men swarming from their tents into ranks. In half an hour the hills are alive with moving columns, and you are watching the morning drill.

" It is afternoon. You have come to visit the camp of the Massachusetts Second. The General had at once pointed it out last evening. You then admired the regularity of its form. You now admire the neatness and order that you find within.

" You go out in front and look over at the opposite hill, where the —— Regiment is in camp. The officer of the day in our camp is administering a punishment. The court-martial had sentenced a drunken and insubordinate fellow to be tied to a tree for one hour three successive days. There he *is tied*. The —— Regiment catch sight of him. At once, in a disorderly mob, they rush to the edge of their hill. They cry, ' Cut him down!' they groan and yell against us. Our guard is called out. Their officers cannot restore order, though they succeed in keeping their men within their lines. The punishment is concluded. Not a man in our lines stirs or speaks. You have contrasted the discipline of the two regiments. You have seen pictures enough, because you want to hear more of this one. Colonel Gordon, as Acting Brigadier, directs the arrest of the ringleaders of the —— Regiment, and of their officer of the day. The next morning, to wit, yesterday, the 3d September, Colonel —— comes to ask that the man may be tied somewhere where the regiment which he *is commanded by* cannot see him. Colonel Gordon says, No. General Banks, on being consulted by Colonel Gordon, directs him to go on. 'Discipline must be maintained,' says the General. Colonel —— then goes to General Banks, and, by what persuasion we know not, wheedles out of him a recommendation to Colonel Gordon that the punishment be inflicted with less 'publicity.' This recommendation comes just before the time for the punishment. General Banks cannot be found in season to give any explanation of his written recommendation. Colonel Gordon makes up his mind to tie the man in the same place and in the same way, come what may. It is done without trouble. But the recommendation from head-quarters has shaken our confidence. This illustrates the difficulties under which discipline is maintained. We are the only regiment that attempts it, and even the officers among our neighbors discountenance the severity which alone insures our discipline. But *our men* are getting, every day, a better tone. They pride themselves on the obvious contrast between their regiment and the others. They submit to the rules out of which this contrast comes. But the fact that the other regiments do as they please aggravates our difficulties and endangers our success. We are beginning to long for the direct command of McClellan, who would sustain our system without fear, favor, or affection. A political education does not favor the direct disregard of consequences which belongs to military command. Yet I do not wish to complain of General Banks. I think he means well, but I fear that he lacks a little either of education or confidence to push things through.

"I have been working away at the deficiencies of our commissariat. I do not hesitate to say that its condition is disgraceful. No organization, and not even accidental and disproportioned abundance, in any direction. A general short commons. This we hope to remedy. But I do not make much progress. In fact, General Banks's division is not officered in the Quartermaster and Subsistence Departments as it should be. But enough of this. We are getting on well, and I only grumble because we might do so much better. To-day, again, the man *shall* be tied to the tree.

"Yesterday morning we had a visit from General Reed, Albert Brown, the Governor's Secretary, and Mr. Dalton, the Massachusetts Agent. They seemed pleased with what they saw. But they only made a flying visit. They brought no news from home, but they brought the tale of Butler's achievement. 'That's the talk,' say I. 'Give 'em unexpected droppings in all along shore. Scatter them with vague dread. Make 'em constantly ask, "What 'll come next?"' General Butler is in luck. He has n't got a big lamp, but he brings it out *after dark*. In the night that surrounded Washington in April, he appeared with his farthing candle: men thought it a sun! Now, again, when the public longs for a glimmer of achievement, he strikes a light, and men are dazzled by even so small a blaze. Verily, opportunity has served him. But the move is in the right direction, and I applaud vehemently. I am just informed that the mail goes immediately, and must close my letter. We hear of a large mail on its way from Washington, and hope to get it to-morrow. It is nearly a week since I had a letter; but if men will go to Darnestown they must take the consequences. Love to all."

"PLEASANT HILL., CAMP NEAR DARNESTOWN,
September 6, 1861.

"DEAR HOWARD, — Advice is cheap. When lost it goes to the moon, according to the old superstition, and does no harm. Hear mine. General Fremont is on his way to Memphis. As sure as sunrise he will go there. Go with him. Now is the opportunity for adventure, for success. Energy and aptitude are in demand. This autumn they will bear fruit. The wheel is entitled to every man's shoulder; offer yours. In other words, pack your trunk, take a few letters of introduction and authentication from the Governor and others, go to Fremont, tell him you wish to serve in his army. . . . . You will do yourself credit, and be in the midst of some of the most brilliant achievements of the war. I have said my say, after reflection, and from a near view of the field.

" Yours affectionately,
" WILDER DWIGHT.

" To LIEUTENANT HOWARD DWIGHT."

"PLEASANT HILL, CAMP NEAR DARNESTOWN,
Saturday, September 7, 1861.

" DEAR MOTHER, — Twice within three days we have been abruptly summoned to get into marching array. Twice has the order been countermanded. This morning at three o'clock I was waked to open my eyes upon the misty starlight by an orderly from head-quarters.

" He brought the order: ' The enemy have broken up their camp at Manassas, and are moving. Get everything in readiness to start. If a signal-light is exhibited at head-quarters, let the long roll be beaten and the regiment get under arms at once.' Colonel Gordon is in Washington. Colonel Andrews gave quietly the necessary orders, and then both he and I composed ourselves to sleep. We have learnt that excitement is useless and unprofitable. Besides, composure is so graceful, and withal comfortable, at that hour. But, seriously, these successive alarms have become the habit of our lives. One of these days perchance the wolf will come. But this morning there are no new orders, and no immediate prospect of a start. Movement must come, however, shortly, and I confess I am impatient for its coming. Just now, perhaps, I can be content to wait. My horse did me the ill turn to fall with me the other day. I was urging him hastily down hill, and he stumbled and went down. He chafed my leg a little, and so I am lying still to-day to get well. To-morrow both he and I will be firmly on our legs again, and it may well happen that we shall both

need them. I was sorry to hear of your cold. It is such
a bad companion for August. You should come and live
in a tent, and then you would cease to have any of the ills
that follow close rooms, warm beds, coal fires, and the other
accidents of civilized life in times of peace. . . . . It is a
sultry morning, and the air moves listlessly through my
tent. I am reclining orientally, and the Doctor has just
been making an application to my bruise. He has also been
chatting pleasantly for half an hour, and so has broken what
little thread belonged to my story. It is well that it is so,
for the life of the past few days does not need a chronicler.
We all expect something coming, but do not know what or
when. I confess I enjoy a few days for the study of tactics
and attention to military matters. The theory slips out of
sight in the tread-mill of daily duty.

I glanced at an article in the Atlantic Monthly this morning on 'The Advantages of Defeat.' I cannot agree to its
positions. American soldiers, — let the fact be plainly
stated, — American soldiers will only become efficient in
proportion as they abandon their national theories and
give themselves up obediently to the *military laws* which
have always governed the successful prosecution of war.
'The incurable habit of insubordination of the citizen,'
as the Saturday Review has it, in a capital article, ' cannot
be transferred to the soldier.'   To-day our army is crippled by the ideas of equality and independence which have
colored the whole life of our people. Men elect their officers, and then expect them *to behave themselves!* Obedience is permissive, not compelled, and the radical basis
is wrong. We have to struggle against the evil tenden
cies of this contagion. When this defect is cured, and men
recognize authority and obey without knowing why, — obey
from habit and instinct, not from any process of reasoning
or presumed consent, — we shall begin to get an army. It
is only necessary to appreciate the fact that, in war, *one will*
must act through all the others, to see that American sol-

7

diers, with all their presumed intelligence and skill, have *the one lesson* yet to learn. So for my preachment. Here appears Colonel Gordon, returned suddenly from Washington. The enemy are moving *somewhither*, and of course he rejoins his regiment. . . . . The obvious weaknesses of delay may drive the Rebels to offensive action. If so, Heaven send them across the river between us and Washington, so that we may have a part in the great battle that crushes them. And yet I cannot believe that any such chance will come to us. Speculation, however, is worthless, on a matter which will have decided itself long before the speculation can reach you."

"PLEASANT HILL, September 10, 1861.
Camp near Darnestown.

"I have had a day or two of horizontal contemplation, enforced by my leg, but now I am well again, and about resuming ' active operations in the field.' You cannot expect that I should give you any stirring news, and had I been on my legs it would only have been for purposes of drill and discipline. After three days of scare, we subside. We keep two days' rations cooked, ready for a march, and there comes to us every day fresh evidence that the enemy are active. Their plan, of course, we do not know, and I have wasted so many good hours in trying to guess that I now give it up. I have had, for three or four days, a chance to read and study quietly, — a thing which has not before occurred to me since I began this enterprise, in April last. I have enjoyed and improved it, and mean to get time always for some of it. Yet it is not easy, in the midst of all the active, practical duties of a life, to secure chances for study and thought, and I have been glad of this. . . . .

"Colonel Andrews, who is in command, is full of life and energy. The want of progress and growth in everything military is a sore trial to him. He works hard for the regiment, and wishes every stroke to tell. I think we do grow better, but when you understand fully what a regiment ought to be, and ought to be capable of doing, you see that we are a long way off from our goal. 'Peas upon the trencher,' breakfast-call, has just beaten, and here comes Colonel Andrews to go to breakfast."

"PLEASANT HILL, September 12, 1861,
Thursday Morning.

"Yes! There they go again! Home, sweet home! And then the maddening suggestion of pleasures and palaces! If our band were malicious and impish, could they insist upon a more discontenting theme? Yet, as sure as there comes a chill, cloudy, morose morning, the band come out to guard-mounting, and fill the air with sighings after home, &c. Now they change; it is Hail Columbia, happy land! Is there not a bitterness of satire in that, even, which alloys the patriotic associations of the melody? Columbia seems anything but a happy land just now, in the midst of rebellion and treason. But the music kindles one, after all. It is the morning that is out of tune, or myself, perhaps. A raw and bitter night, — rainy and chill. The tents blowing down, the rain blowing in, dripping visitors in india-rubber garments sitting down on your bed, a spluttering candle flickering out, and leaving you hopelessly in the dark, a new pool surprising your slipper, a sudden freshet carrying away your dressing-case, the quick, sharp rattle and tattoo of the raindrops, and the tent fluttering with every gusty squall, sleep precarious and uncertain. At last reveillé, and a hoarse, damp 'Good morning' from the Doctor, who speculates grimly, in the next tent, upon the folly of getting up. Yet we do get up, and after breakfast I sit down to write to the tune of home. 'Sich,' as the Doctor is fond of saying, 'is life; and, more particularly, *camp* life.' I happen to have a delicious bit of romance for you to-day; and as the sun is getting warmer, and the rain is drying up, I may get cheerful by telling it. The Chaplain appeared yesterday with the confidential narrative that he had been performing an uncommon ceremony. In a word, he had married a couple! 'Who was the bridegroom?' asks Colonel Andrews, who is still in command. 'Sergeant ———.' It then appeared that the bride came out from Massachusetts to be married, and it had all been ' fixed,' as they phrase it, in a house near the camp that morning, a few hours after her arrival. The Sergeant was to remain true to his duty, and the new wife was to return by the next day's stage. But the romance goes further. The true love had met other ripples in its flow. Malice traduced the Sergeant last spring to his enslaver. She gave him up, and ' he went, and in despair enlisted for a soldier.' The truth came at last to the maiden's mind, and her meditations were no longer ' fancy free.' She loved her lost Sergeant more than ever, and so out she came, and said so plump and fairly, once for all, to the parson, and they were a happy pair again. The Colonel expressed some doubt to the Chaplain, whether it was precisely according to military discipline to get married in camp, but did not take a rigid view of it. Soon after, the Sergeant appeared at the Colonel's tent. ' I should like a leave of absence for three hours, sir.' ' What for, Sergeant?' ' To see a friend, sir.' ' Can't your friend come here?' ' No, sir, not very well.' ' Do you want to be away as long as that?' (severely). ' Yes, sir, I should like *two* or *three* hours' (timidly). ' Sergeant,' said the Colonel, with a twinkle — a benevolent twinkle — in his eye, ' I think I know who your friend is. Would n't you like to be gone till to-morrow morning?' ' Yes, sir, I should, sir.' ' Well, you 've been a faithful man, and you may.' Sich, again, is life, but not often camp life.

"I am busy on court-martial, having been appointed President of the General Court-Martial of this division, — that is, having been designated as senior officer. We sit in the morning, and I am amused to see how kindly I take to the forms of law again. I am getting quite well again of my bruise. but it is good easy work for a lame man. We do not know when we may move, but I am getting to think that orders must come pretty soon now.

"We had a visit from General Banks yesterday before the rain began. The General visited our kitchens, and tasted, with apparent approval, my doughnuts. I say mine, because I regard as, perhaps, the most successful endeavor of my military life, the general introduction of doughnuts into the regiment. It you could have seen the helplessness in which the flour ration left us, and the stupidity of the men in its use, you would hail, as the dawn, the busy frying of doughnuts which goes on here now. Two barrels is a small allowance for a company. They are good to carry in the haversack, and 'stick by a feller on the march.' And when the men have not time to build an oven, as often they have not, the idea is invaluable. Pots of beans baked in holes in the ground, with a pan of brown bread on top, is also a recent achievement, worthy of Sunday morning at an old Exeter boarding-house. The band produced that agreeable concord yesterday, and contributed from their success to my breakfast. Our triumphs, just now, are chiefly culinary ; but an achievement of that kind is not to be despised. 'A soldier's courage lies in his stomach,' said Frederick the Great. And I mean that the commissary of our division and the commissary of our regiment, and the captains and the cooks, shall accept the doctrine and apply its lessons, if I can make them. . . . .

"By the way, do you know that I have grown the most alarming beard of modern times ? I am inclined to think it must be so. It has the true glare of *Mars*, and is, I flatter myself, warlike, though not becoming. I have forborne allusion to it in the tenderness of its youth and the uncertainty of its hue, but now that it has taken on full proportions and color, I announce it to you as a decided feature.

"Dr. —— may be a good reasoner, but he can't reason the Secession army into winter-quarters in Philadelphia.

There is no real cause for depression. Subduing rebellion, conquering traitors, in short, war, is the work of soldiers. Soldiers are a product of time, and so it comes that our mad impatience of delay is chastised by disaster. In the fulness of time, we shall wipe out this Southern army, as surely as the time passes. But we have got to *work* for it instead of *talking* about it. That is all. Between the beginning of this letter and the end is a course of the sun. It has been scratched at intervals, and now I look out of my tent on a glorious sunset, and the music is just beginning for parade."

"PLEASANT HILL, CAMP NEAR DARNESTOWN,
September 15, 1861, Sunday.

"At regular intervals I am prompted to my pen, rather by the desire to think of you at home, than by the consciousness of any story to tell. It is called a hot day to-day. I found Colonel —— and Lieutenant-Colonel —— at Poolesville this morning in a state of intense glow, and crying out at the heat. I find it comfortable, and consider anything short of boiling water my natural element. The force of habit is so strong that my summer on the Potomac has fitted me for tropical life. . . . .

"Colonel —— told us that he had been down the river this morning, and taken a look at the enemy's picket on the other side. And a short conversation took place between our picket and theirs as to the relative forces and skill, &c. This disgusted Colonel Andrews, who tersely expressed the opinion, ' When you see an enemy, *shoot him*.' The shooting of pickets seems to have been voted by respectable authorities to be barbarous. Why, I cannot see. It amounts to this : If you don't shoot, they can post their men securely where they please, and thus attain, without risk, the advantages of outlook and guard which they desire. If you do shoot, they can't choose their position, nor readily secure their advantages. This seems to me conclusive. But *humanity* is a very vague term when applied to war. And we handle these questions very differently from the way in which we shall if the war lasts. . . . . We are looking for a visit and review from McClellan. That will be an incident, and well worth while. The fact is, General Banks has been gradually stripped of his column. General Stone, a regular officer, has been given a separate division at Poolesville, and many of the best officers have been withdrawn from us. General Banks is left without a staff. Has lost much of his artillery and cavalry. . . . . If it were not that I believe that whatever is is right, and that docile submission is the best wisdom, I should regret belonging to this division, as it seems just outside of *the work*. But I am perfectly content with things as they are. When *the time comes* I hope it will find us ready.

" McClellan does n't believe in fresh-sprouted major-generals. That 's clear.

" I guess we shall see him in a day or two, and then perhaps he will open the path to glory to us. He keeps the gates. . . . .

" Coffee-roaster has arrived, and is merrily at work. This is a comfort. Tell father he is the regiment's friend, and I bless him. Colonel Andrews says that I love the Second Regiment first, and my country next. Perhaps it is true. At all events, I care only for its success at present. The call is beating for parade, and the sun is setting. Good by."

"PLEASANT HILL, September 16, 1861.

" I got a letter from you this morning dated Saturday, and full of regret that I don't get your letters. Why, *I do*. Only they come irregularly. Since the gap caused by your cold, I have had my regular journal to cheer and alleviate my life. So don't be discouraged, and above all, don't think that you are writing to the Dead Letter Office. You need not say so to ——, but it would overtax my magnanimity to write to any one in England our news. Their fog must envelop them. ' Can't understand affairs in this country,' is it ? They don't try. It is a plain case enough. The South has been organizing a villanous conspiracy for two years. It is suddenly born, full-armed, as Minerva. We are just organizing our crushing power to put it down. Let England wait patiently, and we will show them that we are a nation, after all. Till then it is idle to attempt to persuade their darkness into light.

" Our court-martial goes on bravely. We hope to get through to-morrow, or next day. But the cases accumulate so rapidly in proportion to our speed of trial, that we do not get the docket clear yet. I was prevented, yesterday, from going on a secret and confidential duty by the fact of the court-martial. If the telegram gives an account of any arrests in the vicinage of Frederick, you may know that nothing but the fact of my being actually engaged in another service prevented my taking charge of a part of that enterprise. I cannot properly speak more plainly of the matter, but events will probably illustrate my meaning, and you will see that we mean to have Maryland under our thumb completely. I confess that I should have enjoyed the duty that I was likely to engage in ; but a soldier has no choice. Every vigorous move of the Federal authority does good. We are in the midst of traitors, and indeed there is no loyalty except *conditional* loyalty in the Slave States. The Baltimore arrests are a capital move. Our life is excited by rumors of a movement by the enemy. I suppose the fact is thus. If the Rebels attack, they will cross between us and Harper's Ferry. Any movement by them will threaten our division, which I hope they mean to strengthen. The circumstance of McClellan's turning his attention to us indicates this as his opinion. I am slow to believe that they will cross anywhere. If they do, we shall have to be the first to oppose them.

" A direct attack on Washington cannot offer them any attraction. I can imagine how strong the pressure is upon them to make a move, and yet I think they have not the power to make it, with any chance of success. We shall see. The sun has come out glaringly, and now we have a threatening thunder-storm coming.

"The coffee-roaster is lovely, and wins golden opinions. At last, also, we have tea, and, indeed, we have waked up our commissary to something like activity. . . . .

"I am glad Charley is going to the war. It will make a man of him. Love to all."

"PLEASANT HILL, September 19, 1861.

"There is no reason why I should write you a letter, except that Captain Abbott is going to Washington and can carry it. With such a motive, let me say, then, that all goes well with us. That the weather is certainly the most trying in the world, — hot, bright, damp-aired, blazing days. Cold, heavy, foggy, shivering nights. If we don't have chills and fever it will be because we take good care of ourselves, which we try to do. The regiment is all right, and improves. My court-martial drags along a lazy and feeble existence. It does severe military justice upon offenders, and one duty is as well as another, though now that I am on my legs again, I should like to resume regular regimental life once more.

"Our officers, and indeed the regiment itself, are very impatient of the quietness of this life; but there is no other way. You would like to see the ovens that the men have built of mud and straw and stones, with the fires blazing from their wide mouths. You would like to see the rich brown coffee come out of my roaster. In short, you would like to see plenty reign as it now does, since the men have got nothing to think of but how to feed themselves. But if you thought again, how little we are doing to teach men to take care of themselves on the march and in active duty, you would see that we are still lame, and probably shall be for many months, until experience has rubbed its lessons into the memory and habits of both officers and men.

" I do not know why I write this, except that such problems and results are constantly occupying my mind.

" You see the exploit at Frederick did not amount to much. The government alarmed the Legislature by making arrests in Baltimore, and by sending up policemen, so that what promised to be quite a Cromwellian stroke was only the seizure of a few straggling legislators, who were frightened before they were hurt. Secessionism, however, is dead in Maryland.

" —— has returned, disappointed that he did not bag more game. I, who was going with him, as I mentioned in my last letter, on this secret expedition to Frederick, am consoled since the result was no larger."

" September 26.

" Cold weather seems to have set in upon us. I hope our Rebel brothers the other side of the Potomac are suffering the same cold nights that we have. Such weather will do more to drive them from Manassas than much artillery.

" There is a lull now. O for a tempest! I am glad Howard seems likely to accomplish his best object. Had he not better use a day in a visit to me on his way West ? "

" PLEASANT HILL, CAMP NEAR DARNESTOWN, September 27, 1861.

" A dark, dull, rainy day without, a calm, quiet, cosey tent within. At peace with ourselves, and *apparently* with all mankind. Such is this Friday morning.

" Yesterday * was a grand day for our army. The orders were issued for its observance by a grand division parade and service, and at eleven o'clock the brigades moved to Darnestown, and formed in a large field for the service. Our friend Mr. Quint gave the address on the occasion. I did not go myself, being detained by the combined influence of a headache and a court-martial. The headache and court-

* The President's Fast Day.

martial have both adjourned to-day, and I think they will not be called *together again*.

"It is said that the division looked very well indeed, and that the Massachusetts Second appeared bright beside the other regiments. This is probably exactly true. We have never been drawn up to face anything else except the Reverend Chaplain, but it is said that the column stood his fire like heroes!

"The impression seems to be gathering force that our term of inaction is drawing to a close. I only hope that when we go across the Potomac, it will be by a grand concerted movement, which will sweep everything before it clean. '*Nulla vestigia retrorsum.*' Not a single *about face* in the whole movement. I think we have reason to be glad that our regiment is getting through the chills-and-fever season so well. The place where we are seems quite healthy, and we suffer much less than our neighbors. By a new division of brigades, Colonel Gordon becomes the Senior Colonel of the Third Brigade, which makes him the Acting Brigadier. This puts Colonel Andrews in command of the regiment.

"I hope soon to hear of Howard's movements, and also of Charley's coming on to join William."

"PLEASANT HILL, Sunday Evening, September 29, 1861, Camp near Darnestown.

"An opportunity presents itself, this morning, to send a letter, and so I write, though I have only to tell you of continued quiet and content.

"And, indeed, it is no easy matter to preserve that happy mental and moral poise in the midst of our present dulness. I think, however, that the regiment was never in a state of more admirable efficiency than it is to-day, and this cheers and satisfies me when I keep it in mind. It is idle, however, to disguise the fact that it is a heaviness to the natural and unregenerate heart to see no prospect of achievement, no opportunity of action.

"I do not hesitate to say, that the winter *must* not set in without deeds that give a lustre to our flag. Volunteering, is it, that is wanted? Show the volunteer that he enters on the path of victory, and the crowd will be immense.

"We heard last night that the report was current that our division had cut the enemy to pieces, or was itself cut to pieces, or something of that sort. If so, and the report ran home by telegraph, you have had a very needless alarm. Never was repose so undisturbed as ours. If you hear such news of us, reflect only, 'It is too good to be true.'

"Your letter of the 23d is just received. I do hope Howard will find success in the Department of the West. There is certainly room for him there, and he has capacity for the place. I have just come in from Sunday-morning inspection. We need for the regiment flannel drawers and flannel shirts. Can you not get up a good package of them, and send them on by Captain Abbott? I see you speak of shirts for the soldiers."

CHAPTER VII.

LETTERS FROM WASHINGTON AND PLEASANT HILL CAMP, NEAR DARNESTOWN.

"WASHINGTON, WILLARD's HOTEL, October 2, 1861.

"THE date will explain the episode in my history, which has relieved the monotony for a day or two. I rode down here to accomplish some business for the regiment, and go back to-morrow morning. . . . . William and I rode over to the forts this morning. They seem strong and uninviting. The enemy, however, will never attempt them. The big battle is not to be fought behind the breastworks of either party. In my judgment, the next severe blow our cause gets will be in Kentucky, whither the theatre of war is moving."

"PLEASANT HILL, October 4, 1861,
Camp near Darnestown.

" I am sitting up to-night, as field-officer of the day, awaiting the hour of twelve, when I make my grand rounds. You may, perhaps, take a half-hour of my tediousness. I wrote a note from Washington. I found William had chosen me a horse, which, though peculiar to look at, was clever to go. In the cheerful phrase of the woman of Kannesch, ' *Il ne sait pas être joli mais il est bon.*' William told me he had written for Charley to come on to his regiment. I hope Charley has already started. He will learn more in a week in camp than in a month at home. Give him my love, and advice to push on for camp with a few good warm clothes and a copy of Tactics.

" Noboby seems even to guess at McClellan's plans. It is against my principle to believe in anything except human *fallibility*. Taking it for granted that McClellan belongs to

the human family, and that he has got an awful work before
him, and *not* seeing evidence of his doing anything in particular, I must say, my impatience gets the better of my hope
now and then.   For instance, when I see Meigs advertising
for gifts of blankets !   Why, are the whole government
asleep ?   If not, why have they not prepared for a *winter*
campaign ?   The roll of the seasons is a phenomenon of
peace.   That, surely, has not taken them by surprise.

"Again, the redundancy of brigadiers disgusts me.
What room have they left for distinction to those who win
glory in the fight.   These *antecedent* laurels cheapen the
very warmest incentive to a soldier's sacrifices.

But enough of croaking.   Though, before I leave it entirely, is not Fremont's fizzle in Missouri enough to make a
saint's amiability *feather*, at least, if not absolutely sour ?
When is the luck to turn ?   I am writing in the stillness of
an almost summer evening, and have got my head full, as
you see, of thoughts that are fruitless.

" I rode back to camp yesterday, and found no end of
work awaiting me.   Among other things, I am detailed on
a board of survey to estimate the damage done to private
property in our army's progress from Harper's Ferry to this
place.   As I am one of those who do not believe in paying
anything, I am, I suppose, a good officer for the post.   The
burdens of war ought, for the most part, to rest where they
fall.   At any rate, these lukewarm, disloyal citizens deserve
nothing but the strictest justice.

" Colonel Gordon is now in command of a brigade, and
he is acting the reformer and reviver with great spirit and
effect.   Indeed, it is cheerful to see the progress our regiments are making in discipline and drill.   The Second
Massachusetts is the example and standard for the others.
General Banks, standing on the hill near his head-quarters,
said to a gentleman in my hearing yesterday, ' That,' pointing to our camp, ' is the best and neatest camp on the con-
tinent.'   Words, I believe, of truth and soberness.   My

visit to Washington tended to satisfy me with our regiment. Good night. I must go out upon a tour of sentinel inspection, which will last till three o'clock in the morning. A soldier's life is always gay."

"PLEASANT HILL, October 7, 1861,
Camp near Darnestown.

" ' Turn out the Guard, Officer of the Day ! ' Such has been the salutation with which again I am greeted this Monday, on my rounds through the brigade. Our field-officers are off on leave of absence, and every third day brings this duty with it. Colonel Andrews has gone off to Washington to see about his appointment. We all hope most strongly that he will not accept it. Indeed, the fear that it was coming has quite depressed me of late. The Colonel is so decidedly the backbone of our enterprise, that I cannot bear to think of losing him. Though I suppose there are some who would have the charity to suppose that I would welcome promotion. But I think that no one ever received an appointment with less of gratified ambition, or will take a promotion, if come it must, with less exultation. The fact is, I foresaw trial and responsibility, and did not crave it. I also deprecated *unwon* laurels and insignificant titles. Something to *work up to* is not just the thing. Though, after all, if one could succeed in really growing to the position, he might well be proud.

" It is eleven o'clock, — a damp, rainy, cheerless night. I shall soon go forth on my rounds. The season and surroundings are favorable to maudlin reflections, and I fear I am falling into them. The next letter I write I will write in glad sunshine and broad day ; not in the flickering twilight of a wind-troubled candle ; but to-night you must take me after sundown. Still, I have cheerful topics. The enemy must soon move or we must, and so the briskness of enterprise is near. Bull Run has given McClellan the liberty to wait as long as he pleases without interference, but he cannot mean to lose October. As for Fremont, I wish him well for Howard's sake ; but the man lacks the one thing we want now, — success. Good reasons for failure are not popular, though they may be undeniable. . . . .

As to stockings for the regiment, we are not barefoot, but stockings do wear out easily, and a regiment uses a great many, and the government supplies slowly. Do not, however, give yourself up to shirts or stockings.

"Here it comes, raw and gusty, and pouring torrents. Well, let it rain. I think I must give up my grand rounds though, and, as it is damp and cold, I will bid you a cheerful good night, and hope for a bright morning.

"It is not so bright a morning after all, but I must be off to Hyattstown, to act on a board of survey; and so good by."

"PLEASANT HILL, MARYLAND, October 9, 1861.

"MY DEAR FATHER, — Your prompt and energetic kindness is truly splendid. I think one thousand pairs of stockings are enough for the present. What we may need, or the government may be able to supply before spring, we cannot now say. Mrs. George Ticknor writes to Colonel Gordon that a number of ladies in Boston desire to form an association to supply the Second Regiment with whatever they need. She will aid you in the stocking direction. The truth is, the government ought to supply every real want of the soldier. I hope it will soon do so. If it fail to do so, we must appeal to benevolence now and then. The principle is a bad one, however, and I do not wish to extend it an inch beyond the immediate necessity.

"One bad effect of appealing to benevolence is, that men will not be as careful of things *given to* them as things *paid for* by them.

"Some frost-nipping compulsion is important to keep them economical and careful.

"I am quite anxious to hear about Howard. I do not so much care whether Fremont is a good or bad general; if Howard gets a footing there he will do well, and will hang on."

"Pleasant Hill, Camp near Darnestown,
October 9, 1861.

" Dear Mother, — I wish I could give you a vivid picture of our excursion the other day on the board of survey. Lieutenant-Colonel Batchelder, of the Thirteenth Massachusetts, and myself went off to Hyattstown to estimate damages done by the army there. The Quartermaster Department gave us a light wagon. We put off our care as we crossed the lines, and left the sentinels behind. We drove to Hyattstown through a pleasant country. The heavy rain had swelled the runs or brooks which cross the road, and in our passage over the last one we broke down. So we left our wagon and took another. On our way back we met the —— regiment, Colonel ———. The Colonel is a lawyer and member of Congress, *not* a soldier. We saw the beauties of moral-suasive discipline. His men on the march during the storm of the night previous had broken their lines. The roadside taverns had sold them whiskey. The whole regiment was *drunk*. A perfect Pandemonium was the scene they presented. We did what we could to help him, but when one soldier, in quarrelsome or pleasant vein, shot another through the body, and a third broke the head of a fourth with the butt of his musket, we thought discretion the better part of valor, and did not wait to see what the fifth would do. General Banks has ordered the regiment back, I believe, and is going to send off another with more discipline and less whiskey. The regiment had been detailed to go to Williamsport on special duty.

" We drove on, and coming near the plantation of Mr. Desellum, whom you recollect I have spoken of, we stopped to dinner. His sister, she who sent me the big bouquet, was at home. She welcomed us cordially, and we were surrounded speedily by a dozen little darkies all of a size. The maiden lady showed us her flower-garden, and her *family* of negroes, and her spinning-room, in which three spinning-wheels were busily twisting the yarn which she was to weave

8

into clothes for her negroes. She showed us also her old family linen, woven by her mother ; and, in fact, introduced us to all the details of farm life. Then she took us into the best room, whose oak floor shone with scrubbing, and whose bright wood-fire felt good. There we had a dinner, and she talked patriotism ; the Colonel and myself listening, and concluding, as we drove away, that we had had an adventure, and found *material* loyalty in Maryland.

" A drive through the wood, across a swollen stream whose bridge had gone, and whose depth made the crossing an experiment of very doubtful success, brought us to camp just as the new moon and evening star had come brightly out of the glow of twilight. There we found Colonel Andrews returned from Washington, having declined the appointment of Adjutant-General, to the great joy of all the regiment.

" We are rigging up very clever fireplaces in our tents, and preparing for winter ; — learning how to be comfortable, which is, after all, the great problem with which my mind engages itself in this *military* campaigning. It is half the battle. I hope we shall have the other half soon."

" PLEASANT HILL, MARYLAND, October 11, 1861.

" DEAR FATHER, — I receive, this evening, your pleasant letter of Tuesday. Also a very kind one from D——. Your compliment from the general commanding is certainly pleasing. But do not suppose that it indicates any success of mine. Remember that the path is a new one, and be content that I shall learn its windings by and by.

Again, D——'s letter indicates the idea that I am likely to be in command here. You will have learned that Colonels Gordon and Andrews are both still with the regiment. This is as it should be, and as I most strongly desire ; and I confidently trust it is as it will be for time to come (I have no wish to emulate the inexperience of colonels whom I see about me). And the *team* as it now is is not too strong for the load. I cannot help feeling proud of the regiment. It never appeared so well as now. But I have no *personal* ambition about it, only an intense longing for its success as a whole. I tell you, good regiments are *great creations*, and I wish we had three hundred of them, as we might have had if everybody had put in briskly at once, as some of us did; but I am overworking my text, as I am apt to do when I get on the regiment.

"You have succeeded in the stockings, I see. Well! they will be a great thing for us, only you must let my patriotism feel *vexed* that private aid should be necessary at this point of time. . . .

"We are building an elaborate stable, thatched with straw, for our horses, and the officers are fitting up tents with cellars and fireplaces, as if we were established for the winter. I think, however, that we shall hardly get ' *to rights*,' as they say, when the order to move will come. Dr. ———, General McClellan's Medical Director, said to me last week, ' I can't tell where you 're to be. What General McClellan knows, no one else knows.' It speaks well for the tonic effect of Bull Run, that the press and people lie down quietly under the thumb of McClellan, and bide his time."

"PLEASANT HILL, MARYLAND, October 13, 1861.

"DEAR MOTHER, — Opie mixed his colors ' with brains, sir,' and with brains we have just done a clever thing near Hatteras. Let us keep the brains at work. As for our own thoughts, they were excited this morning by an order for ' two days' cooked rations in the haversack, and to hold ourselves in readiness to march.' So we hold ourselves serenely and with content, but I do not fear any immediate action. At last, however, with all this cry, the wolf must come.

"The paymaster has been here, and went off yesterday, leaving Uncle Sam's paper money behind, instead of gold as before. . . . . .

" It is a bright and gusty day, and our hillside exposure gives us the full front to the wind. I sit in my tent, this Sunday morning, and keep warm over a pan of coals.

" I was amused, the other day, at an incident of my drive with Colonel Batchelder. We came across a bright-eyed little boy on the road, his pockets bursting with chestnuts, and stopped and took him in, levying on his chestnuts. I asked him if he was for the Union. ' Yes,' said he, with a bright twinkle, ' *that* I am.' ' Why ? ' said I. ' O,' said he, ' that old flag has stood too long to be pulled down now.' I thought that, for a Maryland boy's reason, was a pretty good one. . . . . I am quite anxious to get my buffalo-robe, which Spiegel was obliged to leave in Washington, as the coach would not bring it. The weather is growing colder every day, as it seems. But then we have the cheerful confidence that we are serving our country, you know, which takes the *chill off*."

"PLEASANT HILL, October 14, 1861.

" I was looking, last evening, at the bright gold of the western sky, and the frosty silver of the evening star, and was marking the cold glitter of the moonlight, when Mr. Spiegel appeared with my buffalo-robe in great glee. It was an opportune visitor, and I must not let our quartermaster go to Washington without a line of acknowledgment from me. Tell father that size is anything but an objection. I cannot hope to grow to it, but I will bring it to my model, and compose myself as comfortably as a warrior in his martial cloak. It will be glorious o' nights when we bivouac by camp-fires, as I hope we must soon.

" We have had a glorious October day. Drill in the morning, drill in the afternoon. Questions of suttler's prices, of commissary's authority to settle rations, of quartermaster's allowance of stationery, &c., &c., &c., — the family jars of our little family. I wish I could write you a letter about ' something *in particular*,' but just now there

is ' nothing special.' I think the order to cook rations and
hold ourselves in readiness to march came direct from
McClellan, and was a precaution against an expected attack
or resistance by the enemy opposite Washington.   If so,
that danger has blown over, and we may lie still for another
week.   They have, however, in this division, an organized
secrecy, which covers everything with a drop-curtain.   I received yesterday a letter from Judge Abbott, congratulatory
on my expected promotion.   I hope your ambition did not
wilt when you heard that things stood still.   It is much
better for the regiment that they should, and far better for
me, and I experienced a rebound from my quite decided
depression when I found that the danger of losing our
colonels was over."

"PLEASANT HILL, October 16, 1861.

"I always have an impulse to write when I get a letter,
and as yours of last Friday gladdened me this evening,
I am pen in hand again, though without a story.   No!
I have one, now I think of it.   My maiden lady friend of
the spinning-wheel and flower-garden came to see me to-day.
She and her brother in their best.   I gave them my hospi-
talities, showed them the camp, &c., and made them very
content.   They are full of patriotic ardor.   Its form of
expression is various.   The good lady brought me to-day as
a present, first, two quarts of milk ; second, a pair of roast
chickens ; third, two loaves of bread ; fourth, some preserved
cherries ; fifth, two apple-pies ; sixth, an immense bouquet
of roses and dahlias ; seventh, a bottle of balsam for cuts
and bruises, and ' *other wounds*,' — whether of the heart or
not the stanch maiden did not explain ; eighth, some butter.
I am persuaded that she brought me everything that occurred to her mind as possible.

"The Colonel had quite a joke over my trophies ; but I
noticed he ate the pies, and liked the cherries.   It is refreshing to see two honest country folk loving their flag with
such naïve simplicity.

"They wish 'they could only do something,' and just now I seem to be the object of their baffled patriotism. There is no evading the constancy of their attachment; their love of country will express itself on me. The bouquet, which is half as tall as I am, fills my tent with its fragrance while I write, and it is of an obtrusive and ardent gayety, which seems almost out of season among the falling leaves of October.

"Though I date this letter to-day, it was begun last night, and will progress slowly, I am afraid, amid the interruptions of this morning. One does not see exactly what has been accomplished by living a day in this camp; but he finds, as the hours pass, that something claims attention pretty much all the time.

"I am just now going out to skirmish-drill with the bugle. It is a part of the military duty which I fully understand, and, accordingly, I like to perform it. I hope it won't be long before I can say the same of all parts. . . . .

"Tell Lillie and Charlie P. that I am glad they are knitting for their country, and I should like to come over and take tea some evening."

"WILLARD'S HOTEL, October 21, 1861,
Monday Morning.

"Your letter which spoke of William's bilious fever alarmed my fraternity to such a degree that I got into the saddle Saturday afternoon and found myself here at evening. Yesterday morning I drove out to. camp, and found Colonel Dwight prancing about his camp on horseback, and his regiment at their morning inspection. I took a good look at the Colonel's regiment, and was delighted with it. The Colonel's fever had left him. I had a pleasant day yesterday visiting the fortifications near William's camp. I go back to Darnestown immediately.

"This country needs a government. Every visit I make to Washington makes me feel hopeless. Nothing is done. Not half enough doing."

"PLEASANT HILL, October 21, 1861, 7 o'clock, P. M.
Camp near Darnestown, for the last time!

" I have just time to write you a word.   I galloped up
here this morning in three hours.   Then had a brisk battalion drill.   Then — came the news that Stone was crossing
the river at Edward's Ferry.   We were ordered to report to
General Hamilton, changing our brigade again.   That led
me off to the General's head-quarters, whence I have just
returned with marching orders.   We go to Poolesville to-
night, and cross, I suppose, to-morrow.   I am no believer
in a fight ; but movement is life, and it seems quite like old
times to be in the saddle all day, and then all night again.

" My little gray mustang, which William got for me, took
me to Washington briskly.   I came back at a loose, free
gallop.   The whole division is now on the move.   The men
seem happy as larks.   I am in the midst of questioning and
orders and bustle.   I cannot write any more.   The Colonel
calls for me.   I shall give this letter to Mr. Mudge, who
will tell you all about us.   The Adjutant wants to pack his
pen and ink, with which I am writing.   Mine is all packed.
Good by.   Love to all."

CHAPTER VIII.

"CAMP NEAR CONRAD'S FERRY, October 24, 1861,
Thursday Morning.

"THE violation of every rule and maxim of military law, the exaction of the extreme penalty therefor. Such is the summing up of the massacre near Leesburg. Does it awaken you to the fact that politicians are not generals ?

"But how shall I tell you the story of these trying days ? I wrote a hasty word as our line was forming on Monday night. We marched gayly and willingly off in the moonlight towards Poolesville, at nine o'clock in the evening. We supposed we were to cross at Edward's Ferry, to aid in a victorious advance upon Leesburg. The men marched splendidly. At Poolesville we first met the faint shadows of the coming gloom, — a few stragglers of the Fifteenth Massachusetts. 'Our companies are all cut to pieces. Our captain is shot; our lieutenant-colonel has lost his leg; we have all been cut up,' &c. On we went, more earnestly, and took the road to Conrad's Ferry. Then we began to meet the flying and scattered soldiers. One with only an overcoat, another with only a blanket, another with even less. They all told one story, of flight and death and despair. Still we pressed on. Our men were eager to reach the Ferry. We got there at about three o'clock in the morning. Eighteen miles in between six and seven hours. Then came the rain, and then came the order to stay where we were. The morning broke, — a wild, gusty, rainy morning, — upon our shelterless and weary regiment. The only house near where the regiment stopped was filled with the wounded. As soon as I could get away, I galloped down to the place of crossing. I saw them letting down a wounded man on a stretcher into the canal-boat. It was Captain John Putnam, a clever fellow, of the New England Guards. I turned and went down to the river, meeting on my way a dead one, and, as I passed, one of the soldiers who carried him turned up the face, and said, ' Yes, this is one of the Tammany boys.' I went to the river, to a flat-boat full of wounded ; found Dr. Hayward, of the Twentieth. He said that Lieutenant Putnam, Mrs. Sam Putnam's son, was in the boat, badly wounded. I spoke to him ; he was bright, but evidently sinking. I asked him if I could do anything for him, telling him who I was. He said, eagerly, ' I should like to see Lieutenant Higginson.' I said I would bring him. Then I asked about Caspar Crowninshield, Abbott, Lowell, Holmes. Caspar, they thought, was wounded. Abbott, safe. Lowell and Holmes, both wounded. A little while after Caspar turned up. He was in the primitive costume of his overcoat and drawers, but full of cheery pluck, calm, clear, and a young hero in bearing and aspect. He gave a clear account of himself. I was compelled to go back to the regiment. I sent Lieutenant Higginson down, and did what I could for the men.

" I had been in the saddle about twenty-four hours, and without sleep, and I got into the house among the wounded, and fell asleep on a camp-stool. Soon we were off again to put the regiment in camp under cover of a wood. Just as we got in camp, General Hamilton ordered five companies to go on picket along the river-bank. . . . . The next morning at daylight, still raining, we were ordered to strike our tents, and move back out of cannon range from the river. We came to our present camp. General Hamilton then ordered me to take three companies to the river, and post pickets and keep a lookout. I started. At about three o'clock I returned to report to the General the position of things on the river, when I found General Banks and General McClellan in his quarters. I enjoyed hearing McClellan talk for half an hour. One good remark of his I recall. 'Well,' said he, 'so far we seem to have applied a new maxim of war, always to meet the enemy with an inferior force at the point of attack.' General Hamilton then ordered me to return, and cross to the island at night, and remove some stores which had been left there. I started off again. I got my preparations all made, when an order came, at about eight, P. M., 'Take your companies at once to Edward's Ferry to cross. The enemy is in force there.' I drew in my pickets, and got ready to move promptly, when I was met, just as I started, by a mounted orderly, with a note addressed to the officer in command moving towards Edward's Ferry. 'Return to your camp, and await further orders.' I turned back. The orderly had orders for General Hamilton, and did not know how to find him. It was dark, and I took my horse and rode with him to General Hamilton's quarters. Our regiment had started for Edward's Ferry before the orderly arrived. When they got there, they were ordered to return, and did so. This made the third night of fatiguing marching or guard duty, and to-day they are just done up. My three companies got their rest, however, at the river. It turns out that we were to support Stone, but McClellan suddenly determined to withdraw him, and so the countermanding order. To-night I go back to the river, and go over to the island to remove the government stores. That will give me a lively night again. I ought to be very tired, but excitement makes me feel the fatigue very little. . . . . .

" Providence seems to have watched over the Massachusetts Second, does it not ? It has saved us from Bull Run, and now, from a worse blunder. For what has it reserved us ? I hope and pray for the guidance of a good general, unhampered. I must go back to the Ferry. Good by. Love to all. God bless you."

" I shall try to send you some pictures, though I am too tired to-night for anything but sleep.

" Scene, our old camp ; time, evening. The regiment just getting into marching array under crisp starlight. The men gay with singing and laughter. The camp one huge bonfire of old bedding and tent-floors. Every man in fine marching condition. Again : Scene, the bank of the canal at Conrad's Ferry ; time, eight o'clock the next morning. The regiment huddled in dripping groups, under a driving rain. The men tired and silent. Ambulances of wounded men passing by. Blankets swung on poles, covering the bodies of the slain, and borne along with that heavy, dull tread which betokens the presence of death. Jaded stragglers from the river hurrying back, cold and half naked, to their camps ; the interchange of greetings and tidings. The Colonel and other field-officers huddled under an apple-tree, breakfasting upon a hard-boiled egg, and shivering over a feeble fire, questioning stragglers about the fight. Up comes a Yankee-looking fellow, clad *only* in an overcoat, with that peculiar hunched-up movement which indicates shuddering cold. Dialogue between Colonel Gordon and Yankee. *Colonel G.* Where do you come from ? *Y.* The river. *G.* What regiment? *Y.* Massachusetts Fifteenth. *G.* Did you fight? *Y.* Wal, I guess we did some. *G.* How many times did you fire ? *Y.* Thirty or forty. *G.* What did you do during the day ? *Y.* Wal, at first we was skirmishing along, and I got behind a tree, and I was doing first rate. I come out once, but I see a feller sightin' at me, and so I got in again suddin. Then, arter a while, the cavalry came down on us. I see there wa'n't much chance, and so I just dropped into a hole there was there, and stayed still. Pretty soon we retreated towards the river. We got together there, and formed a kind of a line, and then the fitin' really began. Some fellers came

out near us, and says they, ' We 're Colonel Baker's men.'
' Guess not,' says I. ' Yes we are,' says they. ' I know
better,' says I. ' Let 'er rip, boys ! ' and we fired on 'em.
But 't wa'n't no kind o' use. Baker got killed, and we
could n't see the enemy, and they raked us like death. I
finally come down the bank with the rest on 'em. I see
Colonel Devens there. Says I, ' Colonel, wot 's to be done
now ? ' ' Boys,' says he, ' you must take care of yourselves.'
' All right, Colonel,' says I. And the way my 'couterments
come off was a caution. I swum the river. But I tell you
there was a sight on 'em did n't get across.' *G.* Do you
want to go back again ? *Y.* Wal, not till I get *rested.* *G.*
You 're cold, ain't you ? *Y.* I tell you, I just am. *G.*
Don't you want some whiskey ? *Y.* Don't I ? (Yankee takes
a pull at the Colonel's flask, and expresses himself only
by a long, silent, intensely meaning wink.) Yankee then
turns and sees a shivering figure approaching. ' Hullo,
John ; I never expected to see you again. Wal, I guess
we 'd better go to camp,' and off he moves. The drollery
of the scene I cannot give. I just indicate an outline of
the cool, circumstantial narratives that every other man
would give you. We found none so amusing as this, which
relieved our tedious breakfast. But the men showed no
fear, and, only by an occasional allusion, any sense of the
terrors through which some of them had passed. Their
only idea seemed to be, If there only had been more of us,
how we would have licked 'em ! All accounts agree that
the two Massachusetts regiments fought splendidly, as far
as individual daring and coolness go.

"I sent you off a letter yesterday ; for I must continue
my story without a formal introduction of each picture. I
mailed the letter with the ink wet upon it, and went off on
my duty to the river, to take charge of my picket-line along
the canal. But as tattoo is now beating, and as I put on
my clothes in Washington on Monday morning and have not
yet taken them off this Friday night, I will tell the rest of
my story to-morrow."

"CAMP NEAR THE LITTLE SENECA, Saturday Night,
9 o'clock, P. M.

" He who predicts the morrow in this life has his labor
for his pains. The morrow takes care of itself. Here we
are, and tattoo is just beating again, and we are twelve
miles from our last night's camp. I will go on with my
story. When I got to the river, I began to carry out my
instructions from General Hamilton. They were, to visit
Harrison's Island, which was abandoned by our troops on
Tuesday night, and bring off some government stores. I
found that, owing to the stupidity of the officer whom I had
left in charge at the point of crossing opposite the island,
one of the ropes had been cut, and there was only one rope
left stretching across the river on which I could ferry my
men over. I got my men ready, took the two leaky flat-
boats and moored them well, and waited for darkness. The
night was very cold. In its cover we started with one boat,
leaving directions for the other to follow after we got across
and got things secure. We pulled across silently on the
rope which came up out of the water, and sagged a good
deal with the stream. Just as we got within the shadows
of the opposite bank, the Sergeant whispered, ' Hold on,
the rope has broken.' The men held on by the end, and,
sure enough, it had parted, and we were swinging off down
stream away from the island. There was something laugh-
able in the mischance. We had nothing for it but to return,
which we did, coiling the rope in our boat as we went back.
So ended all visits, for the present, by our troops to Harrison's Island. I was kept on the alert all night by firing up
the river, and got no sleep of any consequence, — sending
and receiving despatches from General Hamilton. At
light, — a bright, golden, October morning, ice an inch
thick, — I visited all the outlooks, and then went back to
camp to report to General Hamilton. After breakfast, on
Friday morning, the Colonel suggested that we should ride
to the Fifteenth and Twentieth.

"I went to see Lieutenant-Colonel Ward. He has lost his leg, below the knee. Said he, ' Major, I am not as I was in Washington.' ' No,' said I, ' you should have accepted my invitation, and ridden up with me on Monday.' We were together last Saturday night at Willard's, and I begged him to wait till Monday and go up with me. He said, ' No, I shall be needed in camp.'

"We then went to the Twentieth. I wish all the friends of the young wounded officers could see them; it was a pleasant picture. In the first tent I visited I found Captain John Putnam. He was bright and in good spirits. I shook his left hand. His right arm is gone at the shoulder. Turning to the other bed, I met the pleasant smile of Lieutenant Holmes. He greeted me as cordially as if we had met at home, talked gayly of soon getting well again. His wound is through the body sideways, just missing the lungs, and following the ribs. Young Lieutenant Lowell, too, in the next tent, was making light of *only a flesh wound* in the thigh. Caspar Crowninshield, whom I found helping Colonel Palfrey, and acting as Major, was as calm as possible. He gave a very good account of the fight; he evidently did gloriously. Only once, when he spoke of the terrible scene in the river after they got in swimming, did he seem to think of the horrors of the scene. Young Harry Sturgis was also bright. He said that Lieutenant Putnam, who was wounded in the bowels, wished to be left, as he said, to die on the field. ' That is the fit place to die,' he said. But Harry took him in his arms and brought him to the river. Young Abbott looked well. Lieutenant Perry is a prisoner, but I think safe, without doubt. So of Major Revere and Colonel Lee. When we got back to camp I got a report from the river that the enemy were quite numerous on the opposite bluff, and that they were putting a field-piece in position there. Though I did not credit it, down I went, and spent the afternoon. We found they had occupied, or rather visited, the island. My glass let me see them plainly in many places, and in others they were within familiar conversational distance. I found they were re-establishing their pickets strongly. I left Captain Curtis in charge, and returned to camp. I found that I was detailed as one of the Examining Board for our division. The Board consists of General Hamilton, Colonel Halleck, and myself. We are to examine the officers as to their qualifications, &c. I cannot approve of my appointment, but as it emanates from the Head-quarters of the Army of the Potomac, I suppose it is all right.

"This morning I was sitting at breakfast, when up rode General Hamilton's aide. 'Major,' said he, 'General Hamilton says you will move your detachment at once.' 'What detachment?' said I. 'The advanced guard and pioneers,' said he. 'I have no orders,' said I, 'and no guard.' 'There is some mistake,' said he. Then up came a lieutenant from an Indiana regiment. 'I am ordered to report to you,' said he. 'Very well,' said I. I went over to General Hamilton, and found the whole brigade was under marching orders. By inadvertence we had not received ours. All the rest of the brigade were ready to start, and our tents were all standing. I went off at once, with my pioneers, and put the road in condition. Here we are in camp. Our regiment was, of course, the last to start. All the others were in motion before our tents were struck. But our regiment passed all the others on the way, and was first in camp to-night. *We can march.* Our night march to the Ferry was perfect. Life is brisk with us, you see.

"I have father's letter about the stockings. After our wretched wet marching, the stockings will be a mercy, I think. Please to tell Mrs. Ticknor that towels, one apiece, will be good for us. I did not think of mentioning them, as, in the seriousness of actual business, the luxuries are lost sight of. The regiment will move to-morrow to the neighborhood of the mouth of the Muddy Branch, near the Potomac. There we are to go into camp for the present.

So ends our week's work. Hard and busy, but not without its use. This morning, as our company on picket-duty came along the canal to rejoin the regiment, the Rebels from the island fired on them several times. They were also busy diving and fishing for the guns which the men threw away in their flight.

The rascals are very saucy over their victory. I think they have the advantage of our men in the chaffing which goes on across the river, though one of our corporals told the sentry opposite him, who was washing his feet, to take his feet out of his (the corporal's) river, or he would shoot him.

"Reveillé will sound at five o'clock to-morrow morning, and at seven we shall be off and away. We are within three miles of our old camp. To-morrow we go somewhat nearer Washington.

"No paper that I have yet seen gives any idea of the fight, as I glean it from various sources. No generalship seems to have been used in the matter. Not a military glance seems to have swept the field, not a military suggestion seems to have planned the enterprise. The men crossed at the worst point of the river; they had only two small scows to cross with; retreat was impossible.

"If you could see how completely this rocky, wooded bluff (of which I have attempted a sketch on the opposite page) overhangs the island and the opposite shore, you would realize what a mad place it was to cross at. If you could see the scows, you would see what means they had to cross.

"Again, the disposition of the troops was wretched. The formation close upon the bluff, and with their rear right upon the river, gave no chance to repair mischance. Also, the thick wood which surrounded them gave the enemy every opportunity to outflank them. If they had meant to fight, they should have rested one of their flanks on the river, and have protected the other by artillery. This would have made their line perpendicular to the river. Their retreat might have been up or down stream. But they could, probably, have prolonged the fight till night, and then run for luck in crossing. Such a position would have been stronger, and retreat would have been less fatal. But they thought apparently the two scows their line of retreat, while, in fact, they were as bad as nothing. There does not seem to be a single redeeming feature in the whole business. They went on a fool's errand, — went without means, and then persisted in their folly after it became clear. . . . .

" It is useless to talk of what *might* have been ; but if you had walked, as I have done, for the past three days on that canal tow-path opposite the bluff on whose crest our brave men formed for a desperate struggle, you could not help discoursing upon the military grotesqueness of the whole action. I have said there is no redeeming feature in the whole case. I am wrong. The determined courage of Massachusetts officers and soldiers is a cheering gleam through the gloom. But Heaven save us from any more such tests of valor. ' The officer who brought you here ought to be hung,' said a Rebel officer to the burial party who went over with a flag of truce on Tuesday to bury our dead. I am afraid that is too true.

" The Rebels, on the other hand, managed finely. They seem to have waited till they had caught a goodly number, and then to have sprung their trap ruthlessly. McClellan's first question was, ' How did our men fight ? ' The answer is plain, — like heroes. If the men were properly officered, they would be the best troops in the world. . . . .

" The blunder and its consequences are of *the past*. The future must be freighted with better hopes. As far as our military position is concerned, except for the loss of life, and perhaps of time, all is as well to-day as a week ago.

" We cannot be thankful enough for the mercy which spared our regiment from having any other share in the movement than to aid in repairing its disasters. I shall not

9

soon forget that night's march, and that gloomy morning. God bless you all at home! We can trust, and must trust, in that Power which will overrule everything for good. Good night. I must get some sleep for to-morrow's march."

CHAPTER IX.

LETTERS FROM CAMP NEAR SENECA.

"CAMP NEAR SENECA, October 28, 1861.

"I WISH you could have looked in on our camp this morning. The stockings came last night. They were spread out under an oak-tree, and the companies were well supplied. The men were radiant over them. The memory of our cold, wet week's marching and counter-marching was still fresh. The chill of the October morning had not yet yielded to the glowing brightness of the sun. The sight of the stockings made us feel warm again. The young officers paid particular attention to the bundle from Professor Agassiz's school. . . . .

"I had no idea that the stockings were so much needed, but the fact is, they are so much better than the ones given by government, that the men are eager for them. The captains all say that there could not be a better gift. We shall await the coming of the shirts and drawers with pleasure. . . . . Collect and keep stockings, if you are willing to do so, against another time of need. Convey, in some form, to the donors, our high appreciation of their kindness. It is *the thing*. And it makes men feel a tingle of grateful pleasure out here, to think they are remembered and cared for at home. Apart, even, from their usefulness, the stockings bring a warming and cheering sensation to the men. That is the *moral aspect* of the present.

"We made a brisk little march yesterday morning, and at noon were in camp again, on a charming spot, sheltered by a fine wood, within the edge of which are the field and staff tents, while the regiment extends out into the open field. We are within a mile of the Potomac. The enemy's pickets ornament the opposite shore, while we adorn this.   The point is near the mouth of the Seneca, and about opposite Drainsville.

" After a week's work, we are again, on this Monday, apparently as far from any immediate active duty as we were a week ago.   I do not know that I can bring myself now to be so impatient of delay as I have been.   It was the itch for a poor kind of distinction that led to the massacre at Leesburg.

" We find, on our return to our old division, that the regiment is reassigned to General Abercrombie's brigade ; and to-morrow we are to move into our new position.   The General places us first in his, the First Brigade.   That gives us the post of honor, — the *right* of the whole of General Banks's Division.

" I have not yet commenced my duties as Examiner of Officers.   We have been so locomotory lately that there has been no time for anything.   A pretty low standard of qualifications will have to be adopted, or we shall have to exclude a great many of the present officers.

" William, I suppose, is down on his old ground again, opposite Aquia Creek, trying to reopen, or keep open, the Potomac.   Well, I wish him luck ; but the leaves of autumn are falling, and we seem to be just about in the same position that we were when I saw the buds first bursting last spring in Annapolis."

"CAMP NEAR SENECA, October 30, 1861.

" We still keep the camping-ground in which we were when I last wrote, and we are enjoying the brightest of October days.   There is a general impression that winter-quarters, or some such depressing movement, is to be the fate of the grand Army of the Potomac. . . . .

" Yesterday Captain Cary took a letter from Colonel Gordon to General Evans in command at Leesburg.   The Colonel was a West Point friend of General Evans, and wrote to ask the fate of our friends of the Twentieth.   Captain Cary took a white handkerchief on a stick as his flag of truce, and crossed the river in a skiff. He went up and down the river, but could find no picket anywhere. After wandering about with his flag for three hours, he came to a farm-house. The man was a Union man. He said he had been twice arrested, and refused to take the letter. He told Cary that he had seen no soldiers for a week, and thought there were none nearer than Leesburg, but he advised the Captain to go back, as he said his flag of truce would not be respected. Cary made up his mind to return. I confess I was very glad indeed to see him back, and considered the expedition a very risky one. . . . .

" We have a beautiful camping-ground here, and are getting it into perfect order for muster to-morrow. The last day of October is our semi-monthly muster and inspection."

" MUDDY BRANCH CAMP, CAMP NEAR SENECA,
November 1, 1861.

" You have your choice of dates, for I think our camp lies between the two, and General Banks uses the former designation for the division, while General Abercrombie uses the latter for his brigade. I hope that we shall cease to have occasion to use either date before the traditional Thanksgiving day overtakes us. Unless we do, it will find us in the wilderness, and in fasting and humiliation. I look to see ripeness in these late autumn days, and I hope that, without shaking the tree of Providence, some full-grown events may gravitate rapidly to their ripe result, even in this ill-omened month of November. Your letter of Monday takes too dark a view of events. I can well understand that, at your distance, our hardships and trials look harder than they seem to us. I do not, in the least, despair of happy results, and the more I think of the Edward's Ferry, or *loon-roads*, or Conrad's Ferry mishap (or, to describe it alliteratively, the blunder of Ball's Bluff), the more clearly it seems to me to be an insignificant blunder on the outskirts of the main enterprise, which, except for the unhappy loss of life, and except as a test of military capacity, is now a part of the past, without any grave consequences to follow. I was well aware that, in writing my first letter, I should give you the vivid, and possibly the exaggerated impressions of the sudden and immediate presence of the disaster. The wreck of a small yacht is quite as serious to the crew as the foundering of the Great Eastern.   But the underwriters class the events very differently.   And in our national account of loss, Ball's Bluff will take a modest rank.

"Should the naval expedition prove a success, and should the Army of the Potomac strike its blow at the opportune moment, we can forget our mishap.   You see I am chasing again the butterflies of hope.   Without them life would n't be worth the living.

"Tell father I have read the pleasant sketch of Soldiers and their Science, which he sent me.   I wish he would get me the book itself, through Little and Brown, and also 'Crawford's Standing Orders,' and send them on by express. This coming winter has got to be used in some way, and I expect to dedicate a great part of it to catching up with some of these West Point officers in the commonplaces of military science.

"We are quietly in camp again, and are arranging our camping-ground with as much neatness and care as if it were to be permanent.   The ovens have been built, the ground cleared, the stumps uprooted, and now the air is full of the noise of a large party of men who are clearing off the rubbish out of the woods about our tents.   By Sunday morning our camp will look as clean and regular and military as if we had been here a month.   Yesterday was the grand inspection and muster for payment.   I wish you could have seen the regiment drawn up with its full equipment, — knapsacks, haversacks, and all.   It was a fine sight.   By the way, why does not father snatch a day or two, and come out to see us?   We are only a pleasant morning's drive from Washington, and I think he would enjoy seeing us as we are in our present case.   D——— would enjoy the trip, too, and they might also pay a visit to William down at Port Tobacco, or wherever he may now be.   I throw out this suggestion.

" To-day I am brigade officer of the day, and I have been in the saddle this morning three or four hours visiting the camps and the pickets on the river.   It has been a beautiful morning of the Indian summer, and I have enjoyed it greatly.   Colonel Andrews took cold and got over-fatigued during our last week's work, and he is quite down with a feverish attack.   Yesterday I found a nice bed for him in a neighboring house, and this morning he is quite comfortable. We miss him very much in camp, and I hope he'll be up in a day or two. . . . .

" ' Happy that nation whose annals are tiresome,' writes some one.   ' Lucky that major whose letters are dull,' think you, I suppose.   That good fortune, if it be one, I now enjoy.

" I have an opportunity to send this letter, and so off it goes, with much love to all at home, in the hope that you will keep your spirits up."

" CAMP NEAR SENECA, Sunday Evening,
November 3, 1861.

" If you had waked night before last in our camp, you would have thought yourself in a storm at sea, with a very heavy northeaster blowing.   By the rattle, and creak, and strain, and whistle of the canvas and gale, you would have believed that the good ship was scudding before the blast.   If you had shivered outside to attempt to secure your fluttering tent, you might, by a slight effort of the imagination, have thought yourself overboard.   When the morning broke, after a sleepless and dreamy night, expectant of disaster, you would have seen, here and there, a tent prostrate, and the wind and rain, for you could *see them* both, wildly making merry over the storm-driven camp.   As the

Colonel stepped out of his tent at reveillé, a big branch from an overhanging tree came crashing down upon it, and broke the pole, and drove into the tent he had just stepped from. 'There's luck,' said I, putting out my own head at the instant. We went out, and found half a dozen of the limping officers' tents flat upon the ground in shapeless masses. Captain Cary said, with an attempt at mirth, ' I woke up about three o'clock with a confused idea that something was wrong, and found my face covered with wet canvas, and my tent-pole across my breast. I crawled out into the rain, and ran for shelter.' By the chill and exposure of the night, I found myself a little under the weather, and I found the weather a good deal *over me.* I was indisposed for breakfast, and the Doctor said, with a meaning chuckle, ' Sea-sick, I guess.' I got my tent secured with ropes and strong pins, and, after considering the best way to be least uncomfortable, determined to go to bed and '*feel better by and by.*' What a day it was! The storm howled and roared, and seemed to tear the tent away from its moorings. I had every alternation of fear and hope, but, to my surprise, weathered the gale. The Sergeant-Major, who is an old soldier and a professional croaker, and whose rueful phiz always appears shining with grim pleasure amid disaster, who says, with a military salute, ' Can't get nothing done, sir, not as it ought to be, sir,' — the Sergeant-Major appeared at my tent with his gloom all on. ' Tent is blown down, sir ; pins don't seem to do no good, sir ; my things is all wet, sir. Never see no storm, sir, equal to this in Mexico, sir.' ' Well, Sergeant, it 'll be pleasanter to-morrow,' is all the satisfaction he gets. The day blew itself away, and, as we had hoped, the sun and wind went down together. This morning a clear sky and bright sunshine brought their gladness with them, and our Sunday morning inspection was a proof that ' each to-morrow finds us better than to-day.' The men came out bright and shining and clean, except an occasional unfortunate whose clothes were drying. 'Got wet yesterday, sir,' was a valid excuse, though not a frequent one. The day was a proof, however, that winter-quarters in this latitude will have to be our resource before many weeks. Tell Mr. —— that I put my feet in a pair of his stockings, and thought of him with the warmest affection. Sich is life, and, more particularly, camp life. To-day we receive the news of Scott's retirement, which has been rumored of late. I did not think that the day would come when the country would welcome his loss. But I think every one is relieved by his retirement. Now McClellan assumes an undivided responsibility, and if he has courage to defy the politicians, he may yet win the laurel which is growing for the successful general of this righteous but blunder-blasted war. What a fame is in store for that coming man. Talk of hero-worship. The past cannot furnish a parallel for the idolatry which will bow down before the man who restores the prestige and rekindles the associations of our dear old flag. You ask in your last letter if my heart does not sink. Sink? It swims like a duck when I think of the future which some of our eyes shall see ; and will not they swim, too, with intense delight, when the sight dawns upon them? For myself, even now, I cannot look upon the flag which we brought away from Boston without a glow and heart-bump, which I take to be only faint symptoms of the emotion that is to come. I augur well from McClellan's new power, and I feel sure that things will go better for it. One will, one plan, one execution. As to the immediate results, I have no opinion. Upon this line of operations I do not look for anything decisive this winter. Yet it is not impossible that the season may favor us sufficiently to allow activity here this month.

" **Monday Evening.**

" I did not finish my letter last night, as there was no mail out. This will go to-morrow. It takes no news, except that Colonel Andrews seems quite to have settled into a fever. The fever is by no means severe, but it may drag slowly along. There is nothing dangerous in his condition, only to be abed is not pleasant, and to be weak is miserable. I have got him very pleasantly fixed, and he has the best care that we can give him. . . . . We have had drills to-day, and the usual incidents of camp life. Our family is having a little measles, but is otherwise well. We have fine, clear weather again, and a bright, hopeful new moon."

"CAMP NEAR SENECA, November 6, 1861.

" ' The war cannot be long. It may be desperate.' This is not prophecy from the closet. It is inspiration from the master of the position. I claim for our General the rare virtue of sincerity, — the fibre of all genuine character. I repose on his statements. Recollect that he wields the causes. Shall he not predict the consequence ? ' I ask in the future forbearance, patience, and confidence.' But not for *long*. If he can compel our people to yield him those, he has already gained a victory like the conquest of a city. ' I trust and feel that the day is not far distant when I shall return to the place dearest of all others to me.'

" Now that 's cheerful. Of course he won't go home and leave us on the wrong bank of the Potomac, — of course he won't go home and leave his lambs to come back wagging their tales, or tails, behind them and him. No ! let us accept, let us hail the omen. ' Youth is at the prow.' ' Pleasure,' God's own pleasure, ' has the helm.' For one, I am ready for the voyage. I take McClellan's speech to the Philadelphia deputation for my chart.

" I am afraid this is in the nature of rhapsody ; but then it is November, and one must live in the imagination, and look over into the land of promise, or he may wither and fall like the leaves about him.

" I wrote thus far yesterday, but the gloomy sky and chilling blasts were so unpropitious, that I thought I would not attempt to resist their influence.   It was a regular heavy, clouded, wet day.   We had as yet no news of the fleet, and nothing to lift ourselves above the influence of the weather.   Last evening we got a rumor of the safe arrival of the fleet off Bull's Bay, near Charleston, after the blow. Upon this vague elation we went to sleep. . . . . I am very glad to receive your copy of Howard's letter, and rejoice that he is in the midst of serious work.   I recognize in his account the inevitable hardships and vicissitudes of his new life.   As part of the Western army, he will undoubtedly see active service this winter, and will perhaps hardly get breathing time, unless he pauses awhile in Memphis to take a look at his old cotton-press.   I am very glad that he is there, and prefer his position in the line to one on the staff, if he is equally well pleased with it.   You say you like to receive my letters, and so, of course, I am most happy to write, but there is really just nothing to say.   Yesterday, for example, all our fires smoked.   My little stove was very vigorous in that direction.   Proverbs are said to be the condensed wisdom of ages.   I recalled that, ' Where there is so much smoke there must be some fire,' and cheerfully hung on to the maxim through the day ; but I felt very little fire.   Then the question of moving the hospital was raised, considered, and settled ; then the increase of measles was croaked and investigated ; then the news came that the patient sick with typhus would die, and at evening he was dead ; and now, this morning, we are preparing his funeral. . . . .

" To-day we have no news but the prevailing and increasing rumor that we shall move, in a day or two, into winter-quarters, or, at least, out of these quarters.   I have a sort of hope that the fates may select our regiment for some Southern service, if we succeed in getting a good foothold on the coast."

" CAMP NEAR SENECA, November 8, 1861.

" Your letter and C———'s and D———'s all came last evening.   I was right glad to see them.   They warmed and cheered

me on the coldest night of our camping experience. . . . .
Colonel Gordon goes off to-day, on a leave of absence, for a
short visit home. . . . . Colonel Andrews is getting better,
but is still shut up, and must be for some time; so I am left
in command.   Of course there will nothing happen but the
quiet recurrence of reveillé, drill, and tattoo, but it is a
different feeling to have the ropes in your own hands.   I am
afraid my last letter was a little dull.   It was written,
towards its close, to the depressing sound of a band rehearsal of the Dead March for a coming funeral.   Such
clouds will overhang one's paper, and leave their shadow.
But they are mere shadows.   Our hope and faith are as
firm as ever, and the world wags on. . . . .

" Tell Mrs. Ticknor that I have no statement of our
wants or wishes to add to those already made, unless it be
for woollen mittens, which would, of course, be gladsome to
the men if they are to stay here, of which we can know
nothing.   Mind, I do not ask for any of these things, but
state the case merely.   Love to all.   Tell —— he is the
dearest fellow in the world."

"CAMP NEAR SENECA, November 10, 1861,
Sunday Evening.

" I have had a quiet Sunday.   Colonel Gordon's sudden
resolution to snatch a visit home has left me alone with the
regiment.   On the whole, I don't mind the care, though
my shoulders are young to it.   A little knapsack-drill keeps
a soldier in marching order, you know, and so of an officer.
There are a good many things to call for care and thought
just now in the regiment.   The care of our sick; the selection of a good camping-ground in place of our present
over-damp site; the problem of keeping warm when air
and ground seem heavy with chilliness; the maintenance
of drills and discipline when so many of our officers are
absent or sick, — not more than half being now present for
duty, — these are a few of the considerations that vibrate

the pendulum of my thoughts.   I have just been out to tattoo, and so, as my ' *little family* ' is put quietly to bed, I am free to write, read, or sleep, as I choose.   Another rainy day yesterday, and the pleasant sun of to-day looked as if he were breeding clouds for to-morrow.   So is November on the Potomac.   If the news is half true from the fleet, why may not a turn of fortune embark us for some Southern shore, and give us a short cut to the tropics ?

" Tell father that he happened to send me just the book I wanted, — Halleck's.   I fancy it is a clear statement of some things it would be well for a major to bear in mind. Our day has been regular and quiet.   Of course, my only purpose is to keep the machine in the same running order as it now is. . . . .

" It is the next morning since I began this letter.   I have been having a long talk with General Banks at his head-quarters.   The General does not seem to know exactly *when* we move from here, but it is clear that our division will not remain here for the winter.   It is astonishing how this army life philosophizes a man.   I think a few years of it would make one ' impervious to the storms of outrageous fortune.'   Colonel Andrews is in a very pleasant house, and is rapidly getting well.   You would be amused to see me drill my battalion.   It only shows we never can tell what we can do.   When I voted for Abraham Lincoln a year ago, I did not suppose I was electing myself into a damp wheat-field with a regiment on my hands ; but that is, apparently, what I voted for.   I only wish all the wheat-fields in the neighborhood bore the same harvest."

"CAMP NEAR SENECA, November 14, 1861.

" I should have written a line at a shorter interval from my last if I had not been full of work.   I decided to move my camp on Tuesday morning, and have given the last two days to making the men comfortable in their new quarters. By some strange mishap, we got upon an unlucky piece of

ground for our camp.   We were assailed by diarrhœa, —
officers and men.   But I think I have made a fortunate
selection of a new ground, and I am myself feeling much
better.   Our whole mess was under the weather.   As I
am left alone in command, I have been obliged to snatch
odds and ends of time to be a little sick in.   Now, however,
we are out upon high, open ground, and have fine, clear
sunshine, and we are all well again.   I do not wish either
to complain or be elate, but I have, this morning, a tranquil
satisfaction in obstacles overcome, and sunshine achieved.
You know there are times when everything seems to get
going wrong.   The Colonel seemed to leave the regiment
just at that moment.   But now we start again.

"We never had a more regular, neat, and comely camp
than we have to-day.   Of course I enjoy that, and I am
trying to keep the machine in good order. . . . .

"If there were no one waiting for me, I should try and
scribble this sheet full, but, in the end, you would know
only that reveillé and tattoo succeed one another naturally ;
that our camp is pleasant, and, I hope, healthy ; and that
to be major commanding a regiment is a busy life, but, on
the whole, a happy one, as lives go.   Love to all."

"CAMP NEAR SENECA, MARYLAND, November 14, 1861.

"Though I wrote you a letter this morning, I may as
well begin another to-night.   The patter of the rain reminds
me that my new camping-ground is to be put to its test.   I
have just finished reading, in the Baltimore Clipper, the
news of the fleet.   Glad tidings !   Such thrusts as these
between the ribs of Rebeldom will make it wince.   Success,
too, gladdens me, independently of its results.   I have got
tired of delay and failure.   Except Sherman's proclamation,
the account all reads well.   That is altogether too mealy-
mouthed.   For one, I should like to go there announcing
that I come as an enemy to waste with fire and sword.
That 's what we mean to do, and I should like the satisfaction of saying so.

" But if calling things by the wrong names pleases the President, and does not alter the things themselves, why, we must put up with it.   An army is a stern fact, and its presence will indicate itself roughly enough.

" The sudden movement of the slaves shows that fire among tinder has *one* effect.   The slight indication afforded by the account of the servile movement is instructive.   I am afraid it upsets my friend ———'s theories.   Indeed, theorizing in these times is very hazardous.   I had rather fight.

" The incidents of my day are not very interesting. Colonel Andrews grows better, but his recovery must be slow.   The attempt to make things go right is an arduous and irritating one always.   In a regiment it is particularly so, because where one thousand men are concerned a thousand little matters will go wrong inevitably.   The net result, when you come to look at it, is often very good, while every ingredient seems to be the wrong one.   But I have no reason to complain of the results, and so I will e'en be philosophical and calm in my observation of the processes.   I am glad to be getting quite well and strong again.   Many of my recent sensations have not been those appropriate to a major commanding.   But now I am getting firm again in my saddle, and can even use the spurs, if desirable. I expect my servant to-morrow.   I shall feel very much like killing a fatted calf for him.   Our rainy night leaves us in very good condition, and satisfies me that my camp is a good one.   I have just finished a chilly breakfast ; have directed some punishments ; have seen to it that the company for picket duty at the river starts in season ; have refused the applications for leave of absence ; have wept copious but unsympathizing tears over my fire, which *will* smoke ; have received the reports of the officer of the day ; have examined the Surgeon's report and the company reports, and reduced the sick-list thirty-two men ; have queried and questioned variously, and expect to do so for an hour longer. I feel exceedingly well and lively, and will close this letter in season for the mail."

"CAMP NEAR SENECA, November 16, 1861.

"The difference between our actions in this war seems to be, that we don't *half do* our Ball's Bluffs, and we do *half do* our Port Royals. Fruit ripe in South Carolina, and no one to pick it. That's the way I read the news from the scene of our late success. Where are the next twenty thousand troops? They should be within an hour's sail of Port Royal. Is it a sagacious military conjecture, that a victory at that point would strike terror and panic to the neighboring cities? If so, should not that conjecture have anticipated the result of which we are just beginning to hear? Should it not have provided a force to enjoy and intensify that panic? I know of a whole division, which, instead of shivering in the mud of Maryland, would gladly be pursuing a panic-stricken multitude with fire and sword. Why not? Of course, we are much in the dark, but my guess is, that twenty thousand good soldiers could to-day enter either Charleston or Savannah. If they could not occupy and hold, they could burn and destroy. 'Rebels and Traitors,' I would head my proclamation. Not 'Carolinians and Fellow-citizens.' Not peace, but the sword. There is cotton to tempt avarice, negroes to tempt philanthropy, Rebels to tempt patriotism, — everything to warrant a great risk. As I read the Southern accounts, they seem to me to indicate the presence of panic. From that, I infer a weak and exposed condition. We shall leave them time to recover their courage, and strengthen their defences. I do not know what is possible to our 'Great Country,' but, possible or impossible, I would pour an avalanche on that shore forthwith.

"You see that reflection and conjecture are the only amusements of our rainy days. So I must fill my letters with guesses and hopes. I advise you to read McClellan's

Review of the War in the Crimea.   One could wish that his pen were free to criticise his own campaign.   Could he not expose, here and there, a blunder ?   Perhaps the answer is, It is not his campaign.

" My new man arrived last night, very unexpectedly to *himself*, apparently ; for he seemed to find obscurity enveloping his path, and to think his advance to this point a great success.

" He brought letters which delighted me.   It was mail night, and I had no mail till John came with his budget. Father seems to speak stoically of ' a long war.'   What it may be *mis*managed into I cannot say, but, decently managed, it cannot be a long war.   The disasters and embarrassments which will follow in its train will be long enough ; the war itself short and desperate, I hope.

" There is something ludicrous in writing so quietly on calm, white paper, without expressing at all the roaring, whistling, wintry surroundings of my present scene.   Our yesterday's rain has cleared off cold.   Real winter this morning.   Ice in the wash-basin, numbness in the fingers, frost from the breath.   I rejoice in the invigorating turn that the weather has taken.   I feel myself much better for it, and I know it must improve the health and vigor of the camp.   But the howling blast is a stern medicine, and even now it shakes my tent so that my pen trembles.   I should like you to have seen the picture our camp presented at reveillé this morning.   I purposely went out without my overcoat, and walked leisurely down the line, as if I were fanned by the zephyrs of June.   I wished to have the men observe that I recognized nothing unusual in our first taste of winter.   Still, in point of fact, it was cold.   Now drill is going on without overcoats.   I told them they must double-quick if they were cold.   The only way is, to hold things up to the sharp line under all circumstances.   It will be a little hard to keep up the illusion all winter, I fear, however. Still, everything requires bracing up constantly.   The virtue

10

of this military life is the importunate recurrence of daily duty. Rain or shine, health or sickness, joy or grief, reveillé knocks ' *œquo pede* ' with impartial cadence at every tent. Its lively and awakening beat thrills a new life through the camp, as the rising sun whitens the glowing east. And then when tattoo at evening *awakes* the men to sleep (for it is not a soothing strain), ' duty performed ' has made them happy, or should have done so, on the authority of the great expounder of the Constitution himself. Such are the consolations of camp life in November. But then, as Dr. Hedge happily observes in a discourse on ' National Weakness,' ' the Rebel power is still unsubdued ; the harvest is passed, the summer is ended, and we are not saved.' True, but we are *not* lost. We propose in the Massachusetts Second to keep Thanksgiving day thankfully, if not for what has happened, at least for what has *not* happened. I have just sent out an order for the provision of Thanksgiving dinners for the men. And I quite expect that turkey and plumpudding will smoke on our mess-pans and exhale from our ovens on Thursday next. I could be content to be at home on that day, but, failing that, I shall enjoy an attempt to extemporize and emulate a New England Thanksgiving in a Maryland camp on the wrong bank of the Potomac. We shall read the Thanksgiving Proclamation, and be as happy as we may. I suppose you will have your usual celebration. I expect to enjoy the unusual honor to come in among the *absent* friends. . . . .

" The pleasure of reading your last letter was somewhat alloyed, I confess, by the pervading strain of eulogy of my own letters. It is all nonsense. The story is a very good one, perhaps ; the telling it is nothing ; and as for ' historical value,' you just wait. Our little events will not be a paragraph in the record which ought to be and must be written.

" Father closes his last letter with the very kind wish that he knew what to send me. I happen to be able to tell him, — viz. a little nice English *breakfast tea.* A good honest cup of black tea would delight me. If you should find that Colonel Gordon has not gone back before this reaches you, pray make him the bearer of a small package of tea.

"I see by to-night's Clipper (it is Saturday evening while I write), that a delegation from Baltimore goes to ask the President for government patronage for the repentant city. This fulfils a prediction I had the honor to make. I see, also, that the landing of our force at Beaufort was a scene of disorder and confusion. That comes of sending the rawest troops to the hardest duty. I am puzzled to know why this is done to such an alarming extent. But tattoo is just beating. It is a raw and gusty night. The air bites shrewdly. I think I will leave that puzzle unsolved, and get within the warm folds of my constant buffalo-robe. Good night. Grandmother will be pleased to hear, before I go to bed, that with one of her blankets I have just made Captain Mudge warm and comfortable in a little attack of illness which has just overtaken him. The soft blanket will be as good as the Doctor's medicine, — better, perhaps. . . . .

"I have just room to bid you good morning, this Sunday morning. I am just ready for inspection, and have no doubt the day will work itself off quietly and pleasantly."

CHAPTER X.

LETTERS FROM CAMP NEAR SENECA.

"CAMP NEAR SENECA, November 19, 1861.

"BY every rule of gratitude, after receiving father's long and cheerful letter this morning, this letter should be written to him. But, as the countryman said of his wife, that what was her'n was his'n, and what was his'n was *his own*, so I fancy I shall talk as freely to both, though I write to only one. Did I not get a letter off on Sunday? I think so. That was a day of bright-blue cold. I gave up church because I had not the heart to keep the men even in a *devout* shiver for an hour. Yesterday I got a little pull back again. I had fully made up my mind to be perfectly well, so it shook my confidence a trifle. I had to keep busy in order to regain it. The day looked rather gloomy. The Adjutant was taken sick, and the Sergeant-Major. So I had to detail raw hands. Three captains were on their backs. The infernal malaria seemed to have wilted every one. Drills were dull, and the hospital over busy. There was a general cheerlessness overhanging every one.

"Just at this moment what does the perverse generalship of our inapposite brigadier but send me an order: 'There will be a review and inspection of this brigade in the large field hitherto known as a division review-ground near Darnestown.' There was hopelessness. Colonel and Lieutenant-Colonel both away; Adjutant and half the captains off duty; myself just between wind and water; every one dumpish. It never rains without pouring. The band leader and the drum-major reported themselves sick at parade. Whew-w-w-w-w! I think it all had a tonic and astringent effect on me. —— sympathized with me in my efforts to repair disasters in season for a *grand review*. I told her that, though things did n't look very bright, *yet* I had always noticed one thing, a dark morning kept growing better, and I was going to *get up* with that faith. I made my arrangements busily last evening.

"This morning was jolly cold. I was busy about all the little formalities and precisions which belong to such occasions, settling them with the various officers to whom the duties belonged. The Acting Adjutant had a little delay which bothered me, but at about ten o'clock the line was formed, — the men all in overcoats, — with full equipment. The morning had mellowed into Indian-summer. After all, the Massachusetts Second did look finely. We marched off briskly to Darnestown, about a mile and a half. The regiment arrived at the large field a few moments late, — the fault of a green adjutant. No great matter, but an annoyance. The rest of the brigade was in line, — my place was on the right. I formed the regiment a little in rear of the line, then rode up to General Abercrombie, who said he wished the whole brigade line changed. This gave me a chance to move our regiment right out in line of battle. I advanced them, and they moved with excellent precision, keeping their line exactly. It was a refreshing turn. The regiment saluted, and then marched round in review, passing round the whole field, and saluting the General, who was at the centre, opposite the front of our line. The regiment marched well, — the distances all well kept, — and wheeled into line again finely. So far, well. Then an inspection, which is a tedious process. The General noticed, what is certainly true, that the men looked *peaked*, dwindled, *pined*. But their soldierly appearance was undeniable. As if to cap the climax of our day's work, the General turns to me and says, ' Put the battalion through a short drill, and then you can take them home.' I might have mentioned that I rose this morning pretty well except a raging headache, and, on the whole, felt brisk. I did not much feel like *shouting* through

a battalion-drill, however.   Still, I did it.   We did it pretty well, too, on the whole.   Shall I tell you what we did ?
You will understand it exactly.   The battalion, as formed for
inspection, was in open column of companies, right in front.
I first threw them forward into line, which went well, then
double-columned on the centre, countermarched and deployed, then repeated that movement at a double-quick, then
broke the line to the left, and wheeled again to the right into
line, then broke to the right by companies, closed in mass
and formed divisions, then column forward and round by
two wheels, closed in mass to their old front, then halted
and deployed column on the first division at a double-quick,
bringing them on their original line.   Then, after a rest,
broke by right of companies to the rear, and so marched
home, having weathered the day.   Now, is n't that a lucid
story ?   Don't you like it ?   It 's just what I did, anyway,
and is n't a bad drill for the inexperience of a headachy
major.   I got home soon after two, having had a hard day
for a regiment so much pulled down as ours.   I put in several good words for us with the Brigadier, and I am in hopes
to whiskey and quinine, or, better still, to transport our regiment into its old health and vigor.   But certain it is, that
hard work, exposure, and Potomac damp have wrought their
perfect work, and we ' need a change,' as the saying is.
Besides, there is this constant picket duty on the river,
watching through damp nights for enemies that have n't a
purpose of coming.   It is the hardest kind of duty, and the
most useless, or rather the least obviously useful, and the
least exhilarating.   I was reading, this morning, an order
from head-quarters about ' amputations.'   ' Pshaw ! ' I exclaimed, to the edification of our surgeon.   ' If they want
to be practically useful, let them pronounce about diarrhœa
and chills : there are no *amputations* in civil war.'   With
such dismal pleasantries we relieve the depression of our
sinking spirits.   But I have the pleasure to know, or to
feel sure, that we are only harvesting now the crop of an

early sowing, and that things grow better. I am very well again this evening. Colonel Andrews now grows obviously better. The Adjutant will go to a house to-morrow for two or three days' rest, and I am inclined to hope that things have just got to their worst with us.

"Perhaps I am giving you an over-dark view. Don't let your imagination run away with it. We are only debilitated, that's all. Nothing dangerous, but annoying. I am only thankful that I am so well, and only troubled that there is so little I can do for the regiment.

"Send us your warm clothes as fast as they are ready in respectable quantities. . . . .

"Tell father I join in his hurrahs, except that I caution him to wait for exploit and achievement before he congratulates his boys, or canonizes their mother *on their account.* It is very humdrum duty they are doing now. It asks only willingness and endeavor, — a good, earnest disposition. If it shall turn out that they can have strength for better things by and by, sha'n't I be glad ! To-day I am only tranquil and hopeful. Our Thanksgiving day will be a great success. I fancy nearly a hundred turkeys : a great many geese and chickens will smoke on our mess-pans ! Then the plum-puddings ! Already the cooks are rehearsing that delicacy in many forms, in anticipation of the grand and decisive movement on Thursday. I think that thankfulness of heart and generosity of good cheer will so exalt and inspirit the regiment that we shall know no more depression or invalidism. At all events, the preparation has a wholesome cheerfulness in it. General Abercrombie to-day said, ' No winter-quarters.' This was direct from McClellan. He also intimated that we *may* go South. That rumor seems to gather and not fade, as most do. It has life in it still, and perhaps it may bring itself to pass pretty soon.

"I am making a long story of my short experiences ; but it is pleasant to write, and, but for a little consideration left for you, I might write on for an hour. As it is, I will write an affectionate good-night, and go to bed.   Before I go, don't let me forget to admonish you to tell Mr. —— that those drawers are as warm as the love of woman, and as constant as the love of man.   Tell him they are my *hope* and *faith* in this great November tribulation.   I will recollect him Thanksgiving day.

"We have a bright Wednesday morning.   I find a chance to send this by Lieutenant Choate, who goes home on a short 'sick-leave,' so I must 'close up promptly.'   What a joke the capture of Mason and Slidell is!   There is fun in it.   Whether there is, also, international law, or not, I don't know.   The luck seems really to have turned lately, and to be going against rebels and traitors.   I was very much pleased to read Howard's letter.   It looks as if he were where he would have a good chance to make a soldier, and to be an active one too.   What an oddity this whole life seems to me every now and then, when I think of it.   Changes and chances are very rapid.   Verily, to be an American is to be everything by turns, and nothing long.

"Speaking of 'nothing long,' what do you think of this letter?   The camp looks white and frosty from my tent, as I look out this morning.   I think I will go to breakfast and warm up a little.   As to my health, it seems firm again to-day, and I have every reason for content.   Love to all at home.

"P. S. — I have reason to believe that the General was quite well pleased with the review.   That is a comfort, under the circumstances."

"CAMP NEAR SENECA, November 20, 1861.

"I have just come in from a walk through the camp at night.   The cooks are busy over to-morrow's dinner.   Picking and dressing turkeys, and preparing the large, glowing ovens for roasting.   The *irregularity* is overlooked, in view of the occasion.   The preparations are so vast that the dinner will be cooking nearly all night.   I shall be able to give you the statistics to-morrow. To-night I only know that it looks as if an army were to be fed with turkey, and another one with plum-pudding. The scene is a busy and gay one. I have also been to see my sick charges. Incongruous scenes for such close association! but we happen to have both pictures at once in camp. Still, I think we grow better, and have only thankfulness and hope for to-morrow."

"Thursday, half past two o'clock.

"Letter-writing after Thanksgiving dinner! What an absurdity! Yet here goes. I must rise on the wings of imagination, invoking also the exhilaration of champagne, to give you a glance at our day. The morning rose red and glorious. The camp was gay, and the men all jovial and willing. Last evening I published an order reciting the Governor's Thanksgiving order, and General Banks's order, and telling the Second Massachusetts that 'Thanksgiving day would be observed and kept by the officers and men of this regiment. There will be religious services at ten o'clock, to be followed by the usual Thanksgiving dinner. It is hoped that the officers and men of the regiment will unite in reviving all the memories and associations which belong to the time-honored home festival of New England, and in public thanksgiving and praise for all the blessings which have followed them since they left the homes which this festival recalls.'

"Such was my programme. At ten o'clock the sun was bright, and the morning like summer. We had a service. The reading of the Proclamation, the singing of praise by a full, deep-toned choir, a jubilant, patriotic awakening, exhortation from our chaplain, then a gay march by the band, which followed the benediction, hastened the steps of the companies as they returned to their quarters. I then immediately got into the saddle and rode off to see the Adjutant and Captains Savage and Mudge, whom I sent yesterday to the hospitable shelter of houses up at Darnestown. Found them all well and happy, and recovering. Came back, visited the kitchens. Turkeys and plum-pudding smoked and *fragranced* from them. Tables were built by some of the companies. A New England turkey-shooting was going on. Companies B and C bore off the crown of victory *and* the turkeys. I then went over to Colonel Andrews. Then I came back to half an hour's business, and so to dinner. A brisk, appetizing morning. But before I speak of our own dinner, let me give you the statistics, the startling statistics of our regimental dinner. Hear it : —

Turkeys.		Geese.		Chickens.	Plum-Puddings.
95	10½ lbs.	76	8½ lbs.	73	95
Weight 997½ lbs.		646 lbs.		164¼ lbs.	1179 lbs.

" In other words, about half a *ton* of turkey, nearly as much goose and chicken, and more than half a ton of plum-pudding. There's richness, as Mr. Squeers would say. The statement shows at once, presumed digestion, appetite, and courage. It is hopeful, — or will it prove the rashness of despair? But then our own dinner, included in this general statement, was as follows : —

" A twenty-pound turkey, etc., and a vast plum-pudding, and no end of apple-pies, etc. I ought to add, that many of the companies had their nuts and raisins and apples. What luxury! We sat down, a small party, — the Chaplain, the Doctor, the Chaplain of the Twelfth, and myself. Tony, or Antonio Olivadoes, our ambitious and clever cook, was radiant over the fire. He had spent most of the night in culinary constancy to his puddings and pies. He invoked attention to his turkey. 'Well now, Major, *considerin'* the want o' conveniences and fixins, I think it 'll taste kind o' good'; and so it did. I opened a bottle of champagne, a present, and gave my toast, 'Luck and absent friends.' So we drank it, and it cheered our somewhat narrow circle. The men are now playing ball, and it will not be long before dress-parade and company duty will replace our Thanksgiving sensations. Never mind, we 've had a good time, and a good time under a few difficulties, which, I think, only sweetened our pleasure. Such is our Thanksgiving chronicle. I like to sit and fancy your home dinner, and to preside, in imagination, over the boiled turkey at the foot of the table. I hope our next Thanksgiving we may be all together; but if not, at least we can hope to be all as thankful as now. Tony, the cook, just puts his head into my tent, with conscious achievement in his eye: ' Well, Major how you like de dinner? I was up all night, — five minutes chopping wood, five minutes cooking, — I did hope it would be nice.' I have just tickled his vanity, and he goes.

" I think I may have a letter from you to-night, but this goes by the mail now. God bless you all at home, and good by."

" HEAD-QUARTERS SECOND MASSACHUSETTS REGIMENT,
Camp near Seneca, Nov. 23, 1861, Saturday Evening.

" Yours of the 19th is in my pocket. The evening has passed pleasantly under its influence. The camp is fast falling asleep.

" I last wrote you just after dinner on Thanksgiving day. The rest of the day went glibly enough. In the evening the men had a brisk dance to the music of the band, and the next morning there were fewer sick men than for two weeks before. Gladness and gayety are good medicines. Friday was a very busy day with me. Among its morning incidents was a visit to Generals Hamilton and Williams. General Williams quite won my affection by saying, apropos of the review, ' The Massachusetts Second is the best volunteer regiment in the service.' ' A man of sense,' was my echo. Our two new lieutenants, Grafton and Shelton, appeared yesterday, and were assigned to duty the next day. They were eager for duty, and promise well. Give Charley the stockings for his men by all means. I rejoice in his effort and success. I am amused to see that the London Times compares Ball's Bluff to Braddock's defeat. That

was *my* first exclamation.   A regular Braddock's defeat!
Who was the Braddock ? . . . .

" I do not expect to come home at all.   While there is
anything to do here, I certainly shall not come.   Indeed, I
do not think I desire it.   Three years or the war, was my
enlistment ; and I am willing to stay with my regiment while
it lasts. . . . .

. This morning's inspection took about two hours.   It was
a thorough one and satisfactory.   We have church this
afternoon, unless it rains, as it threatens to do.

" For one, I have no sympathy with the prisoners at Fort
Warren.   I desire that all benevolence and sympathy may
flow to our loyal soldiers, whose hardship is quite as great.
As for Mason and Slidell, the joke is so good, so practical, so
retributive.   I admire the calm irony with which Mr. Everett wishes them a short residence at Fort Warren.   That
is clever and bright, and politely severe. . . . .

. I predicted church when I was writing this morning.   Lo
it is evening, and the ground white with *snow !*   So winter
steals upon us, and we have a snow-storm instead of divine
service.   Well, camp life has its variety, and is not always same.   I confess, as I look out through the flapping
door of my tent, I think it looks as little like invading *the
South* as any scene I ever looked on.   White and heavy falls
the snow, — I hope on the unjust as well as the just, on both
sides the Potomac !   Now 's the time for mittens with no
holes in the thumbs. . . . . I have quite a long letter from
———.   She is full of the glory and spectacle aspect of the
army and the war, her visit to Washington having taught
her all about armies.   I could give her a few practical lessons that would *unidealize* her abruptly.   Never mind, to
be *illusionée* is to be happy.

" I hope, in view of the dread you express of my going
to Charleston, where they fight ' without giving quarter,'
you will be pleased at the imminent prospect there seems to
be that we shall be snowed into Maryland till spring.   How-

ever, the weather is so fickle, we may have bright sunshine to-morrow."

"Monday Morning.

"Bright and cold. The snow, a thin coating, lay crisp and cold on the ground this morning. The air glistened; my fingers grow numb as I write about it. Our week commences."

"Camp near Seneca, November 26, 1861.

"If you are to have another letter from a major commanding, I suppose it had better be written to-night. To-morrow, I feel sure, will bring back Colonel Gordon, and I shall very gladly shift that burden to his shoulders. There are some objections to holding the reins, very long, of power that you are not to continue in the exercise of; and, though I must say the Colonel has got a very easily managed regiment, and I have had no difficulty in my path, yet the temptation to mould things to your own will is a strong one, not to be indulged in temporary command. On the whole, this is probably better for the regiment, — it is certainly safer for me. The month of November, though we have spent it quietly in camp, has been the most trying one to the regiment in its whole history. I am glad to be able to persuade myself that we stand firmer than we did three weeks since. I hope we shall steadily improve. There is a hopeless desperation chilling one when engaged in a contest with disease. The unseen malaria has such an advantage in the fight. I had rather meet anything for the regiment than the enemy who surprised us in our former camping-ground, and who seems hardly yet to have given up beat. Two weeks ago I had something as much like depression as I ever allow myself the indulgence of. Now I feel quite glad again. This afternoon, for example, a blue, overcast November sky, but a keen, bracing air, we had a lively battalion drill, which went quite well. The regiment turned out full companies, and, altogether, looked its old self — There, I was just in the midst of this last exul-

tant sentence, when what should happen but a knock at my
tent. Enter Captain ———. 'Major, two men of my company are very sick in quarters, and ought to be in hospital,
but there is not room.' 'Well, sir, I can't *make* room.'
Then the same complaint from another captain. I send for
the Doctor. He is abed, having been sick for the past three
days. I send for the Assistant Surgeon. He says, 'Yes, it
is so; but the Brigade Surgeon promises a tent soon. The
measles cases have increased within two days.'

"I require from him a report of every case in quarters,
and a statement of how many sick men ought to be in hospital. This is the nature of the work to be done. To make
bricks without straw. Our sick officers have not yet returned to duty. The Adjutant is still away. I have to look
after everything myself. Still, I do insist that we are getting better. A week on a high piece of ground *three miles*
from the river would put us all on our feet again. But as
long as the morning sun rises only to quicken the fatal
exhalations from this pestilent Potomac, and the evening
dews fall only to rise again with fever in their breath, the
contest is unequal and the victory uncertain. Well, we
can only hope for better things, and be thankful for what
we have. You will see, however, that the constant maintenance of military efficiency under all these circumstances
exacts constant effort. I rejoice in continued health and
increasing strength, and am thankful and happy. I think,
too, that our experience will be a sort of seasoning. One
thing is certain, — we cannot have the measles again!

"I have just come in from my nightly round through the
camp; and, as taps have sounded, all is quiet. I sit alone
in my tent a-thinkin' o' nothin' at all, — and writing about
it, too. Yes, I can tell you about our domestic arrangements, — I mean our mess.

"We have intruded upon an elderly lady who lives near
our lines. She has given us her parlor and the use of her
cooking-stove. Tony is in great feather. He rejoices in all
kinds of culinary eccentricities.

"The old lady, meantime, is repaid by our protection. She confides to me her griefs for the losses of fence-rails and cabbages, of pigs and poultry. This happened when a former regiment was here. Now she is safe. Tony and she observe an *armed* neutrality over the common cooking-stove. This evening she told us the history of Jack Cross, the husband of the lady who owns the house where Colonel Andrews is sick. Jack is in prison — at Fort Warren per-haps — as a traitor. The good lady described his capture. Said she: ' The officers came to me, and says they, " Do you know of Jack Cross's hanging or shooting any one?" " As for shooting," says I, " I 've known him from a boy, and a more peaceable man I never knew ; and as for hang-ing," says I, " I never knew him to hang anything except a big black dog." Which was true, indeed, and I recollect how the dog looked, and he most frightened me to death. But they took him. He was an unfortunate man, but he was a good neighbor ; and a good neighbor can't be a bad man. But this business has got him into trouble ; but I can't seem to understand it nohow. I 'm for the Union and peace before I die.' I think she would have talked till now, had we not left the table, her ideas running in a beaten track of puzzlement and dread. She evidently does not either understand or enjoy civil war.

" I said our camp was still. I ought to admit that the night is full of echoes with the barking cough that prevails, — an unwholesome sound. Good night, and God bless you all at home."

" CAMP NEAR SENECA, November 29, 1861,
Friday Evening.

" 'T is a misty, moisty morning, and cloudy is the weather, — a hunting morning, with no game, however. Mr. Motley and Frank and Mr. Robeson will tempt Providence and trust the rebel highway soon on their way to Washington. I must send you a line by them. As I hoped, and wrote, Wednesday afternoon brought the Colonel and his party. I

was sorry that our bright, clear weather lowered just before
their arrival; and cheerlessness overspread the camp at
nightfall, when they arrived. It was pleasant to see them.
Their visit has been an agreeable one to us, though probably not full of exciting pleasure to them. I have got both
your letters, — the one brought by Mr. Motley and the one
sent by you on Saturday. Your Thanksgiving was as I had
fancied it, and I am glad to get your bright and faithful
picture of it. You will have received, ere this, my account
of the steady improvement of the regiment. You will
know, too, that I am now in perfect health myself, and I
beg that you will put aside all anxiety on my account. As
for coming home, it is now out of the question. I cannot pre-
tend to have felt anything of ' that stern joy which warriors
feel in foemen worthy of their steel,' — but I have a calm
content in the presence of hardship and discomfort, and in
resistance to those influences which assail the efficiency of
' the best regiment in the service.' Again, I feel a satisfaction
in knowing that I am, and have always been, ' reported,' according to military phrase, ' for duty ' on the morning regimental report! Just at the moment when the duty ceases
to be pleasant, I do not wish to have that report changed.
I am aware that these are selfish reasons, and I know also
that it is quite likely things will go well enough without
me. But here I am, and here I stay, for the present.
Colonel Andrews will go on Monday, I hope. Besides, our
Examining Board has been waiting for me to be relieved
from command of the regiment to commence its sittings,
and so I could not get leave to go. *Voilà des difficultés.*
Mr. Motley can assure you of my perfect health. Indeed, I
do not think it would improve it to run home. It would
certainly change my *settled* feeling into an unsettled one,
and so, again, the consequence follows. I think that, to go
to a Thanksgiving party at Mrs. ———'s, and have a chat
with Mrs. ———, or to dine with ——— and his wife, or to see
another pretty Miss ———, or to bid C——— good by as he

starts out, a gay cavalier, to escort his cousin to the dance, or to sit in the parlor of an evening at home, would be fragrant flowers of delight; but then, how soon they would fade, and what a withered nosegay should I bring back to camp with me!

"But I also feel that it would be a galling irritant to go home. The Colonel says you are not awake to the war in Boston. Tameness, irresolution, pity for '*political* prisoners,' — that is, traitors and felons, — talk of restoration by *concession*, pratings of a speedy advance on the Potomac, unmilitary plans for military movements, etc., etc. I have got anything but a pleasant picture of the tone of things at home. Upon my word, I think it would have a bad effect upon the equanimity which I cultivate and desire, to go about much at home. When events, whose progress and logic are unanswerable and persistent, have unravelled the tangled web of your mystification, and taught the good Boston people all about *war*, then, perhaps, it will be safe for one intent on its prosecution and longing for its results to breathe the enervating airs of your placid paradise. Till then, my voice is still for war. Everything here seems to be going pretty well. Camp life has no changes and few incidents to amuse you."

"CAMP NEAR SENECA, November 30, 1861.

"If anything were needed to assure my decision regarding a visit home, it could be found in the experience of the past two days. Yesterday — a rainy day, by the way — I was fully occupied with questions relating to the sick, and, in the afternoon, by a session of the Board of Claims. To-day, field-officer of the day. It has been a bright, windy, drying day, for which we are thankful. A tardy wisdom has at length decided to remove the division of General Banks from its present grotesque position to the neighborhood of Frederick City. Within easy distance, by rail, of Harper's Ferry, of Baltimore, and Washington, the division will there

11

be promptly available for any purpose. It will be placed in a more healthy position. It will be within reach of supplies. It will be so far permanent that it can make itself comfortable for a season. How it will get there is quite another question. The rains of the past week have made the roads almost impassable; and to move a whole division, with its immense trains, a distance of thirty miles, over swollen watercourses and worn-out roads, seems a hopeless undertaking. We probably commence the attempt Tuesday morning. It is certainly a move in the right direction, and seems, to my narrow horizon, made a month too late.

"To-day a part of our sick have been sent off to the General Hospital at Baltimore. Preparations were made yesterday by the Medical Director to send the worst cases from the whole division.

"The order to move the sick down to the canal to take the boat came early this morning. At ten o'clock they were moving; and at five o'clock this afternoon the boat was ready for them. The whole day they waited — two hundred sick men, in wagons and in discomfort — on the banks of the canal. The sight was most irritating this afternoon when I rode down there.

"Just at nightfall they were huddled in, one hundred and fifty men to one canal-boat, the rest sent back for want of room, and the boat moved off. Wretched mismanagement, and I fear great suffering as its fruit.

"In fact, the whole hospital system is a blunder, if not a crime. It wants entire reorganization. There should be no regimental hospitals. What can a regiment do, dragging sick men after it? How can a regiment, with its hospital tent, take proper care of them?

"The proper system would be to have hospitals attached to divisions, all the sick, except trivial cases, sent there, and treated by surgeons who have only that to do. Then the regiment would be free from its greatest embarrassment in the field. Then the sick would not die, as I have seen them do, for mere want of warmth, rest, and nursing. As a matter of organization and unity, as an administrative question, it seems as clear as sunlight; but we work along in a system that did well enough for an army of fifteen thousand men scattered in barracks and garrisons in time of peace, but is utterly inapplicable to a vast army in the field. To-day's blundering movement was, however, bad management, even according to this false system. It stirs one up to see it. But I won't preach on this text any more.

" I hope the war will last long enough to give us an army organized according to all the wisdom and experience of other nations, and carefully adapted to our own wants. What a splendid creation such an army would be! In fact, how plain it is, to any one who watches the progress of things out here, that a soldier is an *artificial* mechanism, that an army is still more so, that for a nation to neglect the art which produces its army is the same thing as for a man to reject the exercises and discipline which promote his vigor. Well, perhaps we shall grow wiser as we grow older; perhaps we shall blunder in some other direction.

" I am in hopes to get Colonel Andrews off to-day or to-morrow, in canal-boat, to Washington. This last sentence is written Sunday morning, the rest being Saturday-night reflections. The day is a dark and threatening one. We shall have a fine march to Frederick!

" I am very well indeed, and there is no news with us. Love to all."

"CAMP NEAR SENECA, December 2, 1861,
Monday Night.

" There is no reason why I should write, except that Colonel Andrews is going, and can take the letter. It is a harsh, cloudy, wind-driven night; and we have detained the canal-boat till morning. We are waiting our orders to march to Frederick. It looks like snow, and altogether there is a cheerful prospect of a march before us! I expect to awake in a snow-storm.

" I am awaiting, with some interest, the President's Message. I shall like to see how he will pronounce a policy. One thing seems to me to be clear. He must leave all political questions to a military solution and settlement. Congress must do the same.

" There is a method in events which must result, I think, in a wise and practical solution of the negro question.

" You recollect the cloister life of the Emperor Charles the Fifth, — the abrupt transition of the proud king from a vast and absolute sway to the solitude and asceticism and self-mortification of the cloister. I want to read the cloister life of King Cotton, — his exile, poverty, and penance. There will be a story of most instructive contrast. It is a story soon to be written. I wonder, too, how Congress will bear our ' inactivity ' this winter. Clear it is that we must be inactive. The mere movement of a division, with its artillery and supply-train and baggage, is a distinct teaching that active field operations are impossible before spring, on this line. So you may continue to think of me as perfectly safe, and as hoping for liveliness with the buds of spring. We shall have tried almost every phase of army experience before we get home, I fancy. . . . . I shall be an early riser to-morrow morning, and so must bid you good night."

CHAPTER XI.

LETTERS FROM CAMP HICKS, NEAR FREDERICK.

"CAMP NEAR FREDERICK, December 6, 1861.

"ALL well. Had a glorious march to Frederick, and have a perfect camping-ground. Will write as soon as I get to rights."

"CAMP HICKS, NEAR FREDERICK, December 7, 1861.

"When I scribbled a hasty note to send by Colonel Andrews, I was looking grimly forward to a snow-storm. That foreboding was premature. In its place, I might have indulged midnight orders to march, and a winter's morning to start in. On Monday night, at eleven, our quiet camp near Seneca was invaded by a mounted orderly, who brought orders for an early start. The night was given to preparation. Colonel Andrews was to go off in a canal-boat at six in the morning. I had planned to escort him. Instead of this, I was obliged to content myself with a hasty good-by at the house, and a careful packing of him and his wife in the hospital wagon, and starting them for the canal. How cold it was! At last we started in good order. The morning was so cold that horseback was penance. I marched on foot, leading my horse. We went, by a new road, toward Frederick. The cold that nipped our ears stiffened the mud, and our path was made easy. A brisk march of seventeen miles brought us to Barnesville, just under the Sugar-Loaf Mountain. The latter part of the way hung heavy on the legs of the men, and they straggled badly. So at evening in the village, whither we went supper-hunting, we found some officers of the —— Massachusetts boasting of the fine marching condition of their men, and alluding to our stragglers. This piqued us. We were assigned the advance, the next day, unless, as General Abercrombie said, some other regiment gets started first !

" I should like to describe our camp at Barnesville. It was on a wooded ridge. The night was intensely cold. Colonel Gordon and I shared a tent, and we put up his stove. The men had good fires. The scene was wintry, and the experience was harsh. The order was issued, ' Reveillé at half past four ' ! ! The men got to bed early. At half past four came the rattle of get up. Our candle was relighted, our stove glowed again, a big fire crackled before the tent, our hastily built straw-bed aided the flames, but the weather kept the keen edge on. We breakfasted on some coffee borrowed from one of the company kitchens, and some bread and cold chicken, — frozen chickens. Soon after half past six the men were all breakfasted, the wagons ready, the line formed. At quarter to seven we were out on the road started. The sun was just showing an intention to rise. The Colonel and I walked. He led off at a smacking pace. Our rear-guard was made up of picked men under Lieutenant Sawyer, an energetic officer. There could be no stragglers. On we went over a mountain road, on, on, on ! The sun came up. It even began to melt the ice a little : still we marched on, till we had made between ten and eleven miles without a halt ! A short rest was all the impatience of the Colonel would allow. Onward again. General Abercrombie here overtook us. ' Great marching,' said he. ' I thought you had missed the road.' He had no idea we could so get the start of him. On along the bank of the Monocacy, — on across the river and the railroad.

" The cars were just coming in. ' Hallo,' says one soldier to another ; ' what 's that ? '

" ' I don't know, it 's so long since I 've seen it, — believe it 's a steam-engine.' The steam-whistle screeched.

We halt just outside Frederick at about eleven o'clock.

Fourteen miles *with knapsacks* in four hours and a quarter! Beat that if you can, over a mountain road.

"The Colonel formed the line in a grove, and the men rested. We awaited orders. But we were so early that the orders were not ready. Two or three hours after, the —— Regiment came along with thin ranks. The Colonel had told our regiment, before starting, that the —— boasted they marched better than the Second. It was that emulation which made us march so well. Now the men enjoyed their victory, and chaffed the late regiment. 'Tell your colonel,' says one, ' that we 'll lend him some of our wagons to help him along,' &c., &c. I marched the whole distance and felt finely. So you may know I am well. We went into camp, after recrossing the Monocacy. Another cold night.

"The next morning, just as the regiment was ready to start on its march to its present permanent camping-ground, we were sitting about the fire on a hillside overlooking our camp, when up came R——. I was delighted to see him, and to hear from home. He made only a short call on us, and left for Frederick just as we started for our new camp. It was Thursday morning. We marched round to the southwesterly part of the city, and struck the Baltimore turnpike. Our camp site was on a wooded slope facing the south and the sunshine. The latter is pouring into my tent as I write, this fine Sunday morning. We were soon busy getting into camp. I have been up to Frederick twice. The first time I went to General Banks's head-quarters, and happened to be invited in at General Shriver's, the Union man of Frederick. I found myself in a parlor, talking to a young lady! What a transition!

"Frederick is a fine old town. Our band-leader already talks of giving concerts there. Our thoughts are all turning on peace and quietness.

"The principal duty will be keeping the men in order, and preventing drunkenness. Yesterday, as field-officer of the day, I was very busy at it.   But had you seen our Sunday morning inspection, you would have seen order, neatness, and system transplanted with no check of growth. Opinions may vary of Colonel Gordon, but his administrative success is testimony enough in his favor.   I wish you could see our camp.   Perhaps you will one of these days.   We have had glorious weather since the cold abated.   It is Indian summer.   At last I have actually caught that evanescent and supposititious season.   We have had the President's Message and all the reports. . . . .

"I hope there will be no hasty and ill-considered legislation about the army.   The volunteer force, as it stands, ought not to be put on the same footing as regulars.   A hasty, extempore, uneducated army made permanent, — what folly !

"CAMP HICKS, December 9, 1861, near Frederick, Maryland.

"To sit in one's tent in the sunshine, and look out through the grove upon a lively and contented camp, is very little like war.   Such is my afternoon's occupation, or want of occupation.   I can hear, too, the music of the Star Spangled Banner, which is just now saluting the flag which has been raised at General Abercrombie's head-quarters near by.

"I went into Frederick this morning, and, as I came over the hill which slopes down to the Monocacy Bridge and overlooks the city and valley of Frederick, I could not but enjoy the scene.   There lay the city, with its spires and buildings clear in the sunlight ; and the whole surrounding valley looked happy with its bright, white farm-houses, and thrifty with its generous barns.

"Peace and plenty were in the landscape.   Yet, six months ago, both were threatened by the terrorism of Secession, and the growing crops then feared a premature harvesting.

"I called, this morning, on the Rev. Mr. ——, a pleasant man.   He was cordial and friendly, and wished me to tell Dr. —— that his present successor at Frederick was true to the flag, and loved his country. The experiences of the past summer have tested his patriotism severely. I also receive this evening by mail a note from Mrs. ——, who is in Baltimore. She writes to ask my intervention to protect her house, which has been occupied for military purposes. I shall do what I can for her, but the plea of necessity is one that knows no law and very little mercy. To-night also brings me what I rejoice in, — two letters from you, one from D——, and a most friendly and agreeable letter from Mr. ——. I could not resist an immediate answer to the latter, it gave me so much pleasure. . . . .

" It has been as warm as summer here to-day, — indeed, most uncomfortably so. But, of course, the change must come soon, and winter will frown upon us again.

" Tell —— he is as right as a tract on the slavery question. Keep it back. Say nothing. Let the war continue to be for the grand purpose which first inspired it, and which has united and quickened a whole people. The inevitable consequence must be the death-wound of slavery ; but that is incidental, and must be natural, not forced.

" CAMP HICKS, December 11, 1861, near Frederick.

" I am building a house this morning. It is well for a young man to get settled in life ; and to build house and keep house may, in general, be stated as the sum of his whole temporal endeavor. My own achievement in this direction will be rapid and decisive. Four trees, as scantling, a board floor on them, and a surrounding pen four feet high, are now in progress. Over this *pen* my tent will be pitched, and I can defy the storm. It is a structure *thought* in the morning and *acted* before night. It is not firmly fixed on earth, and so illustrates the frail tenure of our hold on this sunny camp, again analogizing life itself. It is also just the size for one. In this, perhaps, it is seriously defective, though, in a great part of the earnest en-

deavor of life, it is not bad for man to be alone. At all
events, no military authority indicates a wife as a part of
camp equipage. I have called my immediate business
housekeeping. Let it not be thought that a regiment is
without its domestic cares. They are manifold. To make
the cook and the steward harmonize is more difficult than
to form the battalion in line of battle. I should like much
to greet you in my new house, and have a family party at
the house-warming.

"We are moving, too, the question of a stable for one
hundred wagon-horses. It is a question that will settle
itself shortly. We procrastinate it naturally through this
warm weather; but the cold will soon snap us up again,
and then we shall go to work at it. But this uncertainty
of the future, which every rumor aggravates, does not favor
preparation. Political economists, you know, tell us that a
secure confidence in the quiet enjoyment of the fruits of
industry is a condition of all industrial development, and
without it there is no wealth. We are illustrating that
maxim. 'No winter quarters,' says McClellan. 'Onward!'
howl the politicians. 'You must not draw lumber or
boards,' echoes the quartermaster. Such is our dilemma.
I am attempting both horns by my extempore device of half
house, half tent.

"I did not finish my house yesterday, but this (Thursday)
evening I am writing at my new table in my new house.
It is perfectly jolly. I take great pride in my several ingenious devices for bed, washstand, front door (a sliding door),
&c., &c. I had four carpenters detailed from the regiment.
They gradually got interested in the work, and wrought
upon it with love. The dimensions are nine feet square,
and the tent just stretches down square over it.

"My little stove is humming on the hearth as blithely as
possible. I received last night your pleasant letter of Monday, the first which has come direct to Frederick. This
gives cheerful assurance of a prompt mail. . . . . .

" So —— will be settled before Christmas. He is to be congratulated. He has opened for himself a large sphere of duty and usefulness. This is enough to kindle the endeavor and invigorate the confidence, and so he is fortunate. . . . .

" We have had the development, since our arrival here, of one of those little tragedies that thrill a man with pain. A young man, who came out as a new recruit with Captain Abbott to our unlucky camp at Seneca, was down, low down, with typhoid fever when we were ready to march. Our surgeon decided it unsafe to move him, and so he was left in the temporary hospital at Darnestown, in charge of the surgeon there. After we left, the brigade surgeon of the —— brigade decided to move the hospital *at once ;* packed the poor boy, mercilessly, into a canal-boat with the rest ; took him up to Point of Rocks, and thence by rail to Frederick ; spent nearly thirty-six hours on the way, distance thirty miles. When the boy arrived here he was almost gone. Neglect, exposure, disease, had worked their perfect work.

" It is said, and I see no reason to doubt the statement, that his *feet* were *frozen* when he was taken from the cars ! He died soon after his arrival. You may have seen that the newspapers have got hold of that disgraceful blundering in transporting the sick to Washington. I must have spoken of it in a former letter.

" I consider the Medical Director guilty of the death of our young soldier just as much as if he had deliberately left him alone to starve.

" It is such incidents as this that expose the inefficiency of our whole hospital organization. Alas ! almost every department is equally listless and incapable. But the sufferings of the sick soldier appeal more directly to the heart than other shortcomings.

" Since we have been in camp here we have had a court-martial vigorously at work punishing all the peccadilloes of the march, and the indiscretions consequent upon a sudden exposure to the temptations of civilization and enlightenment, — to wit, whiskey.

"In my tour of duty yesterday, as field-officer of the day, I found that one of the guard posted in the village of New-market had stopped a pedler's cart, and seized a quantity of whiskey intended to sell to soldiers. The pedler was quite ingenious. He packed first a layer of pies, then a layer of whiskey-bottles, and so on. His barrel looked as innocent as a sucking dove on top, but was full of the sucking serpent within. I ordered him to be taken out in the middle of the main street, to have his hat taken off, his offence proclaimed to the people, and the whiskey destroyed. It was quite an effective, and, I hope, terror-striking penalty. . . . .

"It is now Friday morning, — bright, but cool. This fine weather is happiness in itself.

"CAMP HICKS, NEAR FREDERICK, December 15, 1861.

"Another bright, sunny Sunday; the regiment growing in grace, favor, and winter quarters. The band has got its new instruments, and has been piping melodiously in the moonlight this evening. The instruments are very fine indeed. . . . .

"To-morrow morning our brigade is to be reviewed by General ———. Napoleon, as the newspapers are fond of saying, used to precede his great battles and important movements by grand reviews. General ——— is not Napoleon. *Voilà tout.*

"The Colonel, since we got into this new camp, has been doing a good deal of 'rampaging,' and with excellent effect. I think I never saw the regiment in better condition. The relaxed discipline consequent on sickness and the march has recovered its tone completely. We have had a court-martial sitting for several days, and the men have been very generally and impartially punished in their pay. This is good economy for the government, and a sharp lesson for the men.   Each of the divisional departments — the commissary, the quartermaster, the medical — are lame and impotent.

" What do you say to the fact that, but for the activity and *outside* zeal of our quartermaster, we should be in rags ?

" The division takes no care of us ; we go to head-quarters at Washington, and take care of ourselves.   We go to Washington ; but the theory and duty is, that everything comes to us *through* the division department here.

" This has never been true, and, as I said, but for our irregular and enterprising expeditions to Washington, there is little we could get for ourselves.   Again, what do you say to the fact that to-day, but for the activity of officers outside of the medical department, and but for their spending money saved from other sources, our hospital tent would be floorless, storeless, and flung to the breeze ?   Now, however, it has a nice floor, good bunks, and a warm, cheerful stove ; and, yesterday morning, at inspection, looked as neat and comfortable as your parlor.   No thanks, however, to the medical men.   The division medical director don't know to-day that our typhoid-fever patients are not basking in precarious sunshine on the bosom — the cold, chaste bosom — of unnatural Mother Earth, after a sleepless night in the pale shadows of the moon ! !   To be sure, he guesses that the Second Massachusetts Regiment will take care of itself ; but while they are issuing stoves, &c., at Washington, we are buying them for ourselves here.

" Again, a brisk little stove is humming in almost every tent of the companies ; many of the tents are floored : all this, however, with our own money, — individual, regimental enterprise, not divisional or departmental care.   Such is the picture we present.   Add to this that all this outlay and endeavor is adventured by us in the face of a blank uncertainty of the future, an utter darkness, an *outer* darkness, as to whether we are here for a day or for all time, and you have a position that would arouse complaint, if we allowed ourselves to grumble.   We have no hint from head-quarters to guide us.   We have been here nearly two weeks : perhaps we shall get advice when we have finished our action. Advice to *act on* is what we want.   Head, control, direction, will, organization, is what we miss.   I speak only of the sphere in which we move, of this department.   It is a part of McClellan's army, however, and, as such, is entitled to better guidance.   I do not put the fault on General Banks, but on the crippled condition in which his staff and departments are kept.   Of this, however, I am not in a position to be an observer or a judge.   I can speak only of the results which I see.   There is no reason why I should harp on this theme, however.   We get on finely, only I like to make it understood that we do so *over obstacles*.   This is natural, I suppose.

"When I hear, too, all this talk about a 'grand army,' 'the splendid spectacle our country presents,' &c., &c., 'what a terror we should be to England,' 'how ready we are for war,' I know that it is the nonsense of ignorance that men are talking.   'Clear your mind of cant,' says Dr. Johnson.

"I have resumed this letter since last night, and must now get ready for the review this bright Monday morning. Have you read Colonel Harvey Brown's clear, manly, sensible despatch from Fort Pickens? — his statement of results, — fruits of experience ripe and real.   There is a modesty, directness, absence of cant about it that stamp the man a soldier fit for command.   It is refreshing to read such a statement, after General ———'s vaunting return from Hatteras ; after such a telegram as that which chronicled Colonel ———'s braggadocio ride on a cannon from a smart little skirmish near Harper's Ferry, which is called a 'great victory'; after the many magnificent records of routine exploits, which surprise our volunteers into the foolish belief that they are sudden heroes; after the constant record of the movements of my friend ———, who is a first-rate fellow, and doing a good work with too much noise about it. These men seem to be all attempting a '*hasty plate of glory*,' as Colonel Andrews calls it. The simple discharge of duty, and then an intelligent attempt to learn a lesson, and *do better next time*. Let us hope for imitation of this Colonel Brown of the *regulars*. But the Colonel puts his head into my tent and says, ' Major, the line will be formed at twelve o'clock,' and so I must '*prepare for review*.'

Evening.

" There is something gay, inspiriting, exciting, in a fine review. The brigade burnishes its equipments and perfects its uniform. It also puts on its pride and its peacock feathers. All is elation and glorification. Now, though humility is at once a grace and a virtue, its modest worth has no place here. Humility never ' prepares for review,' or ' parades for inspection.' But a regiment does both. So we put on our gayest plumage of pride, with our hats and feathers and epaulettes: the band shone with its new instruments; the sun vied with their splendor, perhaps aided it. The drum-major's silver globe rivalled the orb that it multiplied. Officers and men were ambitious, confident, elate. We were the first brigade to be reviewed, after the others who disported themselves last week, — of course to surpass them. I need not describe the ceremony. Everything went well, except that my horse gave a plunge opposite the General, and slightly disconcerted my salute ; but, as I say, pride was at the helm, and on we went. The Second *did* itself proud. I never saw it march with more steadiness, or keep its line better. After the review a drill was ordered ; and here our regiment proceeded to distinguish and emphasize itself. We had a brisk, rattling, double-quick drill, and were the observed of all observers, and the praised of all praisers ; so that when we came home to read our newspapers, and found that England was going to demand satisfaction and compel the surrender of the ambassadors, we felt all ready for war with England. Still, I cannot believe in all this bluster.

" The right of search and seizure is, on the weight of authority, in our favor. But it is just one of those nice and delicate questions that will affect the mind of the seizor differently from the seizee ; and, on the whole, seems to me a right that ought not to be exercised except in a very tempting case like this one. We must stand to our guns, and England will back down. I hope Charleston has been burnt by its own negroes. That would be a felicity of Divine wrath that could not be surpassed.

" I have received notice from General Hamilton to begin work on the Examining Board to-morrow (Tuesday), the 17th. This will keep me busy for the present ; but I expect quite an amusing time, though perhaps a little monotonously so. I found your letters on my return from review ; one from you, and one from Colonel Andrews. . . . . We want him back ; and the officers and men constantly ask for him, and when he is coming.

" I have only time, this Tuesday morning, before going into Frederick, to bid you good by. Love to all at home. I wish I could hear from Howard."

"CAMP HICKS, NEAR FREDERICK, December 20, 1861.

" It was only the immediate pressure of another topic that crowded out the mention of the arrival of the box of shirts and drawers, &c., from Mrs. Ticknor. They were equally distributed among the men needing them most. They were most gladly welcomed. In size, shape, and substance, they are all we could desire. The gay-colored handkerchiefs warmed the fancy of the men, and were eagerly snatched at. The mittens, too, notwithstanding the finger deformity, were grasped by eager hands. I think it would reward the effort of our friends if they could have seen the opening of the box, and the scattering of the clothing to the companies. The eyes of the men chosen for the gifts glistened, and the eyes of the others fell, as those of children. Indeed, in many respects, soldiers *are* like children ; and the idea that there is a box from home with a present in it is, you know, the crowning joy of childhood. There is a certain flavor to these arrivals, of warmth and comfort, that seems to dwell with peculiar relish on the mind. They make a day glad and cheerful. But I must protest against this form of ' *soldier's mitten*.' Make a good, honest mitten, in which there shall be no aristocracy or seclusion among the fingers, but where they may dwell together in unity. When the man is to use his gun he won't wear a mitten. At other times he wants the old, warm mitten, not this eccentric innovation. By this criticism I do not wish to discourage the sending of mittens of this or any other shape. We want those of any shape. I speak only in the interests of science and truth.

"I wish you could have seen the regiment this evening at parade. We got fresh white gloves for the men to-day ; and the steady line, with its regular and precise movement, the shining brass of the equipments, and general neatness, was a fine sight. Our old uniforms, after all their service, look better than most new ones. General Banks was present, and afterwards came up and admired my tent-house.

"My friend Colonel Geary has gone back to Point of Rocks. General Hamilton is off to Williamsport, and the Board will meet again ' some day next week.'

"I enjoyed Colonel Geary's talk very much. He has seen a good deal of rough life ; was a colonel during the Mexican War, then a Californian, and the last *alcalde* of San Francisco, then a governor of Kansas. He speaks of events of which he was himself no small part.

"Colonel ———, of the Sixteenth Indiana, is a character,— a tall, gaunt Western lawyer turned colonel. He has just returned from a visit to Washington and his home. Speaking of the crowds of officers and soldiers who throng Penn-

12

sylvania Avenue, he said, ' I told my friends if we could only get the Confederates into Pennsylvania Avenue, we could give them an awful thrashing.   I never saw so many officers in my life.   We could thrash 'em to death, sir.'

" I was glad to receive news from Howard.   Glad, too, to find him in service and promoted.   His success is certain, if he holds on.   I shall write to him not to be discouraged, and not to regret being in Missouri.   Halleck will reorganize, correct, discipline the force ; and he will belong to a grand army, and perhaps share in glorious achievement. . . . . It is now Sunday morning, and quite cold.   We have been building a log-kitchen, and are now building a stable.   The government has, I understand, decided to allow us lumber enough to make us quite comfortable. And I think we shall give the coming week to it.   If we are to remain for the winter, I incline to think I shall build me a house, by way of pastime, if not for comfort.

" This fine open weather, which has hastened the month of December to its close, seems made for use.   Perhaps if McClellan could have foreseen it, he would have used it. Now, however, it is too late.   Still, events march, — Kentucky swarming with Union soldiers, and soon to be a battle-field ; Missouri even now the scene of Federal victory. . . . .

" I think the birds of spring will sing Hail Columbia and the Star Spangled Banner all over the South, though the Christmas chimes and carols may be sadly out of tune.   I hope this letter may reach you in season to bring my greeting for Christmas eve.   We can hardly receive the Christmas message, ' On earth peace, good-will toward men,' in any obvious and literal sense this year.   It is said to be the appointed time for a holiday massacre and uprising among the slaves.   It is certain that few Christmas firesides which do not miss a soldier from their circle can gather in our land.   ' Not peace, but a sword.'   Yet I can confidently wish a Merry Christmas to you, and look forward to a happier New Year. We are fighting a good fight ; if only we can be true to our cause and ourselves, we have the right to indulge the brightest hopes and rely on the best promises. God is with us.

" Hang up every sign of Christmas, — the freshest green. Commemorate the message and the Prince of Peace. Gather the Christmas family-circle, and remember the absent ; for family ties are never so close as in these days of separation and trial. Love to all at home. I wish I could send a token to every one, but, instead, must content myself with good wishes.

" Remember me most kindly to all friends. I should like to drop down among you Christmas morning and catch C———, as I certainly should, after my reveillé experience of the past six months."

"CAMP HICKS, December 23, 1861.

" DEAR D———, — I do assure you that your Christmas remembrance has warmed and cheered and brightened this sombre morning in camp. Our wooded camp had been hail-rattled and rain-rattled all night. The half-broke morning was dull with falling snows. The ice-crowned trees bowed their heads and bent their branches, winter-laden. A moaning wind chimed to the ear the sad tones whose corresponding hues darkened the eye. But just as your gift arrived the sun broke, also the clouds. Sun-lightened was the air, and sun-lightened, also, was my spirit. I rejoiced in home memories and associations. And now, the day really is a good day. I expect many empty hours in camp this winter, and hope to fill some of the pleasantest of them with Napier. Unless something more serious than the present threatenings indicate should occur at Falling Waters, we shall probably pass a quiet winter in our present favorable camp. The division is placed here because of the abundant forage of this county and the direct rail communication. I am quite a convert to the wisdom and necessity of taking good care of our army, and saving it up for spring. Events are favoring us rapidly now of their own accord.

" The English question does not yet take shape enough to enable one to judge of it. I have no fear of a war with England. The cause is inadequate. The right of search and seizure is one that I hope we shall exercise sparingly. The game is not worth the candle. Still, I enjoy the joke of the seizure of Slidell and Mason, and am curious to see the ground of England's vigorous protest. England is base and mean in her treatment of us; and if we were only *stronger*, I should enjoy a war with her. As it is, I suppose we must wait, like Dr. Winship, till we have trained a couple of years, and then, perhaps, we shall be up to a fight with her.

" It really seems, this evening, as if winter, Northern winter, had come. If he visits Manassas as he does Frederick, how the Rebels must be shivering in their shoes, if, indeed, they have any shoes to shiver in.

" Howard's position I rejoice in. I quite believe that he will rise in his regiment and see service. I repeat my thanks, and wish you Merry Christmas and Happy New Year ! "

" CAMP HICKS, December 25, 1861, Christmas Morning.

" DEAR MOTHER, — ' A merry Christmas,' said I to *myself*, for want of a larger family-circle, as I put my head out into the morning while reveillé was rousing the camp. And into a brisk, crisp morning did I walk as I stepped from my tent. The moon had not yet lost its flame, though the east was warming to receive the coming sun. A light fall of snow, sent by Heaven to gladden the day, had whitened tents and ground alike. Soon the sun kindled it into a Christmas glisten and sparkle. Yes, the scene was the traditional holiday dress of the season. And now, as I sit and write, my ears are full of the mellow music of Auld Lang Syne from the band at guard-mounting. I believe I am somewhat sensitive to the aspects and influences of air and sky and landscape. This out-door life serves only to quicken and confirm such tendency. I am always apt to thank God for a fine day, through which everything is bright and promising. And Nature having put on her gayest winter merriment, I share her gladness. So I give you all at home a Merry Christmas in this missive, and here's a health to *next* Christmas with *the war over.*

" Yet, even on this merry morning, I have a shadow, which, I hope, is a mere distemper of the fancy. It comes from the sullen aspect of the English news. I start with the faith which I cherish, that there can be no war with England unless she is obstinately bent thereon. There is no adequate cause. But all this preparation, all this arming and bluster, really gives an air of probability to the suggestion that she madly desires to seize the pretext and provoke a contest. I do hope not ; for, with fair play, we are sure, in the opening spring, of rapid, inspiriting, honorable success. Witness McCall's cleverly managed affair at Drainsville. Its conception and execution alike skilful. It contains proof, too, that our superior armament and equipment will tell on every fair field. . . . .

" The incidents of the last year have frightened me out of what little tendency to prophecy I may have had ; but nothing save this cloud from England could dispirit the hope with which I look forward to our coming contest with the Rebellion. . . . .

" Will not our day come for a chance at the enemy? Again I hope. There is no news. I am busy about the Examining Board ; I am assailed by several perplexities within the regiment ; I am ennuied with inaction. But I am well, and, on the whole, content. I am glad you should have a visit from Colonel William.

" My sergeant says : ' I saw your brother, Colonel Dwight, at the office, sir ! He's a splendid officer, sir ! ' So echo I. Love and good wishes to all."

" We are drinking the lees of the old year! It is the penitent reminiscent season. We may look back along the furrow that our little individual ploughshare seems to us to be making. Few of us, indeed, can see that the past retains the mark of our labor. All of us, however, can whip up our teams on New Year's morning, and open a new furrow in a new field, or plough the same ground over again, with new zeal.

" Such is the illusion of hope, and so glad are we to postpone repentance another-year. And, indeed, this bright Sunday morning wins one *hopeward*.

" Since Christmas morning I have been busy with our Examining Board. The work is amusing; but it is also pitiable to see what ignorance and incapacity are to be *weeded* out of the army.

" Yesterday we had a visit in camp from Mr. and Mrs. ———. You recollect charming Miss ———. Well, she shone like a star upon our darkness. Her presence in my tent, which she honored, has left a sort of halo which cheers it still. The first glimpse of womanhood and loveliness I have had for an age, as it seems. The past is so crowded that it seems very distant.

" The Drainsville ' affair ' turns out, in the magnitude of its consequences, a battle and a defeat.

" ' Io Triumphe ' !! McClellan promises Porter's division an occasion, shortly, to show by fighting, as well as in reviews, that they are soldiers. This by his Christmas order. Who knows but my house which I begin to build to-morrow will stand rather as a monument than as a dwelling?

" I must say I think the tonic of victory would be of most happy and invigorating influence. Give me a little of the ' ecstasy of strife.' Bother this constant rehearsal.

" ——— has caught the cavalry complaint, and is off for a

captaincy.   So we go.   The Second radiates its good influence, and every new enterprise borrows our light.

"If we could only have the baptism of battle, perhaps these young men would not be in such haste to leave.   Good by, and a Happy New Year to all at home."

"CAMP HICKS, NEAR FREDERICK, December 29, 1861.

"DEAR FATHER, — I wish you a happy and prosperous New Year, and I wish that I could hope to do something to help make it so.   But, out here in my frontier helplessness, I can only receive favors, not do them.

"It will, I trust, be a happy day for all of us when the regiment has lived its life and done its work, and can return *in peace*.   Such is my dream, though it seems distant. . . . .

"I have just read the capitulation and surrender of Mason and Slidell.   Seward's letter is masterly, his conclusion dignified and perhaps just.   His forbearance to hold on to them because they are not worth it is a stroke.   On the whole, I am well pleased.   What do you think of it ? "

CHAPTER XII.

LETTERS FROM CANTONMENT HICKS, NEAR FREDERICK. — CHARLES-
TOWN, VIRGINIA.—CAMP NEAR BERRYVILLE. — CAMP NEAR WIN-
CHESTER.

"CANTONMENT HICKS, January 5, 1862, near Frederick.

"DEAR MOTHER, — The New Year is fairly open, yet
my pen has been silent.   I would have had it otherwise, but have been prevented writing by a sudden call to
Washington.   There I saw Colonel William, who was as
critical and hypercritical as possible.   I enjoyed his discussions very much.   His spirit and go are delightful.   He will
take his regiment wherever men can go, if they only give
him a chance.   We had a pleasant time, looking over his
books, and talking about war and home. . . . .

"The effect of my visit to Washington was to fill me with
forebodings; but, as I won't stay filled, I am resuming my
buoyancy again.   Yesterday there was a great flurry.   I
had come up to Frederick to church, and was enjoying the
service much.   General Banks was called out of church,
and we found that Jackson was threatening Hancock, and
aiming to destroy the railroad bridges near by.   An order
was immediately issued, 'Two days' rations in haversack,
and be ready to march.'   I did not allow it to disturb me,
but this morning the Third Brigade went off in a snow-storm,
before light, to Williamsport.   We are left quiet; and, as
I consider it all a mere scare, I am glad we were not aroused
by it.

"Winter quarters are pretty precarious, however.   We
are *too far* from the Potomac.   This division is nowhere.
It is liable to go *anywhere,* and hence is unfortunate.   One
regiment of the Third Brigade got back from Williamsport

day before yesterday; now it is off again the same thirty miles through the snow. That's generalship, ain't it? Who is to blame? No one, of course. Bah! . . . .

"I wish you all a happy New Year; and as for us in the army, I wish us all a *fighting* New Year."

"CANTONMENT HICKS, near Frederick, January 7, 1862.

"It is this Tuesday evening my stove is humming in my new house. Talk of luxury! — what is comparable to a log-house, with windows and doors, with shelves and tables, and a large, grand porch for an entrance, and in the Colonel's half of the house an open, old-fashioned, generous, glowing fireplace! You should see the architectural proportions of our new home. You would hardly believe it a week's work of our wood-choppers and masons and carpenters. Yet so it is. I shall hope to send you home a photograph of it. We were within a narrow chance of leaving it the other day, but now we have subsided again into tranquil housekeeping and camp life. I have Colonel Andrews living with me, and, indeed, took the house rather with reference to him than myself. I wanted a roof to put him under on his first taste of exposure. My man John, who is quite a character, takes great delight in the house. He thinks my half better than the Colonel's, though his is somewhat larger. 'It is more *comformblor* nor the Colonel's, sir, and not so desolate like,' is his description of my cosiness. The Third Brigade went off on that alarm toward Hancock; and, as I surmised, the errand proved fruitless. We are, however, gathering hope of progress in the army. This condition of faith in things not seen, and hope without substance, is not inspiriting. The undertone of rumor in Washington was very strong in the direction of activity. I am coming to regard an early advance of our army as a political and moral necessity, whether it is physically possible or not. The achievement of the impossible is the duty and privilege of greatness; and now is certainly McClellan's opportunity.

" Mrs. Ticknor did me the honor to send me a pair of stockings. I wrote yesterday to acknowledge their receipt. The weather, which has been bitter cold, is now moderating, and the tents do not *shiver* as they did."

" CANTONMENT HICKS, January 10, 1862,
Near Frederick, Maryland.

" Napoleon said, ' Marlborough, while he gained battles, ruled cabinets and guided statesmen.' I question much if our General, whatever may be the future record of him as a battle-victor, will ever excite the praise of ruling cabinets or statesmen. My impression, which I cannot shake off, is, that McClellan fails to be master of the whole position. . . . . His admirers all say, ' Wait till he takes the field. He will whirl and sweep his enemies before him like a storm-king.' I hope so ; but meanwhile, in the organizing and preparatory season, whose opportunity is *now*, his impulse is not as widely or as directly felt as I could wish. This seems a tangible and real defect, whose correction ought to be possible.

" It is with such considerations as this that our minds naturally busy themselves at this time. In this seclusion one is apt to get under the influence of moods or rumors, and to exaggerate or create facts ; but I seem, to myself, to notice a great want of tone and confidence in the people and in the army. This may not be so. Certainly, however, Congress is as utterly beneath the emergency as possible.

" After all the flurry of last Sunday, we are again hopelessly quiet. This is exactly according to my faith, and I am sorry that you should have imagined an anxiety for me, as your last letter indicates. Don't mind the telegraph ; you can really judge nothing by it.

" You will see, by the date of my letter, that our *camp* is now changed to a cantonment, by orders from brigade headquarters. The huts and houses have so far outnumbered the tents that this nomenclatorial effort of the General is excusable. Still, we are a camp, in my view, and not a cantonment; though, of course, I date my letter according to the order."

"CANTONMENT HICKS, NEAR FREDERICK, January 13, 1861.

" ' Si le combat est prévu, la troupe se met en grande tenue ; elle doit cette politesse a un ennemi qu'elle estime.'

" Dufour gives this among the rules for combats of infantry against infantry.

" What a charming courtesy ! what French politeness ! Full uniform is the proper compliment to be paid to an enemy that you esteem. After all, none but a Frenchman could have hit upon that rule, or its reason.

" But I have news for you. Was it not Sunday when I wrote ? And I forgot to mention that our band was to give a grand concert on Monday evening. Spiegel, our band-leader, had been ambitious, and the Colonel encouraged him in his scheme. The result was even better than our hope. The hall was crowded. All the beauty and fashion of Frederick were there. Our band showed finely. Altogether, there was *éclat* in the concert. The whole closed with Hail Columbia and the Star Spangled Banner. You would be surprised to see with what hungry ears they listen to Yankee Doodle in this country. Those short-sighted persons who advise disbanding the bands would disarm our army of a great strength.

" I have found to-day that Frederick is echoing the praises of the Massachusetts Second. We even think of a Promenade Concert next week. So do not turn your thoughts in regarding us to the discords of war, but rather to the mellowest harmonies of peace.

" Again, art is giving us repute in another direction. Private D'Avignon, of Company I (a reduced artist, and too good for a soldier), is to have the honor to draw a picture of General Banks. So you see that we are not occupied as your fancy would have us.

" I have a very pleasant letter from you to-day. I think

the question, whether I have found a profession, or only lost one, is premature.   I want no unripe fruit, and I think I must possess my soul in patience and in hope.

"I trust father is not much dispirited.   Let him wait a little longer, and perhaps we shall see something done.

"I enclose you Colonel Andrews's artistic plan of our house. He made it at my request. The dimensions are twenty-four feet by eighteen feet.   It is a wonderful house, and a great comfort this cold and snowy night."

"CANTONMENT HICKS (so called), January 17, 1862.

"I had a corpulent little letter from you, — one actually swelling with agreeable importance.   I hope Mrs. Ticknor's surprise at my acknowledging the present of the stockings was not displeasure.   I thought so long a pair of stockings would bear a short note; and I really wanted the opportunity to express my gratitude for the service she had done us.   You see a letter from no less an authority than George Washington suggests exactly the counterpart of the scheme of benevolence of her association, — an extra shirt for the soldier.

"Life lags along with us.   It has its family cares and its family jars; but, on the whole, all is well; and the lengthening days already begin to promise the coming spring. —— is not right in his idea that I do not want to come home; but I have never seen the time when I could properly do so, and am quite content to wait till such a time.   I should prefer to have activity and success precede my visit.   I am quite busy with my duties on the Examining Board, and there seems no limit to the amount of work provided for us.   The army certainly needs a great deal of weeding out among its officers.

"I find General Hamilton and Colonel Geary very agreeable associates.   The former is really a splendid man, and a fine officer, — educated, self-reliant, brave.   I have great confidence in him, and wish our regiment were in his brigade. General Hamilton is from Wisconsin, where he went a few years ago on resigning from the army. . . . .

" I hope father is regaining his confidence in McClellan. You see the telegraph says that he has persuaded the Congressional Committee into content, after spending the day with them. I think father ought to grant him another lease of hope and confidence ; but for these rascally contractors, swindlers, defaulters, and other leeches I have only hatred and contempt. A vigorous and lively gallows is what this country wants now.

" Any change in the War Department is a change for the better. I should have been glad to see General Banks there, however. I have great faith in his ability and statesmanship, and in his thorough comprehension of this Rebellion. But as a general in the field he has not fair scope for his powers yet. Perhaps it may come, however."

"HEAD-QUARTERS EXAMINING BOARD, January 21, 1861.

" It has rained and hailed and sleeted for the past four days. We are kept under marching orders, but, I think, with no view of an immediate movement, though it cannot be long before we shall be called on to make ourselves useless or useful, according to our guidance.

" I understand your state of suspense as to the army. For myself, I can see no other wisdom than patience and faith. I confess that, now and then, this seems difficult ; but whether McClellan will not vindicate himself is not so clear ; and if, when our army moves, it moves in organized obedience to a single will, the wonder will not be that so much time has been spent in preparation, but that the preparation has been made. . . . .

" While I write this letter, the examination of an unlucky lieutenant is going on. The young man is wandering now through the mazes of battalion drill, and he seems rather lost. I hope this work is nearly over.

" On the whole, bad as the season is, and ominous as the

anniversary on which I write (six months ago, Bull Run), I should like to see some fighting done.

"We have telegraphic news to-day of a 'Great battle and victory over Zollicoffer in Kentucky.' I hope it may not dwindle as Nelson's victory did. I take great comfort in reading the extracts from the Southern newspapers. They seem to write without hope. Love to all."

"CANTONMENT HICKS, NEAR FREDERICK,
January 25, 1862.

"At last we have symptoms of sunshine in our tedious and sullen sky; and at last, also, we have symptoms of breaking light on the horizon of the future. The rout of Zollicoffer (Phœbus, what a name!), of great results in itself, gets its best significance from the confidence it inspires in what may and must follow, if 'alacrity' shall replace torpor, under the quickening guidance of our new War Secretary. I hear the best accounts of Mr. Stanton, and he certainly has the confidence of the country. Indeed, it begins to seem as if we were on our way out of the woods at last. I have had the greatest pleasure in a visit from ———. The Colonel went down to Washington on Monday, and brought ——— back with him. I found him snug in one corner of the Colonel's fireplace on my return to camp in the afternoon. An evening full of talk, and gladdened by a great many home-memories, followed. Unluckily, we are in the midst of our rain and mud, so we could not show our prettiness; but I think he enjoyed seeing a little of the plain prose of soldiering, perhaps as much as its gayer phase. You have no idea of the depressing influence of *mud*, — deep, miry, insidious, hopeless mud. The Slough of Despond is no allegory. The soil of Maryland is very unpropitious, and we cannot find dry ground, at this season, for our camps. Another box from Mrs. Ticknor opportunely brightens this dull time. But it seems that, in this vicinity, we can hardly expect rapid motion just now."

"'FROM GENERAL BANKS'S COLUMN,
Frederick, Maryland, Jan. 17.

"'Nothing of the least interest has transpired for several days past along the line of the Upper Potomac.'

"CANTONMENT (?) HICKS, January 28, 1862.

"I send you the above, clipped from yesterday's paper. It is a wonderfully accurate telegraphic despatch. It is a curiosity of correctness, a prodigy of precision. It states, too, all that I can hope to do for you by way of news. Yet I will not deny that the air is full of rumors, nor that our stay at Frederick is, very probably, to count itself by days rather than weeks.

"This whole region of conjecture is so tracked and trodden by the impatient restlessness of camp life, that I consider it worth little. Yet I wish you to feel sure that, though 'nothing of the least interest transpires,' we keep up a perturbed prophesying, which answers very well to spice and quicken this slow life. . . . .

"I saw yesterday a writing-case that excited my envy. It rolls up very compactly ; and, being composed of narrow and thin pieces of wood, a clamp holds them in place, and makes a tablet of the roll.

"Will you get me a small one ? as I hope to be reduced to a carpet-bag or a saddle-bag very often this summer. . . . .

"I am going to do what I can to reduce living to its lowest terms ; and I hope to be as movable as a small, country frame-house ; which, I believe, is the most restless fixture of modern times."

"CANTONMENT HICKS, NEAR FREDERICK,
January 28, 1862.

"If I write you from my experience, I shall have little to tell of a soldier's life. It is one of the disadvantages of this detached duty that it separates one from the life of the regiment. This I could find more disposition to regret, if

I saw much life now in the regiment ; but, in truth, we are devoting ourselves to keeping warm and dry under every assault of heaven and earth, rain and mud. . . . .

" Yesterday we had a new excitement and amusement. Colonel Geary got up a party to Point of Rocks, by special train, in the evening, to witness his private theatricals. We had a gay excursion. A crowded car of young ladies and old generals ; off we went at about six o'clock. When we reached Point of Rocks, we emerged from the car ; and, amid the clanging, brazen music of the band, piled ourselves into army-wagons, whose sternness was soothed with a little straw. On we went, jolting and laughing, to the camp. There we found an *out-door* stage, bright with hanging Chinese lanterns ; and, in the chilly night, well wrapped up, we shiveringly admired the ' Geary Thespian Corps.' Toodles was very well played ; and, indeed, the acting was successful. We came back by the cars at midnight. Our moving train at the unusual hour, so near the enemy's lines on the other side of the Potomac, set their signal-lights playing, and, undoubtedly, they failed to explain the activity in Colonel Geary's camp by its true cause. In truth, it is an experience, — an open-air theatrical display in January, within reach of Rebel guns, and in sight of Rebel signal-fires.

" General Banks went off to Washington yesterday. Rumor gives him various errands. We only hope that he goes to hear of some movement that he may share or inaugurate. I do not even guess a motive, for my guesses come back on me dishonored so often that I weary of conjecture.

" If the history of the volunteer force for this great war of ours shall ever be written, I can certainly give some very amusing episodes of appointments of officers, and their character and capacity. Our Board continues its weeding ruthlessly. To-day, under the terror even of our presence, were two resignations, — one of a colonel.

" I enclose for you a very *unfair* photograph of my friend

General Hamilton. It does not do him justice; yet it is, of course, a likeness. Place it in my album, if you please. Colonel Geary promises to exchange with me also, so that I shall have the whole Board in my book.

"The association has been such a pleasant one that I shall like to have you keep a souvenir of it. . . . .

"To one who believes in omens, as I do, who hails the crescent with a right-shouldered glance, the battle of Mill Spring is something more than a victory. It is an augury, and it fills me with hope.

"I am scribbling the close of this letter in the rooms of the Examining Board, interrupted by a chat with General Hamilton.

"I give you all joy of Kentucky. Will not father allow his forebodings to be corrected a little? Love to all."

"CANTONMENT HICKS, February 2, 1862.

"A Sunday-morning inspection of your letter, received last evening, prompts me to answer; though it must come out of the blank which is now my book of chronicles. I might write to you, it is true, out of myself. In this case, I should probably exaggerate the thoughts and feelings which spring naturally from the experiences of this new, and, in some sort, intense life. Not that it is now a life of even mental, much less moral or emotional, activity; but I choose the word for its derivative, rather than its acquired significance. The life is *tense*, in the sense of keeping one on the stretch. All the chords seem to be kept at their highest vibratory capacity. With occasional lapses of depressional laxity, this is true; and it gives the meaning to our seemingly dull existence. Action would be a great relief. You good people, who sit at home and ask for a battle with such impatience for result, can only feebly guess at the temper of the army itself. I do not agree at all with some who speak of our being demoralized. I think we are becoming restive, eager, sore; but, I trust, all the more

13

ready and willing for sacrifice, effort, suffering.   I can imagine McClellan himself chafing ' to himself within himself '
while his hand is on the curb.

"But bother reflection ; and of *all* spections the foolishest
is *intro*spection.   I do not care to analyze my present state ;
but I do pray that Heaven has not three months more of
this kind of life in store for me.

"'*Aut cita mors, aut victoria lœta.*'

"You may conjecture, from the above, it has been particularly rainy and muddy this week. . . . . I can call up your
coasting scene, not without envy.   There is youth in it, and
everything young I like.   Our snow here is so undecided
and capricious that it gives no such hope of enjoyment.
And Tug,* too, you say he is depressed.   I can well understand the serious concern with which he must regard his
country's trial.   I hope he will not be doomed to close his
eyes, after a last look at the dishonored fragments of a once
glorious Union.   You must guard his old age till my return.
His life has been one of constant struggle and inquiry ; he
should have an old age of ease and contemplation.   I know
not what fate is in store for him, but few of us can look back
on a life of so many purposes and so much attainment."

"CANTONMENT HICKS, February 9, 1862, near Frederick.

"If I could take the wings of this brisk, sunny morning,
I would certainly fold them on our front-door steps in
Brookline.   Nor would I then proceed to hide my head
under the wings, but, having flapped them cheerfully, I
would thereupon crow!

"But, as the wings and a furlough are both wanting, I
must content myself with a web-footed, amphibious existence
in the mud of Maryland.

"There is a secession song which enjoys a surreptitious
parlor popularity here.   It is called, 'Maryland, — my Maryland!' and rehearses, among other things, that ' the despot's

---

* A favorite old dog, who survived his master but one year.

heel is on thy breast!' If that be so, all I have got to say is, that, just now, the heel has the worst of it. Yet there is a just satisfaction in this morning's inspection of men, tents, and kitchens, — to see how, by discipline, method, and fidelity, there is a successful contest maintained with all the elements. The neatness and order of our camp, in spite of mud, is a ' volunteer miracle.'

" You will be glad to know that the regiment is now in fine health. We already begin to count the days till spring. Of course, it is unsafe to predict the climate. I remember very well, however, that last February was quite dry, and that early in March dust, and not mud, was the enemy I found in Washington. It may well be, therefore, that there is a good time coming.

" Indeed, has it not, in one sense, already come ? Can you blind yourself to the omens and the tendencies ? What shall we say of those statesmen of a budding empire, a new State, which is to give the law to the commerce and industry of the world through a single monopoly ? What shall we say of the statesmen (Cobb, Toombs, etc.) who counsel their happy and chivalrous people to a general bonfire of house, home, and product ? There 's a new industry for a new State. King Cotton is a rare potentate. He proposes to be, himself, his own circulating medium, among other eccentricities.

" Then, too, what admirable inferiority of fortification they succeed in erecting! Will our fleet of gunboats have as easy victories over all their river defences ? and, if so, how far are we from Memphis ? and where is Porter going with his ' Mortar Fleet.' Among the ablest of our naval commanders, he is not bent on a fool's errand. When Jeff Davis sleeps o' nights, does he dream of power ?

" But I 've given you too many questions. In the midst of all this jubilant interrogatory, when will our time come ? Just as soon as the mud dries, without a doubt.

" Our life jogs on here without variety. For the most

part, we spend our time in reading military books and talking military talk.

" I am just now a good deal disturbed by the prospect of disbanding the bands. A greater mistake could not be made. The man with so little music in his soul as to vote for it is fit for — a Secessionist. Marshal Saxe, in introducing the *cadenced* step in the French infantry, says, ' Music exerts a great and secret power over us. It disposes " nos organes aux exercises du corps, les soulagent dans ces exercises. On danse toute une nuit au son des instruments mais personne ne resterait à danser pendant un quart d'heure, seulement, sans musique." ' I have seen many a practical verification of this in the gathering freshness and quickness with which jaded men went on their march when the music called and cheered them.

" Besides, we want the Star Spangled Banner, and its melody, as allies against the Rebel seductions."

"CAMP HICKS, NEAR FREDERICK, February 12, 1862.

" Had n't the little hills better begin to rejoice ? Something ought to clap its hands. What of Burnside ? The luck has changed. Louis Napoleon says he will give us only ' *wishes.*' Good ones or bad, I care not, so they are wishes merely. This evening an order comes to us to furnish, from our regiment, part of a force to man some gunboats on the Mississippi River. That looks like life in the West. It is an outrage on our regiment, of course, but perhaps will help the cause. We send thirty or forty men, — no officers, that is the order. But to go back to Burnside and three thousand prisoners. There 's progress for you ! Yet, in the midst of it all (shall I confess it ?), I have not felt so blue for a month as I do to-day. Exploit, achievement, victory, — but *I not there.* I may feel and express foolishness, and I think I do; but I had rather lose my life to-morrow *in a victory* than to save it for fifty years without one. This inaction and stagnation, in the midst of all the animating news from every quarter, is utterly maddening; and I must yell out my grief in the midst of this general joy.

" There, I have relieved myself a little, and perhaps I can now write reasonably, and with a moderately Christian temper.

" There is some authoritative statement as to the relative merit, I believe, of him who ruleth his spirit and of him who taketh a city. You see that I do neither. When I speak of myself as *not there*, I mean the Massachusetts Second, in whose fortunes and hopes I merge my own.

" I ought, perhaps, to burn this letter, but I 'll send it, I believe. In an hour or two I shall be cheerful as ever, and continue the service of standing and waiting with good heart, I hope."

" CANTONMENT HICKS, February 16, 1862, near Frederick.

" I sent you a howl last Wednesday; but, now that I find there was a plentiful lack of fighting at Roanoke Island, and an equal abundance of running away, I care little about it. Its effect, though, is grand. Still more important is the news from the Mississippi and Tennessee. That ' idolatrous devotion to the old Union,' which the Richmond Despatch so feelingly regrets, we shall hear more from soon.

" We are approaching consummations in many directions, I opine. At times, I almost fear a sudden collapse, and very little fighting after all. Still, I think this can hardly be. It is not to be desired, I think, because of the weak-kneed settlement that would come. I see no good way out of our present difficulties, except through an overwhelming military superiority established *by battles* and defeats. Subjugation, the thing that they fear, is the thing I desire.

" I hope that father begins to revive his faith in McClellan under the apparent culmination of his plans and combinations. But, unluckily, we are a people without faith in men or in principles, I fear ; and that is the most hopeless sign in our condition.

" To-day, we have the wintriest morning of the year. Bright sunshine, however, makes it cheerful; and I look upon it as the last effort of winter. This is not a climate in which winter lingers to chill the lap of spring, and we are all ready for a spring.

" This evening I shall go into church to the pretty Episcopal Church in Frederick.

" Our cook, Tony, came in this morning, in great glee, to report that his pigeon had laid two eggs (and Sunday she lays two). He has several pets, — puppies, kittens, chickens, and doves.

" Hurrah for the Union and McClellan ! "

" CANTONMENT HICKS,
Raining like the recent Federal victories, and dark and cloudy as the Rebel prospects,
February 19, 1862.

" Hurrah for Donelson ! Are not the bricks beginning to tumble beautifully ?

" Glorious Holt has tears of joy filling his eyes. Johnson and Maynard have homes and families again. The ' ungenerous' advantage has been taken !

" Price, too, as we hear to-night, has at last fallen into the trap, and that fox has lost his tail at last. I am thinking that it will be fashionable soon, in rebeldom, for the foxes to go without their tails. In the midst of all this, where are we ? There is not even echo enough to answer the question.

" Tell D—— to keep the money raised by the theatricals for sick and wounded soldiers, and intrust it only to such spending as shall wisely guide it in such channels. . . . . .

" Howard, perchance, has seen service in this Price pursuit and capture. Heaven send him honorable employment. He has the other things needful.

" I have, in my time, heard a great deal said of vital faith and trust in God.   I have observed very little of its practical working in life.   I must say, I should like to have it myself.   The last month has been the hardest one since I entered the service.   Action, action, action, is what we want."

"CAMP HICKS, February 25.

"We are under marching orders, and shall leave very soon for Harper's Ferry and ' *so on*.'   There is an exhilarating cheerfulness in this new life.   I am so *blazé* of sensations that my hope rises feebly.   There may, however, be purpose and exploit in our future, — who knows ?   I have only time to give you greeting."

"CHARLESTOWN, VIRGINIA, February 28, 1862.

"A story to tell, and no time to tell it in.   That is my record.   After tedious waiting in Frederick, with constant threatenings of movement, at last, in the pouring rain of Wednesday night, came the order to be at the depot in Frederick at daylight, to take the cars for Harper's Ferry. So, in the dark, damp fog of Thursday morning, the line was formed, and on we splashed and paddled to the turnpike.   Just at sunrise we entered Frederick.   The band played, ' The girl I left behind me,' and tearful maidens looked a sad farewell.   When we got to the depot, we found no cars.   At twelve, M., we got off.

"Only six hours' delay, caused by the crowding of troops on the road coming from Poolesville.   The day broke clear and cold.   Our Frederick friends saw the last of us, and we were off.   At four o'clock we reached Sandy Hook, and were soon crossing the bridge to Harper's Ferry.   As we entered the town the music swelled out, the men closed up, and on we went, by the Shenandoah road, to the upper part of the town.   We crowded into a few buildings.   An old negro woman gave the Colonel and myself shelter, and we spent the night.   This old woman gave us her political sentiments briefly, thus : ' De Union is broderly love.   Dat 's what de Union is.   Dese yere secesshnists ain't got no sich principle.   In de Union dey do good to one another ; but dese yere secesshnists dey don't do no good to you.   Dey won't help yer out when yer 's in trouble.   Lord bress yer ! dey can't help derselves out, let alone other folks.   I 's for de Union and love ;   dat 's what I 's for.'

    " At three in the morning we were roused up by an order for the regiment to move, ' soon after sunrise,' in a reconnoissance to Charlestown.   In the sharp, windy morning we took up the march.   At Bolivar Heights the force assembled. It consisted of four squadrons of cavalry, two sections of artillery, our regiment, and the Third Wisconsin.

    " Colonel Gordon, as the ranking colonel, was in command.   Colonel Andrews had been detailed as Provost Marshal of Harper's Ferry.   This left me in immediate command of the regiment.   We moved on, over the road by which we had eight months before advanced (!) to Harper's Ferry.

    " When we got near Charlestown, Colonel Gordon hurried on with his cavalry, and all four squadrons whirled down the main street rattlingly.   Half a dozen cavalry scampered out at the other end of the town, on the road to Winchester, and the place was in our grasp.

    " The artillery was posted, commanding the two roads toward Winchester, and our regiment was drawn up in support ; the Third Wisconsin in rear.   We had been there half an hour.   The cavalry had divided itself, and gone out over the various roads.   We then heard that McClellan was coming.   So I drew up the regiment, and he rode the length of it with his staff.   I then joined them, for a moment, to answer General Banks's inquiries, and those of General McClellan.   Colonel Gordon soon came back.   After a consultation, it was determined to remain in the town and hold it.   Our reconnoissance changed to an advance.   I put the bulk of the regiment in the courthouse, — John Brown's court-house.   I was immediately appointed Acting Provost Marshal, and had my hands full all day, attending to the quartering of troops, feeding them (for we were without rations), preventing marauding, posting pickets, &c., &c. It was an awful blustering day. At evening General Hamilton came in and took command. I was in the saddle the first part of the night, on duty, but had comfortable quarters for sleeping.

"At two in the morning, however, there was an alarm. I had to go and get the regiment under arms, also to organize a party for the purpose of obstructing the railway.

"And now, this bright morning (March 1 ; I wrote only a few lines last night), we are busy with a thousand and one affairs. How soon we shall advance I do not know. We are in large force, and shall take no steps backwards.

"McClellan has gone back to Washington, we hear. We know little of our future. The force at Harper's Ferry is increasing. A permanent bridge is going up.

"It takes a little time to organize supplies, but, as the men are fond of singing, ' we are marching on.' The regiment is in fine condition.

"To-day the rest of our brigade, from which we have been detached since the reconnoissance, has marched up.

"We have been mustering the regiment ; and used, for that purpose, the court-room. It was an odd capsize of events that brought about the muster of a Yankee regiment in Charlestown court-house.

"The newspapers, I see, are silent about our movements, or nearly so. I suppose this is under the order of the President checking the telegraph and mail. This order is a sound and healthy one.

"I have had several amusing experiences in this hot secession town in my provost-marshalship. One good lady told me this morning, ' Well ! I hope you 'll be beaten in your next battle ; but you can have the rooms, and I 'll have a fire built directly, as they are rather damp for you.' I thought this charming feminine consistency.

" I think we under-estimate the strength of the secession sentiment and overestimate the Union feeling.   Still, I may speak from the fresh impressions of my recent experience. At any rate, there is a long battle to come after the bayonet has done its work.   Troops have been coming in all day."

"CHARLESTOWN, March 4, 1862.

" The extent to which our regiment has followed the path of John Brown is somewhat curious.   The last coincidence of occupation occurred on Sunday, when the men were assembled in the court-room of the court-house, and listened to our chaplain, who preached from the judges' bench !   This morning Colonel Gordon and I went in to see the cell of Brown in the jail, and also went out in the open field, where, upon a knoll, can be seen the holes in which the gallows was set up.   ' This is a fine country,' said Brown, as he came out into the field which commands a view of this grand country.   ' I have not had an opportunity of observing it before.' . . . .

" This country has been the paradise of debtors, and creditors have seen their mortgages and notes melt away into Confederate bonds, payable ' six months after the ratification of a treaty of peace between the Confederate States and the United States.'   Money has been the one thing in excess, and delusion or terror have made this currency pass readily in payment of debts.   An element which will have some weight when you talk of conciliation is this same currency question.

" Before our arrival, every one had money.   The night before we came to town the bank migrated suddenly to Stanton, and to-day the people are refusing their own money.

" ' Pretty conciliation you bring us,' says one man ; ' why, you won't even take our money.'   This consequence of the ' invasion ' cannot fail to supply an argument to the Rebels, which they will adroitly use."

"CHARLESTOWN, VIRGINIA, March 8, 1862, Saturday.

" We are quite at home in Charlestown now.   We went into camp on Wednesday.   On Thursday I was detailed as brigade officer of the day.

" That kept me in the saddle all day and until night. And now I have a story of a midnight march for you.   It is midnight of Thursday night.   It may have begun to be Friday morning.   I am sleeping in my tent ; my nose alone apprising me that it is bitter cold.   The rattle of an orderly is heard galloping into the camp.   Soon, again, my reviving wakefulness hears the voice of Major Perkins, General Banks's Chief of Staff, talking to the Colonel in the next tent.

" At last I am called.   ' Get the regiment under arms at once, Major,' is the order, ' and move down on the Berryville Pike.'   Colonel Maulsby, who is at Kabletown, near the Shenandoah, with part of his regiment, is reported to have been attacked by Rebel cavalry, and ' cut to pieces.' A force of cavalry, artillery, and two regiments of infantry, under Colonel Gordon, is to move at once, cautiously, to his relief.   It is dark, and *so cold*.   A discussion of the best route ensues.   The regiment is turned out.   I mount my horse and ride down to take command.   In the darkness, it is difficult to see whether the regiment is facing one way or another.   We move down upon the road.   The Sixteenth Indiana follows us.

" After proceeding a mile upon the pike, we turn off upon the ' Dirt Road,' so called, toward Kabletown.   Over rocks, through ruts and mire, half frozen, we make a slight headway.   The artillery cannot proceed.   It is too dark for even safe progress by infantry.   ' Halt ! Build fires, and bivouac till daylight.'   In fifteen minutes, from our position at the head of the line to the rear of it is a succession of bright fires, with groups of men gathered round them.   Down the hill, and along the winding road is one blaze of camp-fires. The sight is a fine one.   At last the morning star rises, like a flame, and the day follows her. We move again, with flankers and advance guard. As we had been sitting about the fire, waiting for day, a teamster of Colonel Maulsby's regiment, who was our guide, had told his story, how the cavalry charged upon them, cut them down, and ' now,' said he, ' Colonel Maulsby and all his officers are either dead or on their way to Richmond.'

" As we drew near to Kabletown we saw pickets and outposts. A company of our regiment, deployed as skirmishers, went down on the field toward them. They withdrew ; but suddenly it appears that they are part of Colonel Maulsby's Home Guard !

" We advance again, when, at a turn in the road, the quiet camp of Colonel Maulsby appears in tranquil unconsciousness. The teamster opens his eyes in blank amazement. We halt. I go on and find Colonel Maulsby, delighted and surprised to see me.

" Then come the explanations. A patrol of our cavalry lost its way, last night, came rapidly in on the camp by the wrong road. Maulsby's men fired, and so did the cavalry. The teamsters and a few of the outposts were panic-stricken, and their terror drew a picture which had little resemblance to the reality.

" In the unlucky blunder, a horse and man were shot. The fugitive teamsters and outposts had led us a pretty chase. The joke and collapse were ridiculous. ' Come in to breakfast,' said Colonel Maulsby. Ha ! ha ! ha ! We are the heroes of Kabletown ! On our return, I told General Banks that Kabletown should be inscribed on our banners !

" We had a night march, and at ten o'clock in the morning we got back to our camp, after fourteen miles of marching over the worst road in the world. Well ! what of it ? There is no harm done, and perhaps this wretched cavalry has learnt a lesson.

" I am writing in the Provost Marshal's office in the

Charlestown jail. Colonel Andrews is still Provost Marshal. John Brown's cell, on the opposite side of the entry, is full of contrabands, fugitives within our lines, most of them to be sent to work at Harper's Ferry. Again I give you an odd retribution from the whirligig of events."

"CAMP NEAR CHARLESTOWN, VIRGINIA, March 9, 1862.

" After finishing my letter to you yesterday, as I came out of the Provost Marshal's office, I saw a sight that I would gladly photograph for you. A large wagon full of negro men, women, and children, overrunning like the old woman's shoe. It had come in from the farm, near town, of some disloyal Rebel. There stood the load of helpless and deserted contrabands ; an embarrassment and a question typifying the *status* of the slave everywhere, as the army marches on.

" ' You see that wagon,' said my friend and quondam enemy, the secession postmaster. ' Well, that is an answer to all your talk of protection and good government.' ' No,' said I ; ' under the government, and with the peace you then enjoyed, there were no such wagons. You had better hasten back under the government, or all your negroes will be in wagons or on foot, whither they choose. War is a rough master, but it has no rules or processes for the enforcement of the slave code.'

" The question meets you at every turn. At the tavern where we stopped for a few days after coming to town were two slaves, — an Aunt Chloe, whose bread and pastry and cake realized Mrs. Stowe's fiction ; her son George, eighteen years old, who waited on table, and whose *free* father is a carpenter in Charlestown. Day before yesterday, on going to town, I found ' aunty ' in great affliction. Her only boy, George, had ' run away.' When General Hamilton went on to Smithfield, George went too.

" He wanted to be free, instead of following longer the apron-string and *status* of his mother. Either his free father or our servants or the change of *air* had 'poisoned' his mind, as our host, his 'owner,' phrased it. I might add case after case.

"The leaven is working ; there is no stopping it."

"CAMP NEAR BERRYVILLE, March 12, 1862.
Ten miles from Winchester.

"A rapid, muddy march brought us to Berryville on Monday afternoon. As brigade officer of the day, I was busy about the outposts of our new position. The only evidence of the enemy was a few cavalry.

"The regiment lay down to bivouac, with the aid of straw and fence-rails. Yesterday I was also busy as field officer, and at one o'clock this morning was glad to leave the saddle for my tent and bed, which had come up at evening. The weather is lovely. Our cavalry reconnoissance went within three miles of Winchester, driving the enemy's cavalry, and taking a few prisoners.

"The best joke of our entry to Berryville I send you in the shape of two newspapers.

"The editor of the Berryville Conservator had the outside of his paper struck off, when our coming led him to strike himself off. Some printers of the Minnesota regiment took up his paper and types and completed the news of the day. The result I send you. It was issued the morning after our arrival. The outside contains the report of Johnson's operations in this valley and at Manassas last summer. The inside records another campaign.

"The date of my next letter, I think, will be in Winchester.

"I hope Howard has had a share in the successes in Arkansas."

"CAMP NEAR WINCHESTER, March 13, 1862.

"At last! My prophecy of yesterday found its fulfilment rapidly enough. Half an hour after my letter went on its way, Colonel Andrews brought the news that Hamilton's and Williams's brigades were in Winchester, as quietly and easily as if no hostile force had ever held it. Jackson left the night before, having held Hamilton and us in check all the previous day by slight demonstrations of cavalry. It is as I have always supposed, though this general exodus from Manassas and the whole line is more sudden than I believed possible. It gives us a stern chase, perhaps a long chase. After lunch the Colonel and I determined to gallop down from Berryville to Winchester to call on Hamilton and see the place, — a pleasant ride of ten miles. We approached the town from the east. The only symptom of fortification was a long rifle-pit, with a few platforms for guns, and one broken gun ' truck,' or ship carriage. We found General Hamilton in command, and in tranquil possession. Jackson cleverly slipped away, carrying with him everything, — guns, stores, men. He had been moving for a fortnight, and has gone to the railway at Strasburg. I think we have lost time uselessly in our over-caution. Our own twenty-four hours' delay at Berryville is inexplicable to me. The effort, I think, should have been made by a movement to Millwood, and so across to the Strasburg pike, to cut off Jackson. A bold game would, perhaps, have bagged him. Still, while the position at Manassas was held, a bold game was too full of hazard. After the broad hint furnished us by the evacuation of Leesburg, however, I think we might have pushed on our intercepting column fearlessly. At any rate, the movement is without brilliancy or effectiveness or fruit, and only postpones and unsettles the time of our success. We got into the saddle again at half past five to return.

"Just at dusk we came near Berryville. Whom should we meet but General Abercrombie. 'The whole brigade is moving,' said he. ' I have a telegraphic despatch from General Banks, that Hamilton is engaged with the enemy at Winchester. Shields has been taken prisoner, and the loss, on our part, is very heavy. We are ordered to march at once to his support.' 'But it's all a mistake,' said we.

'We just left General Hamilton safe and happy at Winchester, and no enemy within twenty miles.' 'Never mind,' said the General; 'I have my orders.' It was no use; he would not let us turn the regiment back, as we desired. There was nothing for it but to yield. We stopped and got some supper, and then followed the regiment, overtaking it at about eight o'clock, as it was crossing a stream. At about ten o'clock, wet and cold, we turned into a field near Winchester to bivouac for the night. A cold time we had of it. To-day we have got into camp near the town. I rode out this afternoon to see their vaunted fort on the road toward Bunker Hill; a poor affair enough. Everything tells me that if Patterson had had courage instead of caution, an army instead of a mob, we should have walked into Winchester last July as we have to-day. But we needed the lessons of that campaign to prepare for this.

"I must not omit to mention the arrival of the boxes of clothing, from Mrs. Ticknor, on Saturday last at Charlestown. They came, like their predecessors, most opportunely. It was the morning after our night march over rough and muddy roads. Our camp was scourged by a blustering and piercing March wind. The boxes opened their warmth upon men who longed for it. Give our cordial thanks to all the ladies whose kindness has done so much for us.

"Great news from Arkansas! Howard is in luck.

"My last night's bivouac, after so many previous sleepless nights, has made me rather sleepy. Our regiment turned into a thick pine wood. Colonel Hackleman's Indiana regiment was just in our rear. They brought along with them the hens and chickens of the neighboring farms, and the feathers flew briskly about their beds. Old Hackleman calls them his 'boys,' and they, in turn, call him 'pap'; and he has a happy, noisy family about him. As they lay by our side last night, I was led to the remark, that Hackleman's babes were in the wood, and *Robbin Henroosts* had covered them with softer covering than leaves. Our regiment is in perfect condition, and the men have really become practised and expert soldiers. Our train came up this morning, and at about one o'clock we went into camp. Before sunset ovens were built, and we had a perfectly organized camp. We may not stay here a day, but everything takes shape at once. The men march easily and rapidly, and I am more than ever pleased and contented with the Second Regiment.

" Have we not a *Monitor* afloat ? Was not her providential arrival at Norfolk an effective admonition to the Rebels ? Check to their king. Private enterprise has done what our Navy Department could not. What a glorious trial trip !

" Just beyond the field in which we are encamped are the remains of the camp of the Second Virginia. An omen, perhaps ; but this peaceable succession to vacant camps has in it little of the element that feeds martial ardor or rewards the ecstasy of strife ! But how silently and surely we are dealing with slavery. The post at which I placed my grand guard yesterday was near a fine old farm-house. Its Rebel owner left with haste, as —— threw his shells with brilliant courage at four men and a threshing-machine which his distempered fancy had imagined and exaggerated into some new engine of destruction. All the negro servants were left in *charge* of the *other property*. This leaving one kind of property in possession of another kind of property hath in it a certain logical and natural inconsistency, which doth not fail to show itself in the practical result. ' Massa 's gone to Winchester. He in a big hurry. Yer 's welcome to the hams and the other fixins. Massa very hospitable man.' So the negro makes free with his fellow-property with every right of succession and enjoyment that belongs to a *next of kin*. Why will he not also learn to make free with *himself?*

" If he fails to do so, it will not be for the want of a good deal of rough but sage counsel from the ' boys ' of the Sixteenth Indiana Regiment, who were posted there. The Hoosiers have very vague notions of property and Rebel

14

ownership at the best. They have not the capacity to rise to the height of contemplating human ownership. A long row of beehives were humming their peaceful labors in the front-yard. I hear that they soon fell into disorder, and that the Hoosiers had a ration of honey! *Sic vos non vobis mellificatis apes !* My Latin may be lame, but the sense is clear.

"I send you a Richmond Enquirer, from the Winchester mail, seized yesterday ; I send you also a paper published by the Twelfth Indiana on their advent to town. It is dull enough, but an odd institution, — a sort of turning of the Rebel batteries against themselves. . . . .

"The origin of General Banks's error about a battle at Winchester, which gave us our night stampede, is supposed to have been in the signal corps. Some one blundered a signal or forged one, we have not yet learned which ; an investigation is going on."

CHAPTER XIII.

LETTERS FROM CAMP NEAR WINCHESTER. — WINCHESTER. — BAT-
TLE OF WINCHESTER. — CAMP BIVOUAC, NEAR STRASBURG. —
CAMP NEAR STRASBURG. — CAMP NEAR EDINBURG.

"CAMP NEAR WINCHESTER, March 15, 1862.

" OF all the platitudes and jingles that ever amused and deluded a chivalrous people, the assertion, ' You can't subjugate a State,' is the wildest.   These people were first subjugated to secession, and now they are rapidly being subjugated back to loyalty.   Subjection is what vast numbers of them sigh for.   If only they were sure that the Union authority would last.   Therein lies McClellan's wisdom.   No step backward, is his motto.   With such tactics, and with a bold and confident advance, I care not whether we fight battles or follow retreats, though the former is far better, we restore the Union.

" I fear the people will regard the retreat from Manassas as a disappointment to our arms, and almost a Rebel success.   I fear that they will think McClellan's preparation and generalship wasted.   A little patience, however, may show that they are wrong.   We have gained an immense moral victory over the Rebellion, and a short time hence we shall begin to see palpable material results.   Only let us not, by a sudden and rash revulsion, begin at once to undervalue our foe.   Nothing but the presence everywhere, in the seceded States, of Union bayonets will accomplish the Union's restoration.   That is a work of some time and struggle, yet it must be done.   The most dangerous heresy seems to me to be the suggestion that the States, having gone out, are to be governed as Territories.   This involves the admission of the theory we went to war against.   Martial law may be necessary within the States for a time ; but the State, as well as the national government, is to be restored, or our contest is fruitless. Changes, rapid and unexpected, are the order of the day. Heintzelman's promotion to a *corps d'armée* leaves open his division. Yesterday, when I went to town, I found that General Hamilton was promoted to the command of that division. He went off yesterday afternoon, regret following him from every one. He is a great loss to us. His departure leaves a brigade vacant; accordingly our regiment is to-day transferred to Hamilton's old brigade, and Colonel Gordon, as senior Colonel, assigned to its command, as Acting Brigadier. This is a pleasing change, and it gives the Colonel room to show himself. It probably, for the present, may find me in command of the regiment, as Colonel Andrews is still on detached duty; but I shall make every exertion to have him returned to the regiment, in justice to him. He has fairly earned the right to the command, and I should not feel content to have him or the regiment deprived of it, though my own personal ambition might be gratified by so desirable a command. I hope I can sink myself in seeking always the welfare of the regiment, and the interest of so faithful an officer and friend as Colonel Andrews. I think more and more, though I am unwilling to write about it, that we missed the cleverest chance at cutting off and bagging Jackson and his force that ever fell in one's way. Caution is the sin of our generals, I am afraid; but military criticism is not graceful, and I will waive it for the present. Yet if you knew how we ache for a chance at fighting, how we feel that our little army corps out in this valley has no hope of it, you would not wonder that a leaden depression rests heavily upon us, as we think of our hesitating and peaceful advent to Winchester. And now why we do not push on upon Jackson at Strasburg passes my limited conjectural capacity to guess. I presume the reason to be that his evanescent tactics would be sure to result in his evaporation before we got there.

" This morning a few companies of cavalry, four pieces of artillery, and five companies of infantry, Massachusetts Thirteenth, went out on an armed reconnoissance, and chased Colonel Ashby's cavalry several miles. The cavalry were too quick for them, and our own cavalry has no more chance of catching them than the wagon train has. They are admirably mounted and thoroughly trained. Where our men have to dismount and take down the bars, they fly over fences and across country like birds.

" General Banks has just gone off to Washington. Conjecture is busy, again, with ' why ' ? My guess is, that we have outlived our usefulness in the Shenandoah Valley, and that we shall make a cut through the gap into the path of the Grand Army. At any rate, nothing more can happen this side the mountains, and I certainly hope we shall not be absorbed into any force that is to be handled by General Fremont.

" Our little town of Berryville is also called, as you may see on some of the maps, *Battletown*, probably with prescient sarcasm on ———'s anticipated cannonade of that peaceful agricultural implement, the threshing-machine. Who shall say that we are not engaged in the noble task of fulfilling prophecy and making history !

" It is now Sunday morning. After two days' cloud and rain, we have bright sunshine. Colonel Andrews comes back to the regiment, and Colonel Gordon assumes his slippery honors as provisional brigadier.

" I should like to go to church with you this morning, even in an east wind. Instead of it, however, I must content myself with thinking of you in my wind-swept camp near Winchester. I see that Governor Letcher appoints Winchester as a place of rendezvous for his new levy of militia. I only wish they would obey his order."

"CAMP NEAR WINCHESTER, VIRGINIA, March 20, 1862.

" I have no sympathy with the strains of peace which come to me in your last letters. Indeed, I am so much dispirited by our inaction, that I have hardly energy for letter writing or elasticity for effort of any kind. McClellan's order, which should be a clarion, is simply an irritant. Here we are, and it is a week since we pitched our tents near Winchester. Daily duty comes with every day. We have had our seed-time and our harvest season, but no fruit. . . . . I presume I love life and home and friends as much as any one, but I would sooner give them all up to-day than have our regiment go home empty. . . . .

"As for Howard, if he closed his eyes honorably on Pea Ridge he has only my envy.

"I hope we may get orders of some kind soon. Even long marches and picket duty, of which we have done too much already, are better than this hopeless idleness in the rear of the vaunted Army of the Potomac.

"If you have any prayers to give, give them all to the supplication that the Second Regiment of Massachusetts Volunteers may find a field whereon to write a record of itself. Do not spend your days in weakly fearing or regretting this or that life, — lives whose whole sweetness and value depend upon their opportunities, not on their length."

"CAMP NEAR WINCHESTER, VIRGINIA, March 21, 1862.

"If you had looked upon our camp at sunrise reveillé, this morning, you would have seen a dreary, wintry picture. The mules gathered closely about their wagons in the scourging snow-storm with sullen endurance, their tails drawn tightly down, and standing in a vicious attitude of expectant kicking. The horses crossly laying back their ears with half-closed eyes and hanging necks. The soldiers standing up to their roll-call in the attitude of the traveller in the spelling-book, against whom the wind is striving to gain the victory of the fable. The ground whiter than the morning's early light, but only serving to darken the tents into a cheerless and gloomy hue. The air itself thick with snow and sleet. The camp-fires just beginning to smoke, and men hopelessly endeavoring to allure a blaze from black coals and dripping wood. The camp-kettles and mess-pans crusted with ice, suggestive of anything else than a warm breakfast. Would you not expect every mind of the thousand men, remembering also their two thousand wet feet, to be in harmony with the scene? Yet, I know not how it is, from some inherent perverseness perhaps, I was in excellent spirits.

"The order has now come to march. Our destination is Centreville, *en route*, perchance, for the enemy. At any rate, I have grown philosophical again.

"I buried hope yesterday, had a glorious wake, and resolved to sink every other wish in the absorbing one of the progress of the war without or with the Massachusetts Second, as it may happen.

"We cross the Shenandoah at Snicker's Gap. The march is one of about sixty miles, and will occupy at least four days.

"General Banks, who has just returned from Washington, seems in good spirits. He gives, however, a depressing account of the Congressional and political folly which continues to assail McClellan. If McClellan were all they charge him to be, their lips should be sealed.

"Every good man will now seek to strengthen the hand and animate the purpose of the General under whose guidance the decisive campaign begins. . . . .

"The weather is breaking away, and promises no very severe penance for our march, though it is not fun that is before us next week. No news yet of Howard, I suppose. It is clear that he has been in one of the hottest battles of the war. You will not hear from me again till Centreville probably."

"WINCHESTER, VIRGINIA (again), March 24, Monday.

"I've only a minute in which to send you greeting. Again are we hurried by a forced march, over rough roads, to see the dregs and *débris* of a battle, — heaps of wounded, dying, and dead. Well, again fortune is against us. We left here on Saturday morning for Centreville. The bridge across the Shenandoah broke, and luckily delayed us. Back we were ordered at midnight of last night. An angry, bitter, well-fought fight followed, yesterday afternoon, upon an artillery duel which had occupied nearly all day. So little did any one know it was coming, that General Banks went up to Harper's Ferry at three, P. M., and the sharp fight commenced at four ! The battle-ground was that on which my pickets had been posted until we left town. It seems to have been an exhibition of dogged courage by unruled and undisciplined soldiers.

" So we go. . . . . The lees and flatness of the sparkling goblet of victory are all that we taste. Jackson and Ashby are clever men. We are slow-w-w ! "

" WINCHESTER, VIRGINIA, March 25, 1862.

" A blue March morning, and I have just returned from the battle-field. A sight to forget. I question much if description of it is well. You may fancy the scattered dead through woods and over hillsides.

" The oddest coincidence of blunders brought about a battle.

" Banks's division had left Winchester on Saturday noon. Shields drew back from Strasburg, and had gone on the back of the town (Winchester). No forces or pickets were on the Strasburg road on that side of the town.

" On Saturday evening there was some skirmishing by Ashby's cavalry, in which Shields was wounded. It seems that Jackson had been informed that every one had left the town. His skirmish on Saturday failed to develop any large force.

" On Sunday, therefore, the fight commenced by our and their artillery. It continued through the day till half past three without any development of infantry on their side. At three o'clock General Banks, supposing it to be only

Ashby's cavalry, with a few pieces of artillery, continuing his system of annoyance, went to Harper's Ferry. But, at about four o'clock, Jackson, with his infantry, attempted to turn our right by sending round over a ridge through the woods. No one was in command of our forces. Colonel Kimball, the ranking colonel of Shields's forces, was, so to speak, in charge of the battle. Shields was abed in town. The staff were galloping about, and the soldiers fought like heroes. General Banks had gone to Harper's Ferry. Jackson had put his artillery on the commanding ridge on his left. He had two regiments of infantry behind a stone-wall in rear of the batteries. Here was the sharp fighting. We sent round our force to turn their position and take their artillery. It was done. Then they tried to retake it. Their force came over a hill, and fired over our men. Our men shot up at them and took them in the head and breast. The woods are torn and shivered by musketry and cannon. Thirty men in Confederate homespun, shot in the head, lie in this wood. Their upturned faces seemed to me looking reproach at Jeff Davis. The fight lasted till dark, when Jackson withdrew, leaving us the field and two pieces of artillery and five caissons ; leaving also his dead and wounded and two hundred and fifty prisoners in our hands.

" Both parties had blundered, — they, by acting on our retreat ; we, by acting on *his* retreat. The upshot is a glorious victory for us. I have just come back from a sad visit to the hospitals ; seeing wounded, dying, and dead, Rebels and Loyalists lying side by side, and receiving equal care. The loss on our side is one hundred or more killed, and two to three hundred wounded. Theirs is nearly three hundred killed and probably five hundred wounded. Everything shows how easy it is to kill a great many men by shooting very often ! Jackson's men, as some of their wounded state, came down expecting to find Winchester empty. They consider our actual movement a feint. Some of their troops marched two days, and came into action late in the afternoon.   I give you my impressions.

"We go to Strasburg to-morrow.   We shall meet no opposition.   We left a *door open*, and in came Jackson. We must not leave another door open.   That's the moral of this story.   The sheer fighting of our men saved us. Good by.   Love to all at home."

"CAMP BIVOUAC, NEAR STRASBURG, March 27, 1862.

"I must write you a line from our hillside-wooded bivouac this bright morning.

"On Tuesday night we made a forced march toward Strasburg from Winchester, to be within supporting distance of General Banks.   We marched till one o'clock in the morning, and then the regiment laid down by the roadside, and built fence-rail fires and rested.   Yesterday morning we came on to Strasburg, where we now await the future. Jackson is supposed to be at Mount Jackson, about fifteen miles from here, with part of his force.   The force was very much demoralized by the defeat and loss.   Their killed, wounded, and prisoners cannot be less than one thousand; three hundred will cover our loss, killed and wounded.   At our bivouac, night before last, a few of the officers, including the Colonel and myself, took possession of a comfortable house, and slept in the ' best room.'   The next morning at breakfast, when the master was out of the room, the mulatto that served us said: ' Jackson took breakfast here day before yesterday.   He told massa that he could not make much, but he should try you again.'   But he won't, think I.   As we marched through Middletown yesterday, whose houses are full of secession wounded, dropped on their march by the retreating army, our band poured out its national music, and there was a somewhat unfeeling sauciness in the swing and tramp of the regiment over the way so lately passed by the panic-stricken fugitives.   At one house near which we rested we found a poor Rebel soldier whom a shell had overtaken in his retreat. One arm gone, one leg nearly so, and the other leg mangled. Poor fellow! his life will be short. By his bedside was a Union soldier of the Seventh Ohio, — the regiment that suffered most, on our side, in the fight. That soldier was nursing and tending the poor wounded man as affectionately as a sister. He had been with him a day, and said he was afraid of being court-martialled if he stayed ; but, said he, ' I can't leave him alone.' Our surgeon, who has been behaving like a trump, gave him a certificate, and advised him to stay. We left him dressing the hopeless wounds.

" At one of the hospitals in Winchester, a Rebel soldier, wounded and suffering, said : ' How kind you are to us! They told us that you would kill us, and kill all the wounded.' Such are some of the lies with which they keep their men up to the fighting point. The women of Winchester began by bringing delicacies for *their* wounded, as they said. After a day, however, when they saw our equal kindness, they began themselves to get a little humanity, and to work for all.

" There is a base and brutalizing influence at work here in Rebeldom, beyond all question.

" The scenes through which I have passed for the last three days remain with great vividness. Take the Winchester court-house as an example. You enter the door, and the vestibule is full of dead. You go in farther, and the court-room is a hospital, in which every variety of wound and suffering meets your eye.

" It is little enough that human aid can do in such a place, but it is wonderful to see the comfort that is given by human sympathy. I noticed one boy shot through the jaw and the back. He had been looking intently at the man next him, when he began some inarticulate address to him. Through the wounded and disturbed jaw he at last made himself understood as saying, ' Do you feel better ? ' ' Yes,' said the man next him. ' Glad of it,' he worked out, with difficulty, and lay back, having imperfectly expressed the sympathy which most men would hardly think he had to spare. Young Lieutenant Crowninshield was walking through one hospital. ‘ Hallo, *Crownie*, how are you ? ’ said a wounded Rebel soldier. On looking at him, he recognized a classmate, named Washington, who left Cambridge a year ago. He was a private in Jackson’s army. His mother and sister were living near Charlestown. The poor fellow was wounded through the lungs probably mortally. What a war this is !

“ An odd incident occurred to one of our regiment. Private Alexander, of Company E, was taken prisoner last summer at Maryland Heights, and brought to Winchester and thence to Richmond. He was released with Colonel Lee, and sent back here to rejoin his regiment. He arrived in Winchester just after we had left for Centreville, but just in season for the battle. He went out on to the field, took a gun from some fallen soldier, and went in with all the bitterness of a six months’ captivity. At the close of the engagement he returned to Winchester, bringing with him two Rebel guns and a Rebel prisoner as his booty and revenge. He thinks he is even with them now. Captain Cary’s company was on duty in Winchester, at the time of the battle, as part of the provost guard. Three of the men got leave of absence in the afternoon and went out to the field, picked up guns, and sailed in. The last that is known of one of them is, that he was seen in the advanced line of skirmishers fighting like a hero. The others, after the battle, returned. So you see our regiment had only four men in the engagement. I believe we remain here quietly to-day. We are on the line of the Manassas Gap railway, but the bridges have been burnt. I think that we shall not be attacked again, nor be able to overtake Jackson, whose movement was against a divided force, and unsuccessful at that. He will not, therefore, assail us when we are reunited. It is a splendid, mild morning. We are camped in a pine and cedar grove facing the south, and resting after a march of sixty-five miles in four days, — awful hard work with very little glory. Those fellows who are put on cars and then shipped to an exploit, with no service in the field, are lucky men. Ours is the labor and heat of the day with no penny as yet. The eleventh-hour men are getting their pennies first! Will there be any left for us? Who knows? Love to all at home. I am writing on your little portable writing-case, which is a convenience. Your letter of the 20th was received last night."

"CAMP FOUR MILES BEYOND STRASBURG, March 28, 1862.

" I had just finished my letter yesterday, and started to mail it, when I was turned back by a hurried order to ' march at once.' Our long roll was beating as I got back near camp, and in a few minutes the line was formed and the brigade in motion through Strasburg. It was reported that our outposts were threatened by cavalry, infantry, and artillery of the enemy. As we passed out of the town we could hear the occasional sullen tone of a cannon. My incredulity was proof, however, against any faith in an attack in force ; so I was not surprised when the brigade was halted a few miles from town, and ordered to go into camp, and send back for its train. It seems that the enterprising and clever Ashby, with his two light pieces of artillery, was amusing himself and exciting us by a slight demonstration. Ready for a rapid and elusive retreat at a moment's notice, he would like to continue his game which he has safely and pleasantly played so long. He is light, active, skilful, and we are tormented by him like a bull with a gad-fly. We chose a fine oak-wood for our camp, and at sunset were quietly in tents again. This morning the sun rose warm and glorious. The singing birds anticipated our reveillé, and we have the sunniest, happiest camp to-day possible.

" I have had an opportunity to hear directly from Jackson's camp yesterday. He is a few miles beyond Woodstock.

He has no tents, and his wagons carry only subsistence, and are ready to move at a moment's notice. His force is four or five thousand men. He says, ' My men have no uniform, they wear multiform.' He keeps Ashby in his rear with his cavalry and two pieces of artillery. His game is a winning one even when he loses. With his small force he detains twenty thousand men in this valley. It seems probable that his attack on Winchester was in pursuance of a positive order from Johnson to make the attack at all hazards, to arrest and detain our force from its intended movement to Centreville. In this aspect it was a success. In my judgment our weakness was in turning back. The force left behind was large enough to take care of this valley. But, indeed, it seems as if we had no plan and no courage or decision. Vacillation is our name. . We cannot take Jackson. If we mean to hold the valley, we should establish our force in position to do so, take the rest to Centreville, and thus perform our part in the campaign. The life that we have led for the week past is a waste of men and of energy. It quells the spirit of our troops, and destroys the prestige of our leaders. My admiration and sympathy go with the gallant Ashby, and the indefatigable and resolute Jackson. With an equal force, the latter would have beaten us at Winchester. Banks, in his general order, speaks of a ' *subtle* ' foe, a most unlucky word for a shrewd observer of our movements. As soon as we give him a chance by dividing our forces or exposing a detachment, Jackson may seize the occasion for an attack. While we remain strong in numbers or position, he will do neither, you may be sure. I hope in McClellan's generalship, and am very glad father gains faith in it. You will soon, as *I know*, hear of movements which show boldness, plan, and decisiveness. The campaign is not to be a timid waiting on the movements of the enemy. I hope events may soon take us to Centreville, where we can feel the direct grasp of McClellan's hand. But I try to be patient, and to feel that ' they also serve who only stand and wait.'   At present we are safe and comfortable enough.   God bless you all at home."

"CAMP NEAR STRASBURG, VIRGINIA, March 31, 1862.

" I was glad to hear, from your letter of the 23d, that you have been doing something, and leading others to do, for the wounded and suffering from Pea Ridge.   You will never appreciate, except feebly and by conjecture, the relief and soothing of which you may be the happy cause.   If, on Monday evening last, you had gone with me into the courthouse at Winchester, and seen the wounded and dying lying upon the bare floor, ' heads and points,' as the surgeon expressed it, the victims at once of hunger and cold and wounds, you would know what could be done with the heart to do and the things to do with.

" Of those people who make a luxury of good works, and are, so to speak, epicures in benevolence, I know not how they could get so much for their money as by coming upon one of these recent battle-fields.

" I rejoice in Howard's safety more than I can bring myself to do in my own.   While you are thinking of the bodily security of your sons, there is one of them who is jaded and depressed by the inglorious military drudgery to which ' the best regiment in the service ' is hopelessly condemned.

" I have just returned from twenty-four hours' picket duty in a cold rain-storm.   The enemy's line of pickets is about a mile from our own.   Ashby brought up his cannon, and threw a few shells at our outposts.   They whistled through the air and fell near us, but were only bravado and insolence. When we go on he will run faster than we can follow. Meantime, the large movements and the decisive actions of the Potomac campaign are probably taking place, and we are stupidly trailing after an evanescent and puny, but resolute, foe.   Bah !   One of our companies is in Centreville, I suppose; one at Snicker's Ferry ; the rest here, drying themselves in the sun after twenty-four hours' hard, wet, useless work, unrecognized and unknown. Whenever the division wants a commissary, or an acting assistant-adjutant, or what not, he is detailed from us. We have not a single full brigadier in the whole *corps d'armée*. Five brigades all commanded by colonels, — unorganized and undisciplined, except a few regiments.

"Do you wonder that I get down in the mouth? It will soon be a year that we have been in service, with nothing to show for it but the effects of the hardest possible work.

"You see I am in no mood for letter-writing. I write because there is a mail going. I shall not write again till I feel better. You need not feel concerned at not hearing from me. I almost feel as if I would not take up a pen again till I could speak of something else than the inglorious details of our present life. Love to all at home."

"CAMP NEAR EDINBURG, VIRGINIA, April 2, 1862.

"I promised not to write you till our monotony ceased. It has done so ; yet the story is a short one. Our regiment started yesterday morning (April 1) to advance. A few shots, as we started, from some of our Parrott guns, scattered the enemy's *vedettes*, and five of our companies, deployed as skirmishers, led the way. The other three companies were the reserve, four hundred yards in rear, and were under my command. The occasional interchange of shots now and then, a rapid rattle of rifle-shots from our skirmishers as they came upon a retreating line of the enemy's cavalry, kept us in excitement till we got near Woodstock. When we came over the hill to that town, spang! went a gun from the opposite hill, and whirr-r-r came a shot over my reserve ; the men ducked their heads a little, and I drew them under the shelter of a bank. Here there was a rapid interchange of cannon-shot ; and when we had shelled out their battery, our skirmishers again advanced, driving their cavalry before them. Just beyond the town we came upon their burning camps, which they had set on fire and deserted.

Again we advanced, and came to the 'Narrow Pass' (so called). Here the bridge over the creek was burning. Our skirmishers put it out.

"The pass is a strong position for the Rebels, and we were not surprised to hear another '*spang*,' and the rushing of more shells. Our batteries got into position, and there was a brisk interchange of shots over our heads, the reserve being in the hollow, and getting an occasional bursting shell near it from *each* side. Here one of our skirmishers came back shot in the breast. As luck would have it, however, his brass plate turned the ball, so that he was not dangerously hurt. Again we went on till we came to this place. Here both bridges, the turnpike, and railroad were burning. We halted a little while before entering the town, and when we pushed on the inevitable '*spang*' assailed us. Our skirmishers drove the enemy across the river, and back into the woods. Our batteries silenced theirs. One poor fellow, in a regiment in rear of our reserve, had his head taken off by a shell. These were the only casualties on our side. Here we paused and went into bivouac; and, after fourteen miles' skirmishing in heavy-trim knapsacks, all our tired regiment went to sleep. This morning there has been a little more shelling. We halt for supplies. We are in bivouac, our tents having been left behind.

"I hope Jackson will make a stand, but fear he will not. Yesterday was quite a brisk, exciting day. The regiment did splendidly, as all agree. I am very well, and recovering my spirits. Love to all."

"CAMP NEAR EDINBURG, VIRGINIA, April 4, 1862.

"We make life musical these hot sunny days with the screeching whir of shells or the sharp buzz and sping of rifle-balls. But the enemy keep at a respectful distance, for the most part, and our own shameful mismanagement about supplies, or some large wisdom affecting other forces, keeps us quiet. Our tents came up yesterday, and we are now in

15

camp again. This morning Colonel Andrews and I have been out 'prospecting' round, as they say in this country.

"The Rebel pickets are in plain sight, just beyond the river, but there is no evidence of any force there, and when we conclude to go on, on we shall go without difficulty. Our advance to this point was made by our regiment in fine style. The men skirmished over a distance of fifteen miles, and did their work well. Neither the musketry nor the artillery delayed or embarrassed our progress, which was as rapid as an ordinary day's march. The impetus and stimulant of pursuit spurred on the march, over a difficult and broken country. At the 'Narrow Pass,' where the Shenandoah and a creek crossing the pike a little below almost come together, but are kept asunder by a piece of rock, over which the road passes with just the width of a carriage path, was the sharpest conflict. It was mainly an 'artillery duel,' as the phrase is. Our skirmishers had learned, however, before this, that, to their deployed line, the shell, though assailing the ear with terror, were sound and fury signifying nothing. Their effect was aimed at the reserves or our artillery, and it really had an unpleasant sound as it whizzed or spanged near us. It is high time that being 'under fire' should be among our '*has beens.*' I am quite satisfied that the order and discipline of the regiment will tell there as it has everywhere else, and our recent experience is a proof of it. . . . . I suppose you must have read General Shields's '*private*' letter about the battle at Winchester. A more barefaced series of Irish romances I never read. The man actually has the effrontery to connect his fortunate blunders into a chain of shrewd stratagems, and with after-event wisdom to glorify himself. The idea of a man in bed, with a broken arm, four miles from the field, not knowing of the enemy's force or positions till four, P. M., directing and guiding a battle that commenced *at once* and closed in two hours !! Pshaw ! It is like Sir Lucius O'Trigger or Mickey Free.

" 'An attack having many of the elements of a *surprise,*'

says General Banks in his order, praising the courage and constancy of the soldiers.

" ' Och, sure,' says our Irish general, turning with a shrewd wink to the public ; ' but it was a sthratagim o' me own.   It 's the clivir *bye* that I am, be dad !   Troth, but I decaved 'em.   And I, too, with only twelve thousand men to me back, and only a brigadier.   It 's I should be major-general at laste, then ye would see.   Gineral Banks, indade ! Och, he 's a foine man intirely, and thrates me well.   But it 's I that inwents the sthratagims ! '

" Possibly there will be truth in history hereafter ; there is none in the present record.

" I advise you to subscribe for or buy regularly the Congregationalist newspaper.   It contains our Chaplain's letters, which I consider very clever and entertaining.

" Is it not about father's birthday ?   At any rate, I may wish him a happy return next year, and may I be there to see."

"CAMP NEAR EDINBURG, April 6, 1862.

" It might be a June morning, by its sunshine and warmth. This broken valley, the ' intervale ' of two sharp, dark-wooded ranges of cuts, itself broken and furrowed by impatient ' runs,' as they call every water-flow in Virginia, *might* be a fitting scene for a pleasure journey.   All the air might a *Sabbath* stillness hold, but another solemn influence is every-where present.   Within a mile of our quiet camp the out-posts of two armies are watching one another.   The cannon and rifle tone break the silence now and then.   If you go down to our line of pickets, you will see the men watching with eager though patient eyes for a *good shot ;* and as the smoke breaks from some cover on the opposite bank of the stream, you may hear a ball whistle near you, and some sentry near by will send his quick reply.   I had quite an animated day yesterday.   As field-officer of the day, I had charge of our line of outposts.   I found in the morning that the Rebel pickets were quite importunate and vexatious.   I

also thought it important to change the position of some of
our pickets ; and, in order to do so, desired to reconnoitre
the ground.   I was soon interrupted in my quiet use of my
field-glass by the whistle of bullets following the crack of
rifles.   The devils had probably worked down through the
ravines.   I moved my horse quietly under cover of a small
house, and could listen to the sound without exposing any
other sense.   I soon changed my position ; and thought,
that, as the road went quite too close to the river, I would
take the field.   But I had not gone far in that direction
when a rapid volley assailed me from behind a straw-rick,
and I was again led to turn back, more especially as some
of the shots seemed to be from some quarter quite too near
for security.   That is the working of these Rebels.   They
work themselves into safe covers, and pop away.   Even their
artillery, from which we have three or four attacks every
day, is often so masked that even the smoke fails to disclose
it.   I leaped my horse over a fence, and made arrangements
for my picket on a line a little less exposed.   But you can
get some idea of the persistency of the devils.   They seem
to act with a bitter personal hate and venom.   In my ride
yesterday afternoon I came to a house about which there
was a gathering of curious soldiers.   The poor woman was
in great trouble.   The Rebel battery had just thrown two
shells through the house, shattering windows and plastering,
&c.   She was in terror, and her husband was away serving
in the army whose missiles had terrified her.   ' Pa is pressed
into the militia,' said the little boy to me.   ' He 's gone
away to New Market.'   Yet these people explain their mis-
fortunes by *our* invasion, not by *their* rebellion.   ' I wish
you 'd move your men away or stop their firing,' said a
young girl to me at a farm-house.   ' *Our* boys 'll shell the
house sure, if you don't take care.'   They cling to their
allegiance to their flying army, — and why should n't they ?
It is made up of their brothers and sons and lovers.   We
find very few men.   Indeed, their *practical* conscription
leaves nothing male and able-bodied out of the ranks.

" But I must not omit to tell you of my revenge on the men who fired at me. The straw-rick stood just in front of a barn. From the hill on which a section of our battery was posted it was a good mark. On my return to that point I directed a few shell to be thrown there. With lucky aim two of them struck the barn itself; and their explosion had, at least, the result to scatter the men within, who were seen to run back to the woods.

" We hear an odd story of an incident in the battle at Winchester. It shows that the Second Regiment has a name in this valley. Probably its long continuance here, and the fact that a flag was given to it at Harper's Ferry, have attracted Rebel attention to it. It is said by some of the soldiers who were in the battle, that when one of the Ohio regiments was broken by the Rebel fire, and faltered a little, some of the Rebels jumped up from the corner of their stone-wall and shouted, ' Where 's Gordon's bloody Second ? Bring it on.' A good deal of curiosity was also expressed by the Rebel wounded and prisoners to know about the regiment, and if it was here. They might any of them have seen it the other day if they would only have *waited!*

" It seems that the Rebels swell their numbers now by a systematic and general compulsion. Such troops will only be an embarrassment to them, I think. But their unscrupulous tyranny spares nothing. An old free negro woman, living in a small hut near our camp, says, ' They took away my son last summer to Manassas, and I 've had a hard winter without him ; but they left me my young son, a poor cripple boy. The other day they come and took him, and my horse and wagon to carry off their sick. He 's a poor, weak boy, and all I 've got, but they would n't spare him to me. I can't help it, but I feel more kind to you all whom I never saw than to them that I was born among.' So she talked on sadly of her troubles.

" Look at another picture of this free and happy people, with their patriarchal institutions. Colonel Gordon stopped for the night at a house near Snicker's Ferry. The master was out of the room, and a mulatto slave woman was busy about the table. ' You are happy, are you not ? ' says Colonel G. ' No,' with a dull, whining, sad tone in her reply. ' Your master 's kind to you, is n't he ? ' ' No, he sold my mother fifteen years ago.' That memory and loss had been her life and sorrow for fifteen years, and it would last. Pretty pictures of pastoral content !

" ' Do not take my corn and grain,' says Mr. Ransom, of Charlestown, a courtly Virginian gentleman. ' I 've a large family of negroes dependent on me, and I must have enough left to feed them, and to take care of my horses and cows till spring. My poor servants will starve.'

" The army moves on ; a week passes, and Mr. Ransom may be seen taking care of his single remaining cow and horse. His dependent servants have taken care of themselves, and Mr. Ransom is rubbing his eyes over the abrupt lightening of his burdens. Let us clear our minds of cant, — pro or anti slavery. There is full as much of the former cant as of the latter.

" It was Sunday when I began this letter ; it is now Monday. We make no movement yet. The Rebel shells have not been thrown among us for a whole day ! so life is a little monotonous."

"CAMP NEAR EDINBURG, April 9, 1862.

" *Scene*, camp, snowing and raining, and blowing angrily; *Time*, Tuesday morning. The Major Second Massachusetts Regiment enters his tent, shaking the dripping oil-skin cap and India-rubber clothing. He discovers John, his John, surnamed Strong i' the arm, or Armstrong, digging a hole within the damp tent to receive some coals from the hickory fire that is trying to blaze without. *John (loquitur).* Sogering is queer business, sir. *M.* Yes, John. *J.* But it 's hard, too, sir, on them that follers it. *M.* Yes, John. *J.* It 's asy for them as sits to home, sir, by the fire, and talks about sogers and victories, very fine and asy like. It 's little they know of the raal work, sir. *M.* Yes, John. *J.* 'T would n't be quite the same, sir, if they was out here theirselves trying to warm theirselves at a hole in the ground, sir. *M.* No, John. Then the coals are brought on, and a feeble comfort is attained. The woods are heavy without with snow and ice. In the afternoon I visit the pickets, and spend a chilly and wearisome day. This morning is again like yesterday. ———, who has shown himself a trump in our recent exigencies, but who has certain eccentricities of manner and speech, came to breakfast this morning, rubbing his hands and saying, ' You would n't hardly know that this was the South if you did n't keep looking on the map, would you ? hey ? What say ? '

" Since I wrote the above I have spent two hours in the hail-storm visiting pickets. This, then, is an invasion of the South, query ?

" We receive this morning news of the capture of Island No. 10, and the defeat of Beauregard.

" Westward the star of — victory takes its way. How long can this thing last ? Is it not collapsing with occasional throes of vigor, and are not these spasms the twitchings that precede death ? I cannot say. But of one thing I am sure, that it will be warmer farther south ; so I wish to go there. It is a week that we have hesitated on the bank of this stony creek ; soon we will move on. Our signal-station on the neighboring mountain can see Jackson's camps beyond Mount Jackson, and his wagons, with teams hitched, ready to move at a moment's notice. We can advance again at any moment, by a prolonged skirmish.

" I wish you all at home much better weather than we have, and the same peace and quietness."

"CAMP NEAR EDINBURG, VIRGINIA, April 11, 1862.

" DEAR D———, — Reduced in my finances : I have not been paid since January 1. Reduced in my commissariat : we are faring on soldiers' rations, our best luxury being hard-bread scouse. Reduced in buoyancy : I have not heard a shell whiz or a bullet whistle for three days. Reduced in temperature : it has been snowing two days. Reduced in aspiration : they have made —— a brigadier ; who now would seek promotion ? Reduced in ardor : rumor says the Rebels are quitting Virginia. Reduced, in a word, in everything, except *size :* the final reduction came, when, on Thursday, April 10, I received, on this outpost of invasion, a note from you out of the midst of such congenial and agreeable companionship tantalizing me with the suggestion that I should join you *last* Monday. I would I had the wings of memory to do it with. But alas ! my face is turned toward the south, and my future is in other hands than my own. . . . . We might have hoped to see you, had not the perversity of General Jackson or the ' stratagem ' of General Shields turned us back from Manassas, whither our steps tended a fortnight ago. Well, there is a sequence, perchance a wisdom, in events, that is better than our plans or hopes. I cannot but rejoice that every day seems to bring us nearer to a military success over this Rebellion. The political solution of our difficulties is quite a more serious embarrassment. I see no wisdom in the government, and seem to myself to be fighting in the dark. One thing, however, is clear, — the more sharp and decisive our victory over their forces, the easier will it be to re-establish a wise government over them. . . . . We have had a very hard time since we came into the field in February, and cannot look for much else at present.''

"CAMP NEAR EDINBURG, VIRGINIA, April 13, 1862.

" MY DEAR MOTHER, — We have been stirred by the news from Grant's and Buell's armies since I wrote, and even more, perhaps, by the attitude of McClellan's forces near Yorktown. This letter can hardly have a rapid flight enough to reach you as soon as decisive news from the Army of the Potomac. I hope large results ; yet, in doing so, I must shut my eyes to everything around me, torpid as it is with the paralysis of — incapacity, shall I say? or mischance? To-day we obey the order of the War Department, and give thanks for our victories. The regiment will shortly be formed for that purpose. The time is a fitting one. It is the anniversary of that sombre Sunday of the dishonored flag which brought us the news of the fall of Sumter. It is also a fit time for McClellan's *coup de grace.* I received yesterday your copy of Howard's letter from Pea Ridge. Its clear description of what he saw and heard and did there is very interesting. After all, I was wiser for him than for myself, and urged him to go to the field where victory has come to be almost monotonous.

" Our life here since I wrote is full of emptiness. Picket duty and occasional shelling. Now and then I go down and let the enemy's pickets fire at me, just by way of keeping up the illusion of war. One of our pickets the other day got hit, but the miss is the rule. Out of this nettle safety we will pluck the flower danger one of these days, but not yet. . . . .

" Since I laid down my pen our service has taken place. I watched the faces of the men, and missed the light which gladdens them whenever *they* are called to action. Veterans in everything but conflict, it only quickens their impatience to hear of other achievements.

" We shall stay here some days longer, I think. Subsistence, clothing, transportation, all limp and halt and stagger.

" We are the most timid and scrupulous invaders in all history. It must be delicious to the *finer* feelings of some people to watch our velvet-footed advance. It keeps me in a state of chronic contempt."

CHAPTER XIV.

LETTERS FROM BIVOUAC NEAR NEW MARKET, VA. — CAMP BE-
TWEEN NEW MARKET AND SPARTA. — CAMP NEAR HARRISON-
BURG. — IN BIVOUAC, OPPOSITE NEW MARKET.

"BIVOUAC NEAR NEW MARKET, VIRGINIA,
Raining from the East.   Easter Sunday, April 20, 1862.

" LOOKING back, it seems an age since we dwelt peace-
fully in the wooded camp near Edinburg.   It was
Wednesday night that our marching orders came.   On
Thursday morning at a quarter before two we had reveillé,
and marched before light, under a pale moon, toward Mount
Jackson.

" Shields's division had gone on in advance.   The day
was a glowing one, and the valley spread itself out before us
like a garden in its fresh green.

" After a short halt at Mount Jackson, which is a town,
and filled with evidences of Rebel occupation, such as large
hospitals, one of them unfinished, we were ordered to march
round to ' turn the enemy's left.'

" Our path was a rough one, through a river, over rocks,
and through deep mud, on, on, on.   We heard occasional
cannonading over toward the centre, where Shields's force
remained drawn up in line of battle, to await our tedious
circuit.   The day was long and hot ; the artillery labored
over the almost impassable road.   I went on in advance,
with some pioneers to aid a little by removing obstacles.   As
we passed through the little village of Forrestville, a party
of young girls sang Dixie to us.   I bought a loaf of bread
there of a woman, and paid her five cents in silver.   ' It 's
too much,' said she.   ' No,' said I.   ' It 's more money than
I 've seen for a year,' said she.   On we go.   We have got
round the enemy's position.   It is dark ; too late to ford the

North Fork of the Shenandoah to rejoin the rest of the army, who have now entered New Market, which Ashby even has left. Tired and foot-sore, we lay down to sleep in the woods. Marching for eighteen hours, and such marching! the bivouac, in the warm, pleasant night is a luxury. The next morning we start again, and ford the Shenandoah, and get on to the turnpike at New Market which we had left at Mount Jackson. The Shenandoah is swift, and up to one's middle. Fording is an exciting, amusing. long task. It is finished at last, and the brigade, led by our regiment, moves through the town of New Market to the saucy strains of Yankee Doodle. We move two miles beyond the town, and bivouac on a hillside. Our tents and baggage are all sixteen miles back, at Edinburg.

"It is late Friday evening before we get bivouacked. Many of the men are barefoot and without rations. Saturday morning it begins early to rain, and ever since we have been dripping under this easterly storm. Luckily, Mrs. Williamson, whose husband is with the 'other army,' and who has a fine farm and a roomy, old-fashioned, ante-Revolution-built house, surrounded by generous barns and outbuildings, swarming with negroes of every shade and size, — luckily, Mrs. Williamson and her six little boys and her aged uncle need our protection ; and, in return, she gives us a shelter for our meals, and so alleviates the adversity which had reduced our commissariat to starvation. Mr. Williamson is a major in the Rebel army. His wife is true to him and to Virginia. The eldest boy, of fifteen years, is a stubborn little traitor. Mrs. Williamson invited us all to tea on the first night of our arrival. She spread a most bounteous meal for us, but hardly sweetened it by the bitterness with which she snarled at our invasion. The general statement that these people are traitors, and deserve all the horrors of civil war, is easy ; but the individual case, as it comes up under your eye, showing the helpless family in their dismay at our approach, can hardly fail to excite sympathy. When we came into New Market on Friday, we met General Banks in high spirits. He complimented our march, and said the Secretary of War had telegraphed thanks to us, &c., &c., that when our movement was perceived, the rear of Jackson's force fled hastily, &c. My own opinion is, and was from the beginning, that the movement was all nonsense, and pretty expensive silliness for us.

"Jackson was ready to run, and began to do so as soon as we began to move. But perhaps we hastened him a little. Here we are, eighty miles from our supplies, all our wagons on the road, our tents and baggage behind, our rations precarious, and following a mirage into the desert. Well, the Secretary of War is much obliged to us ' for the brilliant and successful operations of this day.' So we ought to be happy, and to conclude that glory looks very different to those who see it close to. Our news now is, that Jackson is hurrying to Richmond as fast as possible. We are probably Pattersonized, as General Shields calls it, and shall be too late for any decisive part in what is now expected as the great battle of Yorktown. Still I do not regard it as impossible that the wheel may so turn as to give us a little conspicuousness in the next movements. It is our misfortune not to be in a condition of outfit, transportation, and supply to enable us to do much. We are working, too, on a frightfully long line of operations. Still hope.

"Aha! the clouds begin to break. I wish you a pleasant Easter Sunday. One thing at least we may hope for, that before another Easter day we may be at home again ; for this Rebellion will die rapidly when we hit its vitals. They have not been hit yet, however.

"I wish you could look at our regiment under rude shelters of rails and straw, and dripping in this cold storm. Our shoes and clothing came up yesterday, and this morning we are giving them out. So we are not wholly helpless yet.

"The first night that we bivouacked here a charge was made on our New York battery. A desperate cow swept in upon it, and actually knocked down and trampled on two men before it could be shot.   It was a gallant charge!   You need have no anxiety about us.   We are safe enough.   Our future is uncertain, and we are wet."

"CAMP BETWEEN NEW MARKET AND SPARTA,
Thursday, April 24, 1862.

" When I awoke on Easter morning in my dripping biv-ouac, and looked gloomily at my boots, which, with studied carelessness, I had so placed as to receive the stream from the flimsy shelter over me, and which were full· of water, when, more than all, I poured the water out and put the boots on, I might have known, by intuitive conjecture, that our forces would the next day occupy Sparta.   The storm did not abate until Tuesday, and it left us in hopeless mud and rain.   Our advance is now in Harrisonburg, and Jack-son's force has crossed the gap, and is on its way to Gor-donsville.   'The Valley' is cleared ; and General Banks has been enjoying himself with a 'general order' of congratula-tion, back-patting, and praise, worthy of little Jack Horner, and his thumb and his plum.   Still, one fact is stubborn. Our column has penetrated Virginia one hundred miles, and is very near to important Rebel lines of communication, and has achieved important results with reasonable promptness and without disaster.

" We hear to-day that the freshets of the Potomac and Shenandoah have combined to carry away the railroad bridge over the Potomac at Harper's Ferry.   This will interfere with our supplies, and, I think, hasten our course over the Blue Ridge towards Gordonsville.

" I have enjoyed for the past two days the slight allevia-tion of weather.   Tuesday afternoon the Colonel and I rode through the gap opposite New Market, over the Massannattan Mountain, into the other valley which is bounded by the Blue Ridge.   The road is a graded, gradual ascent, winding in and out.   At its summit is one of the signal-stations, whence the view into both valleys is very fine, and, under the changing, clouded, and showery light, the scene had a great charm, heightened by the camps which were scattered over the green fields of the valley. We descended into the other valley to visit the Third Wisconsin, a regiment of Colonel Gordon's brigade, which is stationed there to protect two bridges over the South Fork of the Shenandoah and another stream.

" Yesterday was a bright, breezy, sunshiny day, tempting one strongly to out-door life, — otherwise I should have written you a word on my birthday. Colonel Gordon and I drove down to Rood's Hill to examine the position which Jackson occupied there. We found it of great natural strength, with a river on either flank, and a broad, flat bottom, over which our approach would have been made.

" We saw one scene in the course of our ride which illustrates the vile tyranny, oppression, and outrage which has been practised by the Rebels here. A neatly-dressed woman, with five little children, — one in her arms, — was crossing the field. We stopped and spoke to her. ' Indeed it is,' said she, ' hard times for poor folks. Jackson took my husband off with him. They gave him his choice to go or death. I expect him back, though, now that you 've got here. He promised to run away the first chance.' Comment on such a ' volunteer ' system is unnecessary. I told you that we were living near the house of Mr. Williamson, and took our meals there. I am now writing in the parlor, which is brigade head-quarters. The husband and father of the family is off with the army, but his uncle, the owner of the farm, an old man of eighty years, is here. He is an intelligent man. He heard John Randolph's maiden speech in Congress at Philadelphia. He sat in Richmond in the Convention to amend Virginia's constitution with Madison and Monroe. His farm here contains sixteen hundred acres, and as he sees his rail-fences disappearing before our camps he recalls how it looked in New Jersey years after Washington's army had wintered there ; not a fence for miles.   This helps his philosophy a little, but he is a bitter Secessionist, though his hope flickers under the blast of Northern invasion.

"One of the most amusing things connected with our movement into this country is the constant and odd exhibition of its effect on the negro.   Day before yesterday our pickets brought in six contrabands.   They had fled from above Harrisonburg, to avoid being drawn off with Jackson's army.   One of them was almost white ; another was of quite mature years, and very much disposed to philosophize and consider and pause over this emancipation question, and act ' for the best.'   I must try to give you a snatch from the dialogue between Colonel Gordon and the negroes ; but I must leave out the brogue and laugh and aspect of the men which made up the incomparable effect.   After asking them where they came from, &c., the Colonel, ' Well, why did n't you go off with your master ? '   *Ans.* I did n't want to go South.   *Q.* The South are your friends, ain't they ? *A.* No, dey is n't no friends to colored people.   *Q.* Well, what made you think we should be ?   Did n't your master tell you we wanted to steal you and sell you to Cuba ?   *A.* Yes, but we don't believe no such nonsense as dat.   De Norf is our friends.   I 've heard all about de Norf, and I never see black men chained together and driven off to de Norf, but I have seen 'em, hundreds of 'em driven off Souf. I 'd ruffer trust to de Norf, and I 'd like to try it.   *Q.* Well, but you can't work and take care of yourself, can you ? Your master always took care of you, did n't he ?   *A.* Bress you, if de nigger don't work, who does ?   De white folks don't do no work.   I 've hired myself out for five years, made de bargain myself, and my master got de money. Yah ! yah ! yah !   And they all laughed.   *Q.* Well, you want to go Norf, do you ?   *A.* Yes.   Then the philosopher, who was named George, reasoned a little more about it.   At last the Colonel said : ' Well, you are free ; you can go where you please.   You ain't slaves any longer, unless you

choose to go back. Now, what are you going to do? Ain't
you going to do something? ain't you going to turn somer-
sets?' The negroes laughed and were exuberant.   'Turn
over, George, turn over,' said the darkies; and down the
old fellow dumped, and went heels over head on the floor
amid a general conviviality.

"That's what I call the practical effect of invasion.
Where the army goes, slavery topples and falls. For my
part, I enjoy it hugely.

"As I write this letter, two men are brought in. They
are just out of Jackson's army. They live over on the
Blue Ridge. A fortnight ago they were hunted into the
woods by cavalry, shot at, and caught and put into the
army. They say that the woods are full of men hiding in
the same way, and that the cavalry are hunting them out.
'The South is fighting for independence,' says Lord John
Russell; 'the North, for empire.' 'No man's liberty of
speech or person is interrupted,' says Jefferson Davis.

"I believe I am fighting in God's cause against the most
diabolical conspirators, rebels, and tyrants in the world.

"The bright sun of yesterday dried the ground so much
that we had battalion drill, and I had the pleasure of drill-
ing the battalion. This morning, however, this treacherous
climate again betrayed us, and it is snowing! for all day, I
fear.

"I rejoice to receive your letter of April 14, just brought
in. It brings me news of Howard and William and home,
in which I delight. I hope William's forebodings are not
well founded, but McClellan must *gather fruit* soon or go to
the wall. Still, silence to all clamor against him, and let
us await the issue. I agree with Howard, that this military
life gets wearisome."

"CAMP NEAR HARRISONBURG, April 26, 1862, Saturday.

"Rain! rain! rain! March! march! march! What
a life! We marched fifteen miles yesterday, in mud and

rain, to this point, and got into camp at night in reasonable comfort, but almost without rations, and now we are busy with the miserable interrogatory of what to eat ?

" Such is our experience. Colonel Andrews is again on detached duty, and, for the past few days, I have been in command. It is impossible to exaggerate the difficulty of taking care of a regiment when the whole Quartermaster and Commissary Departments of the army corps are in such hopeless confusion and debility.

" No other army corps has the obstacles to contend against of this kind that we have. At Yorktown they have the sea, and the Western rivers bear supplies as well as gunboats. Here our wagons cannot bring supplies enough to last until they return from a second trip. We shall be driven to forage from the country ; and I do not see any system adopted wise enough and prompt enough for that effort. But there is no use in croaking ; we shall get out of the woods somehow, I suppose.

" Among other short supplies, we are wholly without newspapers since a week ago. What is the news ? I hope McClellan is silencing his opponents by silencing the enemy's batteries. That 's his best answer.

" Well, the first year of my military service expires this week. It has been a busy one. I am willing to enter on another, but I wish I could see the beginning of the end more clearly than I can. We did n't think the Southern Confederacy had a year's life in it a year ago. They have illustrated the power of able and unscrupulous leaders, and we have furnished some hints, at least, of the weakness of feeble and scrupulous leaders. I am in such a trite and moralizing frame of mind that I will spare you any further prosing.

" We may go on to Staunton, and we may cross the gap to Gordonsville. We can't stay here much longer, and I hope my next letter may give you some guess at our future."

16

"CAMP NEAR HARRISONBURG, April 29, 1862.

"I believe I wrote you a short letter since our arrival here. Written in a northeast storm, perhaps it had a little of the gloom of the sky that overhung it. Let me try what brighter skies may inspire. Sunday morning last broke; yes! broke, and the spell — of weather which had held us so long yielded at last. The snows which we found on the field vanished.

"In the midst of our morning inspection an order came to march at once on a reconnoissance towards Jackson's position in the Swift Run Gap on the Blue Ridge. We got off at about eleven o'clock, with the Twenty-seventh Indiana Regiment. It was our duty to support the cavalry and artillery under General Hatch. We went out on the 'mud pike' to Magaugheysville, or rather *toward* that euphonious town. Such a road! We toiled out eleven miles. The cavalry pushed beyond Magaugheysville and had a brisk little skirmish, in which we took two prisoners and lost one. The Rebels have the bridge that crosses the Shenandoah full of brush and combustibles, ready to burn when we press them. It is reported that Jackson is reinforced by a brigade or more, and that he will make a stand in the gap. If this is so, perhaps we may get a little fight out of him. But I am still of the persuasion which I have always held. Our problem in this valley has always been, the movement and subsistence of our army. The enemy has always been a secondary consideration, though he has kept up a vigorous resistance.

"In the ripeness of time we must cross the ridge and find ourselves close on the flank of that army that resists McClellan at Yorktown. This is certainly the right way. What politics or jealousy or a divided command may confuse us into blundering, I cannot say.

"We have reduced our baggage, and I send home a trunk. The hard pan is what we come down to, and miss only the opportunity to drive twice our force of Rebels from any position they may take.

"I rejoice in the capture of New Orleans, and believe that the 1st of June will show the Rebellion crushed and bleeding.

"Yesterday I was busy all day on outpost duty. On Sunday our regiment marched twenty-two miles between eleven o'clock and sunset : good work. We have met one misfortune since our arrival here. A corporal of Company H, who was a capital man, and a good soldier, marched into our present camp with the regiment, was taken sick the next day of typhus fever, and died within forty-eight hours. This morning he was buried, and I could not help thinking how little of the soldier's reward he would receive, yet how much he deserves.

"We are all well, and hoping to move on toward Richmond."

"IN BIVOUAC MASSANATAN PASS, OPPOSITE NEW MARKET,
May 6, 1862.

"A word with you in the rough confusion of our mountain bivouac.

"Sunday last I should have written, but being a little out of sorts, put it off. In the afternoon we had an alarm, the long roll beaten, and marched toward the front. The regiment spent the night by the roadside. At three, A. M., started for New Market, *in retreat*. Marched all day in oppressive heat and dust, delayed by baggage-trains and batteries. Got into camp at eight, P. M. I was busy posting grand guards and outposts till eleven. At *twelve*, another alarm, and we *marched* again, foot-sore, hungry, weary, in the dark, over the mountain pass. You should have seen the sunrise from the head of the pass. To-day we rest. We found the alarm a false one, owing to the stupidity of General ——— of Shields's division. Our work has been awful and useless *utterly*. My soul is aweary — so, indeed, is my body.

"I could prose you a long story of our experiences ; but to what good ?

"I am well now. We bivouac again to-night. The scenery is glorious, the weather fine. I have two letters from you since I wrote.

"As to ——'s secession friend, let him alone. Colonels Corcoran and Wilcox are still in captivity ; so is Botts and the Governor of North Carolina. Smooth no pillows for traitors.

"Love to all. I am glad to hear such good news of Charley. I hope William is now lucky. Memphis will fall before you get this. Hurrah !

"CAMP NEAR NEW MARKET, VIRGINIA, May 9, 1862.

"After passing three days in bivouac on the other side of the gap, we returned here last night, and went again into camp. . . . .

"Our cavalry made a brisk and bold charge the other day. They are coming up finely under the new general, Hatch. They actually brought in ten men wounded with sabre-cuts ; a thing not before done in the war, and really a most healthy indication.

"Our life in the woods on the mountain was listless, but pleasant enough. I got a letter from Mrs. Ticknor, which I have answered. I hope your funds will all be saved against the wants which weather or battle will surely develop before autumn. It is a pity that your fund should not do its utmost good, and in this direction that work can best be done.

"Just now our own prospects are not such as to give us much claim on home solicitude or benevolence. The Secretary of War has ordered us back to Strasburg.

"Shields, now a major-general ! takes his division across the gap to McDowell. General Banks remains with *two brigades*, one of them ours, at Strasburg. This is the programme.

"With that pitiful force to which Banks's ' army corps ' is now reduced, and at that point fifty miles back of our recent advance, we have no other hope or purpose than protecting Maryland!   A proud sequel, is it not ?

" Of course all this is a severe trial to me,—the severest, I think, of my life.   But equally, of course, I keep a cheerful spirit, and mean to do my best to the end.   Whether the whirligig of time has any revenges in our favor or not we must wait to see.

· " Service is obeying orders, and we are in service.   Perhaps we shall make some effort to get into an active department as soon as things have taken shape.   We certainly shall if we can see any way to do so.   It is rather hard luck for the first regiment recruited for the war, is n't it ?

" We are having very bright, warm weather, and this valley is beautiful under it.   On our night march through the gap, we had sunrise just at the crest of the mountain.   Both the valleys lay beneath us in their morning bath of sunshine, picturesque with camps and wheat-fields and villages.

" Yesterday the box arrived ; the blanket is just what I want ; the stockings went right on men's feet. . . . .

" I wait patiently for news from William.   It may well be that his opportunity will soon come or has come.

" It is a year since our camp life at West Roxbury. What a different year from that to which we then looked forward !

" May the next year be a different one from that which now appears before us.

" Love to all at home."

CHAPTER XV.

BATTLE OF WILLIAMSBURG. — VISIT TO WASHINGTON. — GENERAL
  BANKS'S RETREAT. — TAKEN PRISONER. — RETURN TO REGI-
  MENT.

A T this time Major Dwight received the news of
the battle of Williamsburg, in which his brother
William, then Colonel of the First Excelsior Regiment (New York Seventieth) was repeatedly and
dangerously wounded.

When, in the first accounts, he read that Hooker's
division, to which this regiment belonged, had " suffered severely on the left," he exclaimed : " My
brother William is either wounded or killed."

The telegraph soon brought him confirmation of
the truth of his prophecy.

He obtained leave of absence from his regiment,
and almost at the same hour that his brother reached
the hospital in Washington he was at his bedside.

As he listened with eager interest to the thrilling
account of the conduct of the officers and men of the
First Excelsior, he envied the opportunity so honorably improved, and coveted wounds which were
glorious in his eyes as the reward of bravery and
constancy.

In the absence of military exploit or achievement
on his own part, he took delight in observing that of
others.   At this time he wrote exultingly of his

brother : " He behaved like a calm, bold, constant, obstinate trump."

He now made an effort to obtain for his regiment removal to an active department. Impatient of absence from his post, he soon returned to the Valley, where the opportunity was already on its way which was to give to the regiment a permanent place in history.

No single regiment did more for the credit of our arms in General Banks's retreat before the overpowering force of the enemy than did the Second Massachusetts Infantry. General Gordon, to whose brigade it belonged, says, in his official report : —

" Where all the regiments in my brigade behaved so well, it is not intended to reflect in the least upon others in mentioning the steadiness and discipline which marked the action of the Second Massachusetts, Colonel Andrews."

Of Major Dwight's conduct on the occasion General Gordon says : —

" Major Dwight, of the Second Massachusetts, while gallantly bringing up the rear of the regiment, was missed somewhere near or in the outskirts of the town. It is hoped that this promising and brave officer, — so cool upon the field, so efficient everywhere, so much beloved in his regiment, and whose gallant services on the night of the 24th instant will never be forgotten by them, — may have met with no worse fate than to be held a prisoner of war."

Many were the tributes to his bravery at this time. Captain Quincy, of the Second Regiment, now General Quincy, wrote of him : —

" Our Major Dwight has won for himself the heartfelt admiration of the regiment. His indomitable pluck and perfect *sang-froid* were beautiful.   I watched him on Saturday and Sunday with wonder and delight.   Bullets and death he utterly despised and ignored.   In short, he is a genuine hero." *

The lamented Captain Abbott, of the Second, wrote : ——

" His courage and coolness are worthy of all praise.   He walked about, apparently as unconcerned as if lounging on Washington Street.   His devotion to the wounded is sublime.   He is my hero of the fight.   The men never tire of talking of him and praising him." †

Captain Cogswell, of the Second Regiment, now General Cogswell, in writing an account of the retreat of General Banks's division, simply says : " Major Dwight is the bravest man I ever saw."

No tribute affected him so deeply as that which he received from a wounded man of his regiment whom he was endeavoring to cheer by telling him how well he and his comrades had done in the fight. The man looked at him with tears in his eyes, and said : " Ah, Major, I 'm afraid we should n't have done so well if it had not been for you."

Chaplain Quint, of the Second Regiment, wrote to the family of Major Dwight at this time as follows : ——

" I should not intrude now into your anxiety, your grief, but because your son *was*, let us say *is*, so dear to us.   He had won the universal love of our regiment.   Our hopes

---

* See remarks of Hon. Josiah Quincy at the meeting of the Suffolk Bar, upon the occasion of the death of Wilder Dwight.   Appendix III.

† See also remarks of Hon. Josiah G. Abbott upon the same occasion.   Appendix III.

that Massachusetts will be proud of the late history of the Second Regiment are clouded by the anxiety felt by every man as to the Major's fate. Brought into constant personal intercourse with the men, I have every opportunity to know their feelings. He was always so attentive to the comfort and welfare of the men, was such a friend to every soldier, and was so useful to their needs, that no man could replace him. They *love* him.

" He has been to me a kind friend, in my peculiar office, and I have always relied greatly on his influence and help in plans for the spiritual good of the men. His interest·in our public worship has been great, and it was but a few weeks ago that we were together considering measures for the special improvement of the regiment as to religious plans.

" I hope you have heard that he fell behind the column coming out of Winchester by helping and encouraging along a wounded soldier.

" You will know, of course, how nobly he commanded the little band of skirmishers on Saturday night last, when his small force he formed against cavalry and infantry with entire success ; how his clear, cool, deliberate words of command inspired the men, so that no man faltered, while in ten minutes one company lost one fourth of its number."

An account of his command of the skirmishers to which Chaplain Quint alludes is thus given in the following extract from a letter of an officer of the Second Regiment, dated

" WILLIAMSPORT, MARYLAND, May 29.

" Hardly were we out of town [Newtown] when the ene- my's cavalry and artillery dashed in with a tremendous yell of triumph. They attacked us at once. We fell back with- out any hurry, firing all the time till we got to a little bridge the other side of Cairnstown, when half the regiment made a stand, while the other half got their knapsacks. The

Rebels here closed right round us. They were so near that
we heard every order, and were able to make our disposi-
tions accordingly.

"There was not a word spoken in our regiment, by officer
or man, above a whisper, and it was so dark that nothing
could be seen except by the flashes of our muskets. Finally
we heard the order given to the Rebel cavalry to ' charge.'
A square was instantly formed in the road, and the skirmishers rallied on each side. The Rebels came thundering
down the road, literally making the ground shake. Not a
shot was fired till they were within fifty yards of us, when
Major Dwight gave the order : ' Rear rank, aim ! fire ! load !
Front rank, aim ! fire ! charge bayonets ! ' But the bayonets were not needed. Men and horses were rolled over
together, breaking the charge, sending them back in confusion, and changing the yells with which they came down
on us into groans and screams. This was the last attack of
their cavalry that night."

The following extract from a letter from General
Quincy, of a more recent date, indicates that Major
Dwight's command of the skirmishers was no less appreciated by the Rebels than it was by his own regiment.

It proves, too, that he made no empty boast when
he said of the regiment, some weeks before it was
called to action : " We miss only the opportunity to
show ourselves able to drive twice our force of Rebels from any position they may take " : —

"THE SECOND MASSACHUSETTS.

"NEW ORLEANS, July 1, 1866.
" TO THE EDITORS OF THE BOSTON DAILY ADVERTISER : —
" To the survivors of the old regiment who were present
at its first ' baptism of fire ' in the midnight skirmish of Bar-

tonsville, where, as rear-guard, it covered Banks's retreating column, the following account of the affair, in Dabney's Life of Stonewall Jackson, page 375, will be of interest : —

" ' But as it (the column) approached Barton's Mills, five miles from Winchester, the enemy, posted on both sides of the road, again received it with so severe a fire that the cavalry advance retired precipitately out of it, carrying the General and his attendants along with them, and riding down several cannoneers who had been brought up to their support. So pertinacious was the stand of the Federalists here that the Twenty-seventh, Second, and Fifth Virginia regiments were brought up, and the affair grew to the dimensions of a night combat before they gave way.'

" The ' Federalists ' engaged, as above described, consisted of four companies of the Second Massachusetts, deployed as skirmishers on either side of the pike ; the rear of the battalion being in column by platoon in the road. The skirmish line was commanded by our brave and lamented Major Wilder Dwight. The company most hotly engaged, and whose losses were heaviest, was Company I, commanded by Captain, since Brevet Major-General, Adin B. Underwood. The regiment was unsupported by any other troops. Its friends cannot but be satisfied with the enemy's account of this, its first achievement under fire, — three Confederate regiments being brought against our skirmish line of four companies, and the affair growing to the dimensions of a night combat before the well-remembered ' cease firing ' and ' retreat,' at last rang out from Major Dwight's bugler, and was repeated, in varying cadence, along the line."

The following is Major Dwight's account of the retreat of General Banks's division, as contained in the journal which he kept in Winchester during the week when, reported " missing," he was mourned as dead.

"JOURNAL.

"WINCHESTER, VIRGINIA, Friday, May 30, 1862,
Braddock Street, at Mr. Barnhardt's.

"The first news of an attack on Banks's column reached the camp of the Second Massachusetts Regiment at Strasburg, Virginia, on Friday evening after parade (May 23). The Third Wisconsin Regiment was despatched by Colonel Gordon, commanding brigade, toward Front Royal, to protect the bridges. At eleven o'clock that night we were ordered to pack wagons. After despatching our train we lay down and spent the night in bivouac. No marching orders came. It was understood by us that many of the other trains had not yet gone toward Winchester. At or near ten o'clock, A. M., Saturday, the order came for us to march. As we passed head-quarters on the way to Winchester, it was reported that the Rebel forces were pushing forward direct from Front Royal to Winchester, and we were hurried on, as it was said, to meet them or anticipate them. When we drew near the bridge over Cedar Creek, the battery was ordered forward in haste, and it was said that part of our train at Newtown had been attacked by cavalry. We pushed forward, found the trains halted, and some evidences of panic and disorder. We halted half an hour before reaching Middletown. Then pushed on again. The day, which had been rainy and clouded, grew more clear and hot. The march was through the trains, and a rapid push toward Winchester. Donnelly's brigade was before ours. Between Middletown and Newtown it became evident that our rear was being pressed. The rear-guard had been composed of cavalry and artillery. A large drove of loose horses overtook us near Newtown; one of cattle soon came also; the wagons, also, were crowding the way. Still we pushed on. At about two miles beyond Newtown General Banks appeared, and announced to Colonel Gordon that our advance was in Winchester, and all quiet there. The evidences of panic and pursuit in the rear had been rapidly multiplying, and it had been reported that our train was cut at Middletown by a force coming by the Front Royal road.   The Twenty-seventh Indiana Regiment had been ordered to return to the rear with a section of Best's battery at Newtown. As soon as General Banks announced the entry of our force into Winchester, he ordered the Second Massachusetts Regiment to the rear to protect the train.   The regiment, jaded by their march and fatigue, sprang to the duty.   At Bartonsville, a little more than a mile this side of Newtown, we left our knapsacks, and pushed on.

" As we came near Newtown, evidences of panic filled the road, — abandoned wagons, flying teamsters, &c.   The regiment formed near the edge of the town.   Two companies were deployed as skirmishers on each side of the road.   Two companies were ordered to support Best's section, and the rest of the regiment moved into the town by the road by the flank. They had just entered the town, when the enemy's artillery from the other end of the town threw a few shells at them with skill.   The shell burst directly over the battalion. Colonel Andrews ordered them within the yards on the right of the road.   The skirmishers and reserve moved on, and the rest of the regiment followed, keeping within shelter of buildings.   Before entering the town we had seen cavalry on our right and left.   The line of skirmishers was halted in a hollow just beyond the town, and the reserves and battalion kept within the town.   The artillery of both sides kept up a rapid fire.   It was, perhaps, five, P. M., when we turned back.   We held the position till sunset.   At the edge of the town, on a door-step, was a half-eaten pile of corn.   The man of the house said Ashby's horse was eating there when we came into town.   I fed my horse with what was left.   This was the only forage, I believe, taken from the enemy.   Before we withdrew from Newtown we set fire to the abandoned wagons.   It grew dark rapidly as we withdrew.   I had a detail of two companies, A and C, as a rear-guard.   One platoon of each company was deployed in the fields, on each side of the road. The reserves were united within the road. The enemy soon followed our retreat. As they came in sight of the burning wagons their yells and shouts were demoniacal. Expecting an attack by their cavalry upon the rear-guard, I prepared for it. When we came near Bartonsville a halt was ordered, to pick up the knapsacks. We could hear the yells of the men coming on. Soon the sound of approaching horses was heard. The growing darkness, confused by the glare of the burning wagons, compelled us to trust our ears. I drew the line of skirmishers into groups near the road, formed the reserve into a square, and directed the three bodies, so formed, to pour their fire upon the approaching cavalry at the command from me. The cavalry came on. The fire was ordered and delivered. The cavalry went back.

"Their advance seemed checked. I rode back up the hill over which the cavalry had come, but could hear no sound. It then became necessary to draw in and relieve the rear-guard, to enable it to take its knapsacks. At the foot of the hill on which we had been posted was a little run which the road crossed over a small bridge. The rear-guard was drawn in across that run, together with Company B, which had come out to their support.

"Company I had been ordered to report to me as a rear-guard ; Colonel Andrews stating that he thought the pursuit checked. Company I came down near the run to wait there till the knapsacks should be taken and till the column should move. Hardly had they got there when I could hear voices beyond the run. It had been reported to me that orders were being given to infantry. I heard a voice saying, ' There they are ! there they are ! in the road ! ' As a few shells had been thrown at us when we were in position beyond the run, I thought the enemy might intend some such compliment, and I directed the company which was in column by platoon to break back against the roadsides. The doubt was soon scattered. A galling and severe infantry fire opened on us.   Company I replied at once, and with admirable coolness and effect.   In spite of their inferior numbers, and of the wounded falling about, they kept their position and maintained their fire.   I sent back to Colonel Andrews for support, and parts of Companies C and B in the clover-field on the right of the road soon opened a fire that relieved us speedily.

" Company I, however, had lost eight or ten killed or wounded in this sudden and vigorous attack.

" We withdrew slowly, the column having now got in motion again.   The enemy pressed us only a little way ; then all was quiet.   When we came to a brick house our wounded were carried into it, and a halt was ordered till ambulances, which were sent for, could be brought back for them.

" I posted a line of sentries across the road and in the fields, and posted the reserve of Company I within that line, and the regiment was taking some rest, while Dr. Leland * was busy dressing the wounded in the house.   After about half an hour the sentries reported sounds as of an advancing column.   Upon going back, I found that I could hear it, and so reported to Colonel Andrews.   Colonel Andrews expressed an unwillingness to leave the wounded unless we were compelled to do so, and ordered me to return again. I did so ; and leaving word with my sentinels to fire at once upon hearing or seeing anything suspicious, I was on my way to report to Colonel Andrews that the enemy were certainly approaching, when I was stopped by a fire from the direction of the sentinels.   Immediately a sharp and extended line of fire opened from the enemy's skirmishers close upon us.   The column moved at once, as soon as it could be got in order.

" Our sentinels and reserve from Company I stood their ground under a second severe fire.   Part of Companies B and C were rapidly deployed, and we moved on in retreat. Part of Company D, under Lieutenant Abbott, was un-

* Dr. Francis Leland, Surgeon of the Second Massachusetts Infantry.

luckily left behind on our right, where they had been deployed as flankers. For a moment they were between two fires, but the fact was discovered in season to avoid disaster. We were compelled, however, to leave Dr. Leland and the wounded prisoners in the hands of the enemy. The enemy pursued us closely beyond Kernstown. Soon after passing that village, I drew in the skirmishers, and followed the column rapidly. We passed our cavalry picket at the tollgate. Between twelve and one o'clock the whole regiment lay down to a dreary bivouac just outside of Winchester on the left of the road.

"I met Colonel Gordon on the road, and went with him into town. He sent out his Adjutant, Lieutenant Horton, to attend to the posting of pickets. We went to see General Banks. I had only a few words with him. I told him the nature of the pursuit, and intimated the opinion which I had formed, that an attack would be made at daylight. I got no orders nor any intimation of any plan or purpose for the next day. I went back and lay down by a small fire for about an hour.

"Soon after three o'clock, A. M., Colonel Andrews requested me to go into town, to hurry out some ammunition for our regiment. I saw Colonel Gordon, but could get no ammunition. When I came out of Colonel Gordon's room I met a messenger from Colonel Andrews, saying that an attack seemed imminent, and there was no general officer on the field. As I went back to the regiment I met Generals Williams and Hatch, and gave them the message. I then went back to the regiment. I found Colonel Andrews and Colonel Ruger together. I said to the former : ' Ought we not to take possession of that ridge ? ' pointing to the one on the right of the road. Colonel Andrews said, ' I have already selected it, but where is Colonel Gordon ? ' I replied he was coming. The regiment was formed, and Colonel Gordon, on his arrival, sanctioning the position, the regiment moved by the flank, across the road, and up the hillside.

" We had just crossed the road when a Rebel regiment, in line (Fifth Virginia), appeared on the ridge, showing that they had anticipated us.

" As we moved up the hill Colonel Andrews told me to ride forward, to examine the position. I did so. A fire from some sharpshooters saluted me, and I could see a battery and some regiments opposite the position that we were advancing to occupy. Meantime, Cothren's battery opened on the Fifth Virginia Regiment, and scattered them out of view. The Second Massachusetts moved on to its position, and took the line of a broken stone-wall, the right of the regiment resting on the crest of the hill. The rest of the regiments of the brigade formed on our left down to the pike. The battery was posted on a rise of ground behind our regiment. The Second Massachusetts was ordered to lie down. Part of Company D was deployed on the right as skirmishers. There was a warm fire of artillery and musketry on our position. The three right companies kept up a brisk fire on the battery and infantry opposite ; rising and lying down again. Colonel Andrews and I dismounted. We could see one of the enemy's guns deserted. The enemy's pieces, I have since found out, belonged to the Rockbridge artillery. Our fire drove them from their guns, and I have also heard that their loss at this point was considerable. Soon, however, their fire ceased, for the most part, to annoy us ; though their battery and ours kept up a rapid interchange over our heads, with more or less effect on both sides.

" I happened to notice one or two mounted officers of the enemy pointing and gesticulating in the direction of our right flank, and suggested to Colonel Andrews whether they did not mean to send round a force to flank us. He seemed to think it probable. There was a stone-wall on our right and in front of our line about thirty yards or forty. Colonel Andrews ordered Companies D and I to deploy forward to that wall as skirmishers to protect that flank, and also to

17

observe and harass any movement of the enemy like the one anticipated. At about this time a sharp fire of grape and spherical case, as I suppose, began upon the wall and the field in rear of us. I have since found out that the guns of the Rockbridge artillery were ordered to divide their fire between this wall and the battery to prevent our pushing a regiment up to the wall.

"I went forward to the wall, dropping occasionally, as I saw the flash of the enemy's guns, to avoid their somewhat importunate projectiles. It appeared that the expected movement had commenced. There was one piece of low ground where the enemy's flank was exposed in their movement. They then passed behind a wooded knoll which covered them. Colonel Andrews ordered me to go to Colonel Gordon to report the movement. I did so, finding him in a hollow in rear of the centre of the brigade. He directed me to return, and ascertain in what force the enemy were moving. I went out to the wall, and ascertained that two or more regiments had already passed. Our skirmishers were exposed to a sharp fire at the wall. I reported the fact of the number of the enemy moving on our right to Colonel Gordon. He told me to tell Colonel Andrews to throw back the right of the regiment, and he would send up a force to support him. He also directed me to see that some of the artillery moved forward and to the right to play upon the enemy at this point; I was busy attending to these matters.

"One of Cothren's pieces was brought forward, our skirmishers were withdrawn from the wall, the Twenty-seventh Indiana and Twenty-ninth Pennsylvania moved up to our right. I had dismounted to go down toward the wall, and was directing the officer in charge of the piece where his fire could be directed with most effect, when I heard a cry. I turned and saw that the Twenty-seventh Indiana, which had just opened its fire, had broken and was running. I saw that the enemy were pouring up the hillside and round on

our right.   I saw, also, that the Twenty-ninth Pennsylvania
had broken and was following the Twenty-seventh Indiana.
The enemy were coming on at a run, with yells, but not in
any regular order.   The officer commanding the piece said
to me, ' What shall I do ? I have got no support for my
gun.'   ' Blaze away at 'em,' said I.   ' I shall lose my gun,'
said he.   ' Well,' said I, ' you must do as you choose.'   I
turned and found that our regiment was withdrawing.   I
could not see my horse anywhere, and so I followed on foot.
As we passed off the hill the enemy rose on its crest.   Their
cracking and whistling fire followed us closely.   I recollected
an unmailed letter in my pocket, and preferring to have it
unread, rather than read by hostile eyes, I tore it up as we
went down the hill.   A few of our men would turn and fire
up the hill, reloading as they went on.   I delayed a little to
applaud their spunk.

" But the flight before me and the flight behind me are
not reminiscences on which I like to dwell.

" We passed down into the edge of the town.   As I came
along, a young soldier of Company C was wounded in the
leg.   I gave him my arm, but, finding that he was too much
injured to go on, advised him to get into a house, and went
on.   The regiment was forming in line when I reached it.
Before I had time to go to the left, where Colonel Andrews
was, the regiment moved off again, and I followed.   It now
became a run.   A fire began to assail us from the cross
streets as well as from the rear.   I turned in at the Union
Hotel Hospital to get on to the next street, but found the
same fire there.   Just as I was near the edge of the town
one of our soldiers called out to me, ' Major, I 'm shot.'   I
turned to him, and took him along a few steps, and then
took him into a house.   I told the people they must take
care of him, and laid him down on a bed, and opened his
shirt.   I then turned to go out, but the butternut soldiery
were all around the house, and I quietly sat down.   ' Under
which king,' &c.   A soldier soon came in and took me

prisoner. I made friendly acquaintance with him. He went with me for a surgeon for my wounded soldier, and also to pick up the overcoat which I had thrown off in the heat. I soon went down with my captor to the Taylor House, where I found Colonel Bradley Johnson, First Maryland Regiment, who took charge of me.

" As I came back through the streets secession flags were flying from many of the houses; the town was full of soldiers and rejoicing. I found many of our soldiers prisoners in the court-house yard. I was busy about the wounded, and was allowed to go out to get a dinner.

" In the afternoon I went upon the field with some of the prisoners of our regiment and buried our dead : two of our own regiment and two from some other. They were buried under the cedar at the right of our line on the hill, and I read a portion of Scripture over their open grave.*

" In the evening I went up to the Academy Hospital, where I found Major Wheat of Wheat's battalion, who took care of me, and with whom I passed the night, and who treated me with the utmost kindness and courtesy.

" The next morning (Monday, May 26) Major Wheat took me, together with Colonel Murphy, to breakfast at the Taylor House. There I saw —— Pendleton, of General

---

* Four years later, almost on the very anniversary of this burial, friends of Major Dwight sought and found the consecrated spot. They were guided thither by a man from the immediate vicinity, who, when asked if he remembered, on Sunday afternoon, after General Banks's retreat in May, 1862, seeing a Union officer with some of his men, under a Rebel guard, come out upon the hill yonder to bury four Union soldiers, replied, " I should think I ought to remember it ; I helped to dig the graves." The cedar had been recently cut down, but the stump remained, and beside it were the four graves. The bodies had only the week before been removed to a soldiers' cemetery in Winchester, and those who visited the spot stood, as Major Dwight had stood, over the open graves. The form of the bodies was distinctly visible, and outside the graves were portions of the blankets in which they were wrapped, the visor of one of their caps, and other relics of them. Nearby was the " broken stone-wall," behind which the two of the buried men belonging to the Second Massachusetts had perished, and within sight were all the most interesting points connected with the battle and the retreat.

Jackson's staff, and through him sent in a request to General Jackson. First, to see him; this was refused. Second, to send information, by a flag, to our friends of our number of prisoners, wounded, and dead; this was refused, on the ground that General Banks, after the battle of Kernstown, took no such step; and, as the aid said, ' If it had not been for our private sources of information we could have known nothing of our wounded and prisoners.' Third, for a parole for our soldiers who were suffering from want of food; this was also refused on similar ground to the former. Fourth, then for a parole for myself, to enable me to board at some private house in Winchester; this was granted.

" I went to the house of Mr. George Barnhardt, on Braddock Street, where I had stopped when we were in Winchester before.

" I was at the Union Hotel Hospital on Tuesday morning, May 27, where our wounded were being collected, when I was delighted to see Colonel Kenly, of the First Maryland, from Front Royal, wounded with a sabre-cut on the head, but not dead, as reported. The Colonel came with me to Mr. Barnhardt's house, and has been with me ever since.

" On Wednesday, May 28, I attended the funeral of Sergeant Williams, Company F, who died on Tuesday morning soon after I left him. General Jackson gave permission to eight of the Second Massachusetts prisoners to go out with me as an escort for the burial of their companion.

" The number of killed, wounded, and prisoners of the Second Massachusetts may be approximately stated thus : killed, eight; wounded, thirty; prisoners, ninety.

" Our men have suffered from want of food, but only because the Confederates had it not to give them.

" The wounded are doing well, and are in fine spirits. Company I, especially, is in fine spirits.

" It should not be omitted in the record of the scenes of Sunday, that, in the retreat through the town, citizens fired from the houses upon our flying and straggling soldiers.

" Within an hour after the Rebel occupation of the town, Confederate flags were flying from windows, the women appeared gayly dressed on the streets, with Confederate colors, and wearing also little flags. The houses were vocal with ' Maryland! my Maryland!' and ' The Bonnie Blue Flag!'

" There is little doubt, however, that the Rebel loss far exceeded ours. The hospitals are crowded with their wounded. They lost, also, many officers. Their wounded are much more severely wounded than ours. I have heard that the official reports show the loss on Sunday to be ninety-six killed and one hundred and ninety-two wounded.

" I got, from conversations with various officers and soldiers, certain interesting facts connected with the pursuit and retreat. I inquired about the charge of cavalry near Bartonsville. ' Who was it ambuscaded us there?' was their inquiry. And it seemed, from further conversation, that it was a serious interruption of their advance, and a cause of loss to them. It led them to bring forward their infantry, which gave us a fortunate delay to get our knapsacks. At General Jackson's head-quarters I saw the Lieutenant-Colonel of the Fifth or Second Virginia Regiment. He asked, with interest, who it was that was at the run near Bartonsville. I told him I had that honor. He said that he had three companies deployed there of his regiment, and he added that he did not care to fight us again in the dark. Privates of the Fifth and Second Virginia reported that Jackson told them they should be in Winchester on Saturday night. The Fifth and Second are from the neighborhood of Winchester, and were coming home. Some unexplained cause led Jackson to hold them back at Newtown, otherwise they would have attacked us there.

" In the battle on Sunday morning, it was Taylor's Louisiana brigade that went round to our right. Wheat's battalion was a part of that command, and he told me about the movement. Jackson had a very large force, eight or ten thousand men, moving on the pike. On our left was a part of Ewell's force, which engaged the First Brigade. One of their regiments (a North Carolina regiment) suffered severely from the fire of the Fifth Connecticut; but their force swept into the town even before the Louisiana brigade turned our right.

Jackson's forces were so jaded and worn down that they could not keep up the pursuit. The infantry was halted about four miles from town. The cavalry continued the pursuit. The colonels of the infantry regiments kept sending word to Jackson that their men could not keep on. Jackson had been marching his men without baggage, almost without food, from Franklin, where he had engaged Milroy. He crossed the Massanattan Gap at New Market, kept up the Valley at Front Royal. The number of his forces must have been between twenty and thirty thousand. It consisted of Ewell's and Johnson's (Edward) and his own command. They pushed rapidly on, and were promised that they should go into Maryland!

"The young soldier who took possession of me was on foot, but he told me he belonged to the Second Virginia Cavalry. 'Where is your horse?' said I. 'He was shot last night when we were ambuscaded,' was the reply. Then I informed him that we shot him.

"To-night (Friday evening, May 30) there is every evidence of alarm and retreat on the part of our captors. We are expecting every kind of good news, and hoping that they will be too late to carry us off on their retreat.

"To-day (Saturday, P. M., May 31) they have loaded all their wounded into wagons for transportation in their retreat.

"Colonel Kenly and I have been paroled this afternoon. Colonel Kenly's wound in the head improves daily. Most of the prisoners, officers and men, marched off this Saturday morning.

"I have furnished bread and some vegetables to our

friends at the court-house every morning. Now that they
have gone, I fear that they will suffer, perhaps for want of
food.

"Lieutenant-Colonel Cunningham, Twenty-first Virginia
Volunteers, who has just taken my parole, tells me that his
regiment was on the hill opposite our position.

"'Your battery was splendidly served,' said he; 'and
your line of sharpshooters behind the stone wall on your
right picked off every officer of our regiment who showed
himself. Seven or eight of our officers were wounded by
them. We fired spherical case *over* the wall at them, and,
at last, round shot *at* the wall from the Rockbridge artillery.'

"*Saturday evening, May* 31. — The streets are quiet to-
night. We await events.

"The parole under which I have been quietly living at Mr.
Barnhardt's since Monday involved only this restraint: con-
finement to the corporate limits of Winchester, and the duty
of reporting every morning at ten o'clock at the office of
the Provost Marshal. We have fed on rumors, speculations,
fears, hopes, falsehoods, and sensations, but have felt none
of the constraints of captivity. The parole which I have
given to-day is, not to serve till exchanged, and I may 'go
at large.'

"Mr. Barnhardt, a big Dutchman, who has lived over
seventy years, as he says, 'just for good eating,' returned
from market Wednesday morning. 'No market,' says he.
'Butter forty cents, eggs twenty-five, lamb twenty; and
all because the Confederates is here. I could ha' sot down
on the market-steps and ha' cried, as sure as you sit there
in that there *cheer*.' To-night his nervousness has reached
that point that he has gone to bed 'a'most sick and down-
hearted.' He is a Union man. 'I was born a Union man,
I have always been a Union man, and a Union man I'll die,
and the Devil can't make nothing else of me.'

" *Sunday noon*, 12 M., *June* 1. — We have been listening two hours to the sound of cannon in the direction of Strasburg or Front Royal. A report comes in, that Milroy camped at Wardensville Friday night. Another now comes, that Shields and Milroy are between Middletown and Newtown, and Gustavus Smith is in their rear. *Quien sabe?* What a week of rumor it has been! First Ewell was at Bunker's Hill to cut off Banks; then our troops had crossed the river; Wheat was in Hagerstown; the bridge at Harper's Ferry was burned; then Cooper and Dix were in Charlestown with large force; then Shields was at Front Royal; then Richmond was taken; then we were repulsed; then Banks was within four miles of town; then Fremont was in their rear, &c., &c., &c. We speculate, discuss, study the map, &c. This morning a scout has been sent out towards Martinsburg, to General Banks, to say that nothing but a thin veil of Stewart's cavalry covers this town. We wait the ' careful ' advance of some Federal flag from somewhither.

" *Sunday evening.* — A thunder-storm is sharply rattling over us. Hope is still deferred. The sound of cannon hushed at about noon. Rumor says, Milroy has been driven back, and Jackson is pushing beyond Strasburg. It adds, that he orders hospitals to be prepared for his wounded here. No news from our front. A foolish doctor from the hospital tried to fire up the engine to go to Charlestown, but was prevented by the citizens, with whom he has had some altercation. A guard is now placed over the hospital again. We are not ' out of the woods,' and had better not halloo yet, though we need not be scared by owls! Would that Banks or day after to-morrow were here!

" *Monday morning*, *June* 2. — No news. We are endeavoring to get a wagon to go to Martinsburg, and, if successful, will be off at once for ' *our lines.*' "

"WILLIAMSPORT, MARYLAND, Monday Evening,
June 2, 1862. At last.

"Soon after my last words, Mr. Barnhardt, with corpulent and puffy energy, came up stairs. 'Well, will you go this morning?' 'Yes.' He had previously told me, when I asked him about a wagon for Martinsburg, 'O, it worrits me, it worrits me!' Now he said, 'I've got a wagon for ye, yes I have, already!'* Sure enough, a contraband and his cart were at our door in half an hour. Dr. Stone† and I started at once. Colonel Kenly bade me good by and God speed.

"Now for impudence and liberty! On we rode. Four miles, and then came the halt that we dreaded. Two mounted citizens pragmatically inspected our paroles, and at last let us go. Then two cavalrymen, whom we dissuaded. Then we were shouted at to halt! Two mounted men, with bowie-knife, revolver, carbine, and sabre, said, 'You must turn back.' Our hearts sank, but we took out our papers, reasoned, persuaded, and, as Providence would guide it, led them to respect our paroles, and let us free. They said, 'We will go back to town and ask again.' On we went, and, with only another halt, but with every nervousness of anxiety, we got to Bunker's Hill. There the harness broke, and again we looked to the rear, but on we went again. 'What is that?' 'Our cavalry?' 'It must be'; and sure enough down they charged upon us, and we were, in an abrupt transition, at once within the Union lines. I cannot describe our thankfulness and heart-swell.

---

* After Major Dwight left Winchester, some of Mr. Barnhardt's neighbors, who were Rebels, said to him: "You'll have to suffer yet for keeping your Major so long, and then helping him away." "I told them," said the brave old man, "that they could n't rob me of much if they took my life, for I was 'most eighty year old."

† Dr. Lincoln Ripley Stone, then Assistant-Surgeon of the Second Massachusetts Infantry, who would not abandon the hospital in his charge at Winchester, was a prisoner. He was paroled; the parole to be a free release, if at Washington he could secure an agreement that surgeons should not be liable to capture; which was accomplished.

" We reached Martinsburg.   Then our contraband and colored driver, entering into the spirit of our pursuit, agreed to put us through to Williamsport.   We crossed the river, met Brown's * wagon.   Brown's ready grin and constant delight prepared me a little for the enthusiasm of the regiment.   I cannot describe their welcome.   God knows, I should be proud to deserve it.   I have never known greater happiness or thankfulness than to-night.   Good by, my dear mother.   I go to Washington to-morrow.   I will come home when I can, and tell you all."

He could not describe the welcome of the regiment.   Another, an eyewitness, has attempted to do so.   In order to appreciate it, one should understand the state of mind of the regiment concerning him during the previous week.

The first account of him after he was missed came from one of their number, who affirmed that he had seen him, during the retreat, in the streets of Winchester, on foot, surrounded by Rebel cavalry, with his sword raised.   To the excited imagination of the witness, it seemed that the Rebels succeeded in taking his life on the spot.   This account was received without question at first ; and, although reliable men afterwards testified to having seen him at a later hour uninjured, yet as day after day passed without any tidings of him, the first impression was not removed, and their feeling was, that he was among the killed.

" It was in the dusk of Monday evening, June 2, just after parade, while officers and men were in or about their tents, many talking of the Major and his probable fate, that a stir was perceived among the officers.   The lamented

* George H. Brown, Regimental Wagoner.

Captain Cary was heard to exclaim, ' Good heavens, the Major ! ' as he rushed forward. Then the Major was seen running, on foot, towards the regiment. The officers ran to meet him. More than one lifted him in his arms. The men ran from their tents towards the limits of the camp. They could not be restrained : they broke camp, and poured down upon the Major with the wildest enthusiasm.''

At this time our informant left the scene to telegraph to his family the news of his safety.

"On my return to camp," he says, " the scene of noisy excitement was changed for one of profound calm. The regiment was drawn up around the Major, who was reading to them from a paper which he held in his hand. Not a face there but was wet with tears. He gave them the names of those of their comrades who were prisoners in Winchester. He told them who were wounded, and the nature of their wounds. He told them of their dead, and of the burials, upon which even the Rebels of Winchester had looked with respect. Then he said, ' And now do you want to know what the Rebels think of the Massachusetts Second ? " Who was it ambuscaded us near Bartonsville ? " asked a cavalry officer of me. I replied, " That was the Massachusetts Second." An officer of Rebel infantry asked me who it was that was at the run near Bartonsville. " That was the Massachusetts Second," said I. " Whose," asked another officer, " was the battery so splendidly served, and the line of sharpshooters behind the stone-wall who picked off every officer of ours who showed himself ? " " That was the Massachusetts Second," said I. On the whole, the Rebels came to the conclusion that they had been fighting the Massachusetts Second, and that they did not care to do it again in the dark.' "

The next day he wrote from Washington : —

" DEAR MOTHER, — I send you my journal.   You will see by it that I became a prisoner by carelessness, mixed, perhaps, with good-nature.   D—— is with me.   I stay here to see about my exchange, &c.   I am sorry you had so much anxiety for me, but thankful to be able to relieve it.   Love to all.   My reception by the regiment is reward enough.   I must get back to them."

Two days later he telegraphed from Washington as follows : —

" Have order for exchange with Major Davidson at Fort Warren.   Shall come home at once and arrange it."

CHAPTER XVI.

RETURN HOME. — PROMOTION. — FORTRESS MONROE. — REJOINS REGIMENT. — LETTERS FROM CAMP NEAR CULPEPER. — BATTLE OF CEDAR MOUNTAIN. — LETTERS FROM CAMPS NEAR TENALLY- TOWN AND ROCKVILLE.

AFTER having, as he supposed, successfully accomplished, in Washington, an early exchange, Major Dwight hastened home, where he arrived at midnight of Friday, June 5.*

That home "received its dead, restored to life again." Must he go forth a second time to danger and to death? Patriotism faded under the temptation to hold him fast.

On the evening which followed his return he was entreated to consider the possibility of his resigning from the army. He had served there faithfully for the past fourteen months, he had helped to create one of the best regiments in the service, he had at last enjoyed the long-delayed opportunity in the field, and had improved it honorably; could he not now feel that he had done his part in the war? Could he not now, in conscience and in honor, return to civil life, where a career of usefulness was open to him, and to the home where his presence was so much needed? Every argument was urged which might possibly lead him to regard this as the path of duty. He listened patiently and in silence to all that was

* See Appendix I.

said. When the last word was spoken, he calmly, and in gentlest tones, replied : —

" The last year has been the richest of my life. For the first time in my life, I have been sure, every day, that I was doing good. I have worked hard in the profession of the law, and gained cases for people, and they have been very grateful to me, but I never knew with certainty whether I had done them good or not. Now I know, every day I live, that I do good to those poor fellows in our regiment, and I shall not give it up. I would not if I could, and I could not if I would, with honor.

" Then, as to my life, my experience at Winchester taught me *that* is God's care, not mine. I took no care of it then myself. I was all the time in front of the line ; I went forward into the most exposed positions possible. I saw a dozen men take aim at me. They did not hit me. I was as safe there as I should have been at home. And I shall be so again, till God's time comes to take my life. When that time comes, I am perfectly willing to give it up."

He ceased speaking. Personal selfishness was rebuked. He was never again asked to reconsider the purpose to which he had dedicated himself.

Much of his first day at home was given to a visit to Fort Warren, whence he returned buoyant with the hope of being soon exchanged for Major Davidson, who, in accordance with the arrangement made by Major Dwight at Washington, left the next day for Richmond with the expectation of speedily accomplishing that object.

Some days later he wrote to his brother Howard as follows : —

" DEAR CAPTAIN, — How are you ? I 'm prisoner of war.

It seems to run in the family.* I hope you won't have it.
I wish that you may find a speedy end of your service in the
West. I have had a very pleasant week at home, but am
very impatient to be back to the regiment."

He was indeed an impatient "prisoner of war."
On being reproached for so reluctantly yielding to
the necessity of remaining at home, he said : —

" You do not doubt, do you ? that this is all very pleasant, — being here, having an easy time, amusing myself, —
it is all very pleasant ; but *it is not the life for me.*"

After two weeks, brightened by the kind attentions
of friends, in the course of which he received his promotion as lieutenant-colonel of his regiment, he prepared, on the evening of June 22, to leave home the
next day for Fortress Monroe, where he believed he
should find his exchange accomplished. In the course
of his preparations he said, incidentally, that he did
not expect to live to come back again, adding, " And
I do not much care whether I do or not. What I *do*
care for," said he, and the earnestness and vigor of
his manner as he spoke will never be forgotten, —
" what I *do* care for is to have an opportunity to find
a field, and to improve it honorably."

The next day, as he left home, his parting words
were : " Mother, *you* believe in God ; that's the best
advice I can give you."

There was nothing new or strange in receiving this
counsel from his lips. Even from boyhood he had
been accustomed to express, under circumstances

---

* Colonel William Dwight, Jr. was taken prisoner after the battle of Williamsburg.

calculated to call it forth, his trust in the overruling providence of God, and his sense of the duty of constantly and cheerfully recognizing it. Yet, "his faith," to borrow language which has been otherwise applied,—"his faith transpired not in outward professions, but in his actions; in the uprightness, the moral elevation of soul and spirit which sent him straight forward, without turning to the right hand or the left. His faith, in the literal sense of the word, is known to us only through his works."

Judge Gray showed his appreciation of it when, after his death, he wrote : —

"I have never known a man who seemed to hold in juster proportion his duties to himself, his friends, his family, his country, and his God. If all men were like him, there would be less discussion of the comparative merit of faith and works."

On the 30th of June he wrote from Washington as follows : —

"I have just returned from Fortress Monroe. Our relations to the enemy are so complicated and uncertain that I could accomplish very little. The only hopeful sign is, that my major did not return with the rest. I had a pleasant enough visit at the Fortress.

"I go to our camp near Winchester to-morrow morning, and shall be absent a few days. Now is the season of rapid changes, and I hope for a change for the better.

"Speculation or prophecy will be disaster or fulfilment before this reaches you, so I will say adieu.

"Hope and pray. If all goes smoothly for me, I shall see you again for a few days next week. But I fear even a longer delay. Love to all."

18

He arrived in Brookline during the following week. This second return, without hope of immediate exchange, was too severe a trial to him to be a source of unalloyed pleasure to those who welcomed him. His home was no longer with us. His home was with his regiment, where, during his recent visit, he had seen how much he was needed. We missed the gladness which had animated him on his first return. We saw how hard he found it to be resigned to the dispensation which held him back from the performance of those duties that were forever knocking at his heart.

Yet there are bright spots to look back upon, even in this last visit. Among the pleasantest to him were Commencement and Phi Beta days at Cambridge, which he enjoyed with his accustomed zest.

The following is extracted from an eloquent tribute paid him, after his death, by a distinguished writer.* It contains a vivid picture of his appearance on the latter occasion : —

" At the dinner of the Phi Beta Kappa Society, of Harvard University, in July last, after General Devens had made a stirring speech, and Holmes, in a clear ringing voice, had chanted the fiery music of his battle-lyric, ' Never or Now,' and the other speakers had all obeyed the imperial impulse of the hour, there was a sudden and loud call for a young man who was trying to escape from the hall, — the only retreat he ever willingly attempted; — and, at last, yielding to the summons, he turned and fronted the company with a bright, ardent smile, while, amidst the shouts and thunders of applause, the President introduced him as

* George William Curtis.

Lieutenant-Colonel Wilder Dwight, a prisoner of war at large upon his parole. The heroic aspect, the burning words, the passionate appeal he made for honor and liberty, we shall none of us forget.

" And now that he shall be seen no more, we remember him as he stood there, the express image of that dauntless daring, that blithe earnestness, that religious faith, by which alone the great victory is to be won."

On Monday, A. M., August 11, he received the news that his exchange was effected. At the same time he heard of the battle of Cedar Mountain, in which his regiment had lost so heavily.

Every true soldier can appreciate the bitterness of his feeling at hearing that his regiment had been in action without him. The loss of his friends who had fallen cut him to the heart. He suffered as he had never suffered before. Some hours were given to visiting the friends of the wounded and the killed, and to making arrangements for serving them ; then he left us, never again to return.

His premonition that he should not live to come back had seemed to gain strength with every passing day. He often expressed it naturally and cheerfully. The evening before he left home he talked of it more seriously, casting his view forward into the future world. He would have us prepared for what was to come.

Those who met him on the last sad morning saw in his face what he felt. To more than one he said, as he took leave of them, " It is the last time."

Yet, his anxious thought was not now for himself. He was bearing others' burdens.

"I took it hard this morning," he said to us in parting. "I feel better now. I shall get back and help those poor fellows, and that will be a comfort." And with a look full of love and care, and "God bless you!" on his lips, he was gone.

On reaching camp he wrote : —

"CAMP NEAR CULPEPER, VIRGINIA,
August 13, 1862, 9 P. M.

"I have a chance to send a line, but hardly time to write. A sharp, sudden half-hour's work, under desperate circumstances, has crippled us sadly, as you must have heard only too well. My return has been simply sad and bitter.

"Of the hopes that may be indulged, I think these are accurate. Major Savage, a wounded prisoner, and Captain Russell, unwounded, taken while caring for Major Savage. Captain Quincy, a wounded prisoner, able to walk off the field. Lieutenant Miller, a slightly wounded prisoner. You know of Robeson, Grafton, and Oakey. Lieutenant Browning is also wounded severely, but not dangerously. Our loss in killed, twenty-seven ; wounded, one hundred and four ; missing, thirty. There will be many deaths from wounds.

"Our five brave, honorable, beloved dead * are on their way to Massachusetts. She has no spot on her soil too sacred for them, no page in her history that their names will not brighten.

"The regiment looks well, but O, so gloomy! I have much to tell, but to-night, after the fatigue and stress of the last three days, cannot write.

"As for myself, I look *forward*. Love to all."

* Captain Edward Gardiner Abbott, Captain Richard Cary, Captain Richard Chapman Goodwin, Captain William Blackstone Williams, and Lieutenant Stephen George Perkins.

Two days later he wrote : —

"CAMP NEAR CULPEPER, VIRGINIA, August 15, 1862.

" I have fallen into camp life and its spirit quite easily. It is the virtue of duty in the field that it is persistent, inexorable, exacting. It is the virtue of the military life that it is busy and ardent. Both these considerations urge themselves on me as I sit down to write in cheerful temper, while there are so many reasons for heaviness and sorrow.

" Our crippled regiment turns out to its duties and parades as if nothing had happened to it, while its thinned ranks and vacant posts tell the story of its trial and losses, — of its glory too.

" Yesterday morning I spent with Colonel Andrews in visiting our wounded, and doing my possible for them. It is hard to see some of the very best of our men disabled ; but their pluck and cheeriness are delightful. The regiment behaved wonderfully, but the position into which they were ordered was a hopeless one.

" After dinner General Gordon and I rode out to the field of battle, and I examined it thoroughly. I shall write out and send you a full account of the position and the action. The scene was full of interest. I went to the spot where Cary fell and lay till he died on the following day. I found, too, where our other officers fell. The evening was spent with Professor Rogers, Mr. Dean, Mr. Shaw, and others, who have come out to get tidings of our officers.

" This morning we have had a grand review (the first occasion of my putting on my sword as Lieutenant-Colonel) of Banks's corps. As we passed out to the field our bands played a dirge, and we paid a marching salute to Colonel Donelly, who had just died of his wounds, and was lying in a house in the town. Then to the field. The loss of the corps is about two thousand five hundred. Their work was done in a few hours, and all you can say is, the enemy went back, but their loss can hardly have equalled ours.

" This afternoon I am on duty again, so that I have no time for writing you as I could wish. I hope something can be done to recruit us up to an approach to our former numbers. Nothing can ever make good our losses. Cary and Goodwin and Grafton were all too sick to march, and went up to the battle-field in ambulances, rushing forth when their regiment was ordered forward.

" All these and many other memories I could write if I had time. Love to all at home. I am well, and most happy to be back here."

Again he wrote : —

" CAMP NEAR CULPEPER, VIRGINIA, August 17, 1862, Sunday.

" The battle of Cedar Mountain, or, correctly, Slaughter's Mountain, or, in common speech, Slaughter Mountain, seems to be proclaimed by General Pope, accepted by General Halleck, and, probably, welcomed by the country, as one of the most obstinate, desperate, and gallant contests of the war.

" It is claimed loudly and with argument by both sides as a victory, and therefore lacks the best test of success, namely, to prove itself. It failed to be decisive. What Jackson intended by his move across the Rapidan is known, perhaps, to himself. If he meant to hurt and to get hurt, he succeeded. If he meant anything further, he failed. But he left a sting behind him.

" The right wing of Banks's army was certainly hurled into a storm that wellnigh wrecked it. The field of battle was well chosen by the enemy. From the slopes of Slaughter's Mountain on his right, whence he commanded the whole field and viewed it at a glance, to his left in the wood the enemy were strong. Our men attacked, and held them back most gallantly.

" But you must get the outline and details of the battle from other sources. I will attempt to follow my regiment as it went into action *without me*, in its hot and toilsome march from Hazel River to Culpeper, where it arrived on

Friday at midnight, and bivouacked near its present camp, in its weary and feverish approach to the field on Saturday, and in its sharp trial as the day closed.

"The regiment marched from Culpeper about six miles to the field, and arrived soon after noon. It went into position on the right, on high ground, in the edge of a wood. There the men waited, rested, and lunched. The battle was going on, on our left and centre, mainly with artillery.

"At last, and after five o'clock, P. M., the sharper musketry on our right told that they would probably be called on. Suddenly Colonel Andrews got an order to move immediately to the support of Crawford's brigade, then engaged in a wood about one third of a mile in our front. General Crawford, it seems, had, with mysterious wisdom, and without full examination of the field, pushed his brigade out into an open wheat-field, bounded on two sides by woods which the enemy was holding. There he was, suffering and perishing, at the moment the order came to the Second. Colonel Andrews moved them, as ordered, at a double-quick, down the hill, across the field, through the bog, over the ditch or ' run,' up a steep hillside, and into a wood dense and thickly grown, on, on, on till out they came upon an open field, of which I give you a sketch on the opposite page.

"The regiment was a good deal disordered when it got through the woods. It marched out through a gap in the fence into the open wheat-field, in which the recently cut shocks of wheat were standing, as indicated on the plan. It was formed under a fire from the woods *opposite*, but soon brought inside of the fence, and ordered to lie down behind the fence. A few words more about the ground.

"The open field is not level; there is a swell of the ground, which falls off gently toward the enemy's side, and becomes a marsh ; but as it approaches the enemy's wood, it rises again rather suddenly, and the hillside thus made is densely wooded.

"On this wooded hillside the enemy were piled up. The

woods indicated on the plan on the right of the open field are a low, bushy growth, hardly taller anywhere than a man, but so very thick as to be a perfect cover.

" Recollect that the enemy held this approach to our right.

" When Colonel Andrews entered the woods through which he came to this open field, he met dismayed soldiers of Crawford's brigade, saying, ' We are beaten ! ' Crawford had driven his brigade, before this, at a charge, across this field, or tried to do so, and the fire from both directions upon them proved very destructive.

" The Second took up a position behind the fence, as I have said. Captain Abbott, with his company as skirmishers, had advanced beyond the fence into the field, but were subsequently withdrawn.

" Colonel Andrews had, in front of him, the enemy in these woods, and could see only the flash of their guns. Still, he suffered very little. Soon he was ordered to move down toward the right farther, which brought him quite close to the low wood. At this time he got an order to charge across the field.

" He said it was impossible, and General Gordon, whom he went to see, agreed with him. Colonel Andrews declined to do it, saying it would be simply the destruction of the regiment.

" It afterwards turned out that the order had been misunderstood by the staff-officer who gave it. General Crawford's brigade, it must be remembered, had retired from the scene before Gordon's brigade came up to the field. Gordon's brigade of three regiments, part of one of which, the Third Wisconsin, had already been engaged in Crawford's first charge, were alone in this position, and without support. Soon after this Colonel Andrews saw a Rebel line advancing diagonally across the field. He at once opened a file-fire upon it from our regiment. Gaps opened, the Rebel line wavered, and became very much broken. While this was going on, and when it seemed that this advance might be checked, a fire opened from the woods in which we were, on our right flank, and even in rear of it. Colonel Andrews found that the troops on our right, of our own brigade, had been driven back. This first fire, on our flank, killed Captain Goodwin, commanding the right company, and dropped half of that company. Colonel Andrews then ordered the regiment to fall back. At this time the fire upon us was from front, from beyond our right, diagonally, and, most severely of all, directly upon our flank. The enemy were in overwhelming force, and we were left alone.

" Under a fire of this kind no troops can stand or live. This flank fire cannot be replied to without a change of front or a supporting force. These were impossibilities. Under a storm of bullets which our thinned ranks (for then our heavy loss was suffered) attests only too strongly, the gallant regiment withdrew, leaving one third, nearly, behind.

" The trees in the wood remain to testify to the severity of the fire. There and then, within a few yards of the fence, fell Goodwin and Abbott and Williams and Cary and Perkins, and many a fine soldier by their sides. The colors were shot through and through, the staff shattered and broken in two, the eagle torn from the staff, but Sergeant George, of Company A, the color-bearer, brought them off in safety and in honor. As soon as the regiment, in its retreat, came outside of the wood, it was re-formed by Colonel Andrews near the point where it had entered. The whole time since it entered the woods was little more than half an hour. Many of the men, besides those actually hit, had stopped to give aid to the wounded or dying, and so the regiment was a mere fragment.

" It went back to a point near its original position, and near a house, which at once became a hospital. Colonel Andrews describes the feeling with which he then discovered the losses. Of the captains, seven went in, and one only,

Captain Bangs, came back. Of the lieutenants — but you know the record. At first it was thought and hoped that our list would be of *wounded*. Alas! how speedy was death. The regiment was soon moved toward the centre; and it spent the night, in presence of the enemy, on outpost duty. During the night there was some confusion and fighting. One of our sentinels took five of the enemy's cavalry with skill and courage. His name is Harrington, Company E. I had noticed him previously, as a bold, cool man.

"Among the incidents of the fight, Corporal Durgin, one of the color-guard, was approached by three Rebels, as he was looking for Major Savage. He at once called out : ' Adjutant, bring that squad here. I 've got three prisoners.' The men hesitated ; one struck him with his musket, when Durgin doubled him up by a thrust of his rifle, shot a second one, while the third ran away, and Durgin ran too.

"Colonel Andrews's horse was shot twice ; once in neck and once in shoulder. Major Savage's horse was shot after he dismounted, and he was subsequently wounded. Captain Russell stopped to help him, and was so caught. Captain Quincy, too, was wounded and taken.

"On Monday morning, the enemy having drawn back, our burial-party went out. Cary was found, as if placidly sleeping, under an oak near the fence. He had lived until Sunday. His first sergeant, Williston, was at his side, alive, though severely wounded. He had watched with him, and when the Rebels took from him all that was valuable, Williston begged the men to give him Cary's ring and locket for his wife, and their hearts melted, and he was happy in giving them up to be sent to her.

"Abbott wore a proud, defiant, earnest look, as when he fell, with the words on his lips : ' Give it to that flag, men !' pointing to the Rebel emblem opposite. Goodwin and Williams and Perkins too. Cary and Perkins and Goodwin went to the fight in ambulances, being too sick to go. Goodwin had to be helped along into the fight, but said, ' I cannot stay when my men are going.'

" It was a sad burden that was brought back to our bivouac on Monday.

" I have twice visited and examined the field, and tried to live over again the scene, that I may share, as far as possible, the memories of my regiment.

" I was seeking, by description, the spot where my dear friend Cary fell and died, and was in some doubt about it, when my eye caught, among the leaves, a cigarette paper. I knew at once that it must be the place, and looking farther, I found some writing with his name on it. These had doubtless fallen from his pocket.

" I took them as mementos, and cut also a piece of wood from the stump on which his head rested. These I have sent to his wife.

" Our chaplain was busy near the field with the wounded all night. His fidelity and constancy in remaining there after our forces withdrew deserve recollection.

" This morning we have had service, and the camp is now under the influence of its Sunday quiet. There are a good many questions about the fight, and the responsibility of it, which I will not discuss. It seems a pity that we pressed them on our right. The darkness was so near, and the night would have given us time to concentrate our forces. But it is as it is. No troops ever encountered a severer test, and our regiment behaved nobly. *Voilà!*

" To-morrow we shall have our muster, and account for our losses.

" We may, probably, be here some time, to repair our losses. I went out to dress-parade this evening, and as I marched to the front, with *five* other officers, to salute Colonel Andrews, our griefs seemed heavy enough. The Third Wisconsin Regiment, so foully slandered by some of the newspapers, behaved gallantly, and did all that men could do.

" Tell Colonel William, of Williamsburg, that Crawford pushed his brigade out into that open wheat-field without skirmishing at all on his right, and never sent a skirmisher into the bushes and low woods on the right of the field.

"We were rushed up at a double-quick to his support, and occupied the ground that he had just lost. Bah! then it was too late.

"I send you a memorandum of my wants on a slip of paper. The weather has been cool for several days; the nights even cold. I am in excellent health, and I hope you are well and in good spirits.

"Colonel Andrews's behavior in the fight is the admiration of all.

"My love to all at home. Write me, and send me every scrap about the regiment and our lost brave men."

"IN BIVOUAC NEAR RAPPAHANNOCK CROSSING, August 20, 1862.

"I had hardly finished my last letter when marching orders came. We had a night's bivouac Monday, a tedious, dusty, broiling march yesterday, and another bivouac last night behind the Rappahannock, which is now between us and the enemy, who were, I suppose, themselves awaiting us beyond the Rapidan. I have no spirit for speculation or prophecy, only an aching for result and fulfilment. . . . .

"Lieutenant Mills has reported for duty, and finds himself very busy. He comes at the moment when we need every officer's service. He will do well. Last evening when we came on to the field, I found Private Kent Stone waiting for me, looking bright and earnest. He came on in charge of the new recruits from Washington; and as soon as we were established, he marched his recruits into our field, and they were assigned to their companies. I advised the Stones to go into Company C, Captain Cogswell, and they will be well cared for there. . . . . There is nothing to tell. I suppose our movements are for the purpose of effecting a junction with McClellan's forces, which are, at all events, expected by us.

"This is the end of my week since joining. It has been a full one."

At this time a prohibition was put upon the mails, and Colonel Dwight was unable to send home his usual journal until September 3, when he wrote from Washington : —

" After an experience of sixteen days here, I am humiliated, exhausted, yet well and determined.

" The history of Pope's retreat, without a line and without a base, is a military novelty.   We lived on the country, with a witness, — green corn and green apples.   Twice cut off by the enemy, — everything in discomfort and confusion.

" Forced marches, wakeful bivouacs, retreat, retreat.   O, it was pitiful! and now a whole city full, here at Washington begins to feel our presence.   Bah !

" The regiment has behaved well, the brigade has behaved well.   Charley's accident was funny.   He was taken from his horse in a *mêlée*, but Colonel Taylor assures me unhurt and lively.*   It is the family luck.   I will write more when I can, and when I have been to sleep.   I am perfectly well, and in as good spirits as can be expected.   Have got a large mail to-day.   Thanks for letters.   Love to all at home. Keep ——— there.   The service is not for the young ; and though the race seems to be to the swift, the battle is not yet to the strong."

"CAMP NEAR TENNALLYTOWN, MARYLAND, September 5, 1862.

" I wrote you a hasty scrawl in my hurried visit to Washington, just to assure you of our safety *at last*.   That was Wednesday.   We went into camp near Fort Albany, and within a mile of the Long Bridge.   Yesterday we got marching orders again ; crossed the Potomac at Georgetown, and came out here on the Edwards's Ferry and Darnestown road, about eight miles, and are now in camp. . . . .

* Lieutenant Charles Dwight, of General Sickles's staff, while leading a charge on the enemy, was taken prisoner during the battle of Bristow Station, August, 1862.

" We suppose that we are to go up the river towards
Edwards's Ferry. You would, perhaps, like to have a record
of our life since we occupied the line of the Rappahannock
till to-day. It has been so tense and corrosive that I am not
yet in tone to write an account of it. Our week on the
Rappahannock was a series of marches, countermarches, vigils,
pickets, wet bivouacs, always within sound, often within
reach, of the enemy's cannon, moving under the hissing
importunity of flying shells and round shot. One morning
at Beverly Ford we took a position from which our forces
had been driven two previous days. Colonel Andrews and
I breakfasted under a tree with shell and round shot moving
merrily about us. We held the position. On Monday night
we lay under arms within half a mile of the battle in which
Kearney and Stevens fell, near Fairfax Court-House. The
fight was a fierce one. During most of it a violent thunder-
storm raged fearfully. I can only leave you to imagine the
scene. We were all night under arms, wet through, and
without fires. The worst night I ever spent. Tuesday
night we came in last over the Warrenton Pike, — the very
tail of the Grand Army, as we had been before.

" Our risks and chances have been great, but we were not
in either of the fights about Manassas or Bull Run. I am
glad of it. Unsuccessful battles we have had enough of.
I have been too busy to get news of Charley. We have
been on the march for eighteen days. Colonel Taylor's
account of the matter was encouraging. I met him by
chance on Tuesday. Inquired at once for Charley. His
answer was, 'He is on his way to Richmond.' I was taken
aback. Under all the circumstances, you may regard him
as lucky.

" I hope he will be paroled without being taken to Richmond.

" Our recruits have had a hard time. It is an illustration
of the folly of our whole system of organization and recruit-
ing, that we should have dragged one hundred and fourteen

unarmed recruits through all this business.　But I will not
begin about follies.　The events of the past three weeks are
incredible.　Disaster, pitiable, humiliating, contemptible !
Love to all at home.　Now that we are in Maryland, I suppose the absurd order stopping the mails will be rescinded.
I shall write again as soon as I can."

"Camp beyond Rockville, Maryland, September 7, Sunday.

" It is a hot, sunny, breezy afternoon.　We are in line of
battle with Sumner's corps, as we have been ever since
yesterday noon.　The air is full of rumors, but my opinion
is firm that the Rebels will not cross *in force* into Maryland.
If they do, and if our hearts have not really died within us,
then we shall be fit to strike them.　We want SOLDIERS,
SOLDIERS, and a GENERAL IN COMMAND.　Please notice the
words, all of them ; for the history of the past fifteen months
is the sad record of that want.　Nothing surprising happened
in Virginia.　The force brought against us was not larger
than our own, was equally fatigued, and, still more, without
food.　But we allowed them, — impotently and with fatal
blindness, allowed them to outgeneral us.　We ignored what
was passing under our eyes, denied the familiar maxims of
military science, blustered up to the moment of defeat, and
then fled back to our base.

" ' No line of retreat.'　' No base of supply.'　' No strong
positions.'　What is the issue of that policy ?　A starving
army hunting lines of retreat upon the firm base, and up to,
and within, the strong fortification of its capital.　We stood
on the banks of the Rappahannock a week, while the enemy
steadily pushed his columns up the other bank, and through
a well-known mountain pass upon our rear.　O, it is heavy
to see life and hope and peace and honor withering away
daily under such influences !　Nor do I see any evidence of
tone or wisdom in power anywhere. . . . .

" It has come back to McClellan !　I met him as I went
into Washington the other day.　His manner was gay, con-

fident, elate. His staff were jubilant. Again he takes the reins, and what do you expect? I must hope, though I know not why."

Once more he wrote from Washington : —

"September 11, 1862.

" I am here now two days getting arms for our recruits. All is reported quiet beyond Rockville, and I do not return till to-morrow.

" Charley is spoken of as having shown gallantry and conduct. His career is an honorable one."

CHAPTER XVII.

BATTLE OF ANTIETAM. — WOUNDED. — DEATH. — BURIAL.

THE few lines from Washington with which the preceding chapter closed are the last we have from Colonel Dwight until those written on the morning of the battle of Antietam, in which he fell. From others we have an account of the intervening days. Mr. Desellum,* whose farm, four miles beyond Rockville, was passed by our army on its way to Antietam, writes : —

"After the disastrous experience of our army in General Pope's retreat, and its pause behind the fortifications at Washington to recruit, it again advanced.

"Amidst the perils and dangers thickening around us, the friend of Colonel Dwight, Colonel Batchelder, of the Massachusetts Thirteenth, rode up. He informed us that Colonel Dwight was alive and well, would soon be up, and had determined, in conversation when at Arlington Heights, to call and see us. The news animated us. How characteristic of the man, to think of obscure friends while surrounded by the horrors and dangers of the battle-field.

"Colonel Dwight, with Colonel Dalton, called upon us as expected. The time and circumstances will never be forgotten. Immense armies were in motion, the Colonel in haste : none knew the danger better than he, or was more ready to meet it. But oh ! the inroads upon the Colonel's health by unmitigated service ! He had undergone ex-

* See page 86.

cessive fatigue, and was then tortured with pain. Riding up, apparently indifferent to suffering, all hastened to meet him. His first remark was, ' Where are all the spinning-wheels ? Are they going yet ? ' A cordial greeting followed. He called all the colored children up to him, showed them to Colonel Dalton, asked them questions, and amused himself with their replies. He then gave us a narrative of the regiment and himself, after which sister and myself, waiving all formality, stated our domestic troubles occasioned by the war, to which he patiently listened, and kindly replied.

" It was evident he needed rest and refreshment, and while enjoying both he requested his ' friend of the spinning-wheel and the flower-garden ' to show Colonel Dalton her domestic manufactures of linens and woollens.

" He appeared to feel a momentary relief, and in conversation was animated. While sister was trying to administer to his comfort on a couch he remarked with a pleasant smile, ' How well you know how to make me feel comfortable ! '

" In a short time he felt refreshed, and determined to press forward. I implored him to stay a few days with us, at least, to recruit his shattered health ; entreaties were vain. He well knew the terrible ordeal before him, and said, with emphasis full of meaning, ' *I expect active service !* ' He appeared to have but one wish, — his country's good, — to which health and all other considerations were subordinate.

" Bidding sister, colored children, and all a final farewell, he remarked to me, ' Come to our camp at Damascus,' and ' I wish you to correspond with me by letter.'

" Mounting their horses, Colonel Dwight, as he rode away, politely and gallantly bowed and waved his hat three times to sister.

" I went a short distance with them, speaking as encouragingly as a full heart would permit. At the gate the final parting ; he rode away.

" With subdued feelings, I could only invoke the Divine protection in his behalf.

" Onward he went through pain and suffering, severe marching, privation, battle, victory, wounds, and death."

Chaplain Quint writes : —

" On the 12th of September, Friday, Lieutenant-Colonel Dwight, who had for some days been in Washington on business for the regiment, rejoined us.   It was near the close of the day, and his horse bore marks of his haste to find us. We were near the end of the day's movement, and he and myself, with the ambulances, were some half a mile behind, while he told me what he had done and learned.   He soon rode on and joined Colonel Andrews.   He had been suffering pain in the early part of the week from a carbuncle on his face, and was still weak.

" At night he slept in a tent with Colonel Andrews, Dr. Stone dressing the face.   In the morning, after sunrise, we left our camping-place, and soon after noon reached the vicinity of Frederick.   After camp was in order Colonel Dwight, Colonel Andrews, and myself rode into Frederick, where Colonel Dwight was joyfully welcomed by the numerous friends he had made the preceding winter.*   He always *made* friends, he never *lost* one.   On Sunday we marched to the eastern slope of the Blue Ridge ; a most fatiguing day we had, and it was past midnight when we lay down supperless.   Colonel Andrews, Colonel Dwight, Dr. Leland, and myself were side by side.   We anticipated a battle ; but the enemy had left during the night, and in the morning we crossed the ridge, passed through Boonesboro', and bivouacked.   We rode together nearly all day, and at night my arm touched him if I moved.   He was cheerful as ever, but far from well.   On Tuesday morning his blanket and mine were put together on rails so placed as to insure a

* See Appendix IX.

shelter from the sun, and we read and wrote letters* until a sudden order to move preparatory to going into action. We moved about a mile and a half, were drawn up in position, but only artillery fire was had, and at night we camped. He was so weak that Colonel Andrews and myself urged and induced him to lie in an ambulance which Dr. Leland offered. He entered it reluctantly. We had not been quiet over an hour when orders came to move. He and myself again rode together, generally in silence. It was half past ten when we halted, and his last march ended. Near by were some wheat-stacks. We took a little and lay upon it ; Colonel Andrews, Colonel Dwight, and myself together. He said but little, and we slept until about five, A. M., when we were roused by cannonade. Our corps was speedily moved towards the front, but a little distance off."

At this time Colonel Dwight wrote, in pencil, to his mother as follows : —

"Near Sharpsburg, September 17, 1862. On the field.

" Dear Mother, — It is a misty, moisty morning ; we are engaging the enemy, and are drawn up in support of Hooker, who is now banging away most briskly. I write in the saddle, to send you my love, and to say that I am very well so far."

Chaplain Quint again writes : —

" Colonel Dwight was as active and efficient as ever. It was not for several hours that our regiment went into action. Of the action others can tell infinitely better, as I was caring for the wounded who were brought to the rear.

" I am told of his bravery and daring, — that after our regiment had captured a Rebel flag he galloped up and

---

* Whatever may have been written by Colonel Dwight on this morning was lost in the confusion which followed the battle of Antietam, and never recovered.

down the lines with it in his hand, waving it amid the cheers of the men, reckless of the fire of the enemy.

"Colonel Andrews was with him as he was shot, and will tell the circumstances.

"His last act before receiving the fatal wound was to walk along the line of the regiment, which was drawn up under the shelter of a fence, and direct the men to keep their heads down out of the reach of the enemy's fire."

Colonel Andrews writes : —

"Lieutenant-Colonel Dwight was mortally wounded within two feet of me. He had just come from the left of the regiment, and was about to speak, when the ball struck him in the left hip. He fell, saying, 'They have done for me.' He then complained of intense pain. The ball also wounded him in the left wrist. The regiment soon fell back a short distance, and men were ordered to carry him, but the pain was so intense that he refused to be moved."

Here, while alone upon the field, under the fire of the two armies, he took from his pocket the note which he had written in the morning, and added to it the following : —

"DEAREST MOTHER, — I am wounded so as to be helpless. Good by, if so it must be. I think I die in victory. God defend our country. I trust in God, and love you all to the last. Dearest love to father and all my dear brothers. Our troops have left the part of the field where I lay.

"Mother, yours,
"WILDER."

In larger and firmer characters, across the opposite page, he wrote these words : "All is well with those that have faith."

The paper is stained with his blood, and the scarcely legible lines show with what difficulty he accomplished this last effort of a life filled with acts of fidelity and love.

We next hear of him from Private Rupert Sadler, who crept up to him at great risk. He writes : —

"After we had got out of the reach of the enemy, I went out to see what had become of Colonel Dwight. When I got near the road, I had to crawl on my hands and knees. The Rebels had not advanced any, and I saw a horse which I thought was the Colonel's. While I was examining it a squad of Rebels saw me, and began firing at me. I laid down behind the horse until they stopped. After I had looked about for a few moments I saw a man with his head lying on a rail. I felt that it was the Colonel, and I hurried to him. It was as I thought. I gave him a drink of water, and asked him where it was he was wounded. He said that his thigh-bone was shattered. I saw his arm was bleeding, and asked him was it serious. He said, "It is a pretty little wound." I saw two of our men coming, and I called them over. The Rebels saw them, and began firing. After the firing had ceased Colonel Dwight wanted us to go back to the regiment. Said he, 'Rupert,* if you live, I want you to be a good boy.' I wanted to bind up his wounds, but he said it was ' no use.' He gave me a paper that he had been trying to write on, and the pencil. The paper was covered with his blood. I gave them all to Colonel Andrews, except the pencil ; I have that now. He then gave us directions as to carrying him. We lifted him carefully, and carried him into a cornfield. In the evening I was detailed, by

---

* This brave, devoted boy, then a private of Company D, did not long survive the friend and benefactor for whom he so freely risked his life. Soon after the battle of Antietam he was made color-corporal. He was killed in action at Gettysburg on the 3d of July, 1863, while carrying the colors.

Colonel Andrews, at Colonel Dwight's request, to go and take care of him. I was with him until he died."

Magee, one of the men who helped carry him from the field where he fell, says: "When we first came to him to lift him up he said, 'Boys, don't think that because I am wounded I feel any less spirit than I did before, for I feel just the same.' We were looking for an easy place to put him down, when he said to us, 'Put me down anywhere, boys; any place is good enough for me.'"

He was here joined by General Gordon, who writes:—

"As Wilder was brought back from the fatal spot to the wood that skirts the battle-field, I rode to his side. He had just been laid under a tree, the blanket in which he had been carried under him. As I reined up my horse his eye met mine, and he almost exultingly saluted me. At this moment bullets whistled over our heads, shot and shell crashed through the trees; the wood was no longer a safe place for the wounded: I said, 'I must have you immediately removed from here.' He replied with heroic firmness, 'Never mind me; only whip them.' . . . . I ordered six men to take hold of the blanket and carry him to the rear, where he could be cared for. I would have gone myself, but my command had no other leader. I never saw my friend again. I am sincerely a mourner that I shall meet him no more on earth. I can also rejoice that such an example is left me."

Chaplain Quint writes:—

"My servant found me and told me that Colonel Dwight was wounded. I immediately began to search for him; but, though I was in the saddle, could not find him for an hour. I then discovered him with friends in the garden of a hospital somewhat in the rear. He was lying on a stretcher, covered by a blanket, with his eyes closed, and quite pale from loss of blood. As I kneeled down beside him he opened his eyes and smiled, as he took my hand: 'Is that you, Chaplain?' said he. I expressed my sorrow for his wounds; and, doubtless, he saw my deep feeling in my face, for he immediately added, in a coaxing tone, 'Don't feel bad'; and with a firm look and natural smile, said, '*It is all right, all right.*' I replied, 'I thank God you feel so cheerful.' When he added, 'Now, Chaplain, I know I'm done for, but I want you to understand I don't flinch a hair. I *should* like to live a few days, so as to see my father and my mother; they think a good deal of me; especially my mother; *too* much (this was said smilingly), but, apart from that, if God calls for me this minute I'm ready to go.' Colonel Andrews soon came, and, bending over him, yielded to the grief which overwhelmed him. Colonel Dwight threw his arm around his friend's neck, and drew him down to him, saying, 'Kiss me, dear, don't take it so hard, dear fellow, don't take it so hard; think how much better it is that I should be lying here than you, who have wife and children at home.' He then talked with him freely on the subject of the day's fight, and other matters. He said to him, 'I want it distinctly understood that, in dying, I have no personal regrets; my only regret is, that I cannot longer serve the cause.' He gave him the history of the boy Sadler, who had been his charge before the war, and for whom he now asked Colonel Andrews's sympathy and care. He said, too, that he should like, if he had strength, to prepare something which might be read to the regiment from him; adding, with a smile, 'if it is military to do so.' He also told him that he wished a soldier's burial; and, turning to me, he said, 'I do not like display, but I think this appropriate, don't you?' I replied that I did. He afterwards enlarged upon the subject, saying, 'I have lived a soldier, I die a soldier, I wish to be buried as a soldier.' He wanted the papers from Sadler. I sent for them and obtained them.

"It was determined to try to move him to Boonesboro'. I had already sent for an ambulance before Colonel Andrews came. When it arrived we lifted him upon the stretcher into it, but at the first movement of the ambulance the pain was so intense that we had to cease the attempt. We took him out, and replaced the stretcher in its old place in the garden of the hospital.

"I found that he could be moved only on the stretcher, so I sent for a detail of men at our wagon camp, some miles distant. While waiting for them he said but little, only adverting now and then to some item of business for the regiment which he wished attended to. I lay down beside him."

At this time he was joined by Lieutenant James Kent Stone, of the regiment, who afterwards wrote to his father * as follows : —

"I watched by the side of Colonel Dwight, on the ground among the wounded, on the night after the battle, and the next day I helped carry him three or four miles on a stretcher, and helped place him in the bed where he died. As I sat by him in the night he took my hand, and talked with me for quite a long time. He said he hoped to go home once more, and see his friends, and talk with you, before he died. He tried to look on the bright side, to speak in an earthly way ; still, he was prepared calmly to meet the worst, and was ready to die there where he was. He looked upon you as his minister, and wished me to give you his last message, if he never saw you. I will render his words as nearly as I can. He was ready to die. He looked back upon the past with many regrets for failings and for misused opportunities, yet still, with the self-respect of a man who has tried, on the whole, to do his best ; as for the future,

* Rev. John S. Stone, D. D., then rector of St. Paul's Church, Brookline, Massachusetts.

there was but one hope ; no putting forward of one's own claims, but reliance on the merits of *Another*. ' You know what I mean,' said he. When he had finished, wishing to go to sleep, he took a drink of water from me, and pressing my hand, said, ' Good night, dear boy. I hope your future will be as bright as it promises and ought to be.'

" The men admired Wilder Dwight more than any other officer in the regiment. They talk often of how he rode along on the battle-field, laughing and cheering, rallying them on. Hal * and I feel that the one great friend we had in the regiment is gone. All are kind, but there was none so true as the Colonel."

Chaplain Quint continues : —

" After our men arrived it was too late to move him any distance in the darkness. I sent for an ambulance, satisfied that the best thing to do was to place him inside for the night, where he would be sheltered from the dews. When the ambulance arrived we carried him to it, having placed it in a good position, and arranged it as well as possible. The men lay around it, and he was well sheltered. At daybreak we lifted him from the ambulance, and Dr. Leland dressed his wounds."

Lieutenant Stone again writes : —

" When his wounds were dressed he examined them in a most cool, naïve manner. Looking at the hole through the forearm, he said, ' Now that 's a very neat little wound ; a *proper* wound ; but the other (pointing to his thigh) won't do so well.' By this time Dr. Leland had found a farmer, named Thomas, who owned a substantial house † about

---

* Henry Van Dyke Stone, a younger brother of Lieutenant Stone. Eager to serve their country, these young men waited not for commissions, but hastened to join the Massachusetts Second as privates during the dark days of August, 1862, which immediately followed the battle of Cedar Mountain.

† When, four years later, friends of Colonel Dwight visited this house, and

three miles off, where the Colonel could have a good bed and be well cared for. It was determined to carry him thither. Twelve men from the new recruits were detailed for the purpose. He divided them into six parties, who relieved each other by turns. During the journey of three miles and a half he called out the reliefs himself. At one time one of the third relief carelessly stumbled. It jarred him very much, and he said, ' Third relief, to the rear ! Now, boys, put on my best team.' We were obliged, in one place, to ford a rapid stream about two hundred feet broad. It must have caused the Colonel great pain in crossing, but he did not show it at all outwardly. He was generally silent, but he now and then spoke pleasantly to the men, asking them their names and occupations. Once he asked us if we had had any breakfast. Upon our answering no, he said, ' Ah ! *young* soldiers. An old soldier would never have left his wagon-camp with his haversack empty.' One incident I must not forget. As we were passing through a piece of woods we met a man with a Rebel flag which had been captured the day before by one of our regiments. Rupert Sadler got him to show it to the Colonel. It was the State flag of the First Texas. The names of the various battles in which it had been borne were inscribed on it. Colonel Dwight read off the names : Seven Pines, White Oak Swamp, Ethan's Landing, Gaines's Farm, Malvern's Hill, &c. As the Colonel read the last name Hal called out, in

learned from Mr. Thomas's own lips that he was a whole-souled Union man, they told him that they were grateful to know that Colonel Dwight did not die under the roof of a Rebel. He replied : " I think it most likely that if he had been taken to any house nearer the battle-field than mine it would have been to a Rebel's. I was almost alone here as a Union man through the war; but when they threatened me with the loss of my property, I always told them I 'd never be afraid to stand by the flag."

Mr. Thomas was, withal, a good Christian, and did not omit to mention that morning and evening prayer ascended from his dwelling during that day and night of suffering. In giving his religious views, he said, " I belong to the United Brethren." It was evident that he was of the Good Samaritan order, who would find a brother in any one to whom he could do good.

the same tone of voice, ' Boonsboro'.' ' Good for that man ! '
cried the Colonel ; ' if I knew who he was I 'd give him a
dollar.' But Hal kept still. At one time one of the men
asked where the rest of the regiment was. Colonel Dwight
called out, ' Who asked for the Second Regiment ? I 'll tell
you where the Second was *yesterday*. In the foremost front
of the battle fighting like men ; and we *drove* them, boys,
drove them ! ' "

Drum-Major Kesselhuth, of the Second Regiment,
wrote to a friend after the death of Colonel Dwight
as follows : —

" I was with Colonel Dwight, and helped to dress his
wounds. The morning after the fight, while going to join
my regiment with my drum-and-fife corps, which had been at
work with myself in the hospitals, we met him, lying on a
stretcher, on his way to Boonesboro'. He stopped us, and
requested, as a last favor, that we would play him the Star
Spangled Banner once more. As we played, he raised himself up, suffering terribly, for he was mortally wounded.
When we had finished he thanked us ; and, repeating the last
line of the song, he said, ' I hope that glorious old flag will
wave over this whole country again. So may it be. *So
shall it be*.'

" He died a true patriot. Would to God the whole army
was officered by such men as he ! "

Chaplain Quint says : —

" On the morning after the battle, when the men were
carrying him to the house where he died, as we passed the
Fifteenth Massachusetts Regiment, which had been badly
cut up, and was drawn back by itself near the hospital, he
asked to have the flag waved again before his dying eyes.
During the journey, if water was given him, or any other
service rendered, his old ' thank you ' was never omitted.
Indeed, the night before in the garden, he repeatedly sent his

servant and others to relieve the poor wounded men around him, while in pain himself; it was like him. On the journey, it was found necessary to make two long rests.''

Lieutenant Stone continues : —

" It was between one and two o'clock when we reached Mr. Thomas's house. It was a brick building, airy and comfortable. We carried the Colonel into a bedroom. As he was very much fatigued by the journey, we left him awhile to rest. In a short time we were called in to help lift him into bed. By following his own suggestions, we succeeded in placing him in bed without his suffering in the process. I could see that he had failed very much since the morning. He was very pale, and his eyes sunken. As we lifted him he said, ' Now, boys, steady and true ! steady and true ! ' These words he repeated a great many times. Having arranged him comfortably, we at once turned to leave the room ; but he roused himself and said, ' Wait a minute, boys ; you 've taken good care of me, and I thank you very much. God bless you ! ' This was the last I saw of our dear Colonel. We then partook of a dinner which the Colonel had promised us while we were carrying him.''

" That afternoon," writes Chaplain Quint, " he suffered considerably ; the pain in the limb was great. The next morning I had no thought but that he would live several days, although he was very weak ; he seemed quiet ; the blinds were kept closed, and I allowed no one to enter. But *he* felt that he should not see any of his family. He spoke of it, and of the time required, and spoke of the probability of William's being near. In the morning he sent a despatch asking his father to hasten. This was the *third*. The first I found he had sent the first day, as I was writing one myself. The second was for a surgeon. ' They tell me,' said he, ' that I *may* recover. I do not believe it, but still it is my duty to leave nothing undone.' Various little matters he had seen to. Some delicacies came from Frederick, and he sent thanks for them. Letters were brought, which he read. About ten he seemed considerably weaker ; but it was not until near noon that a marked change took place. I was in the kitchen directing the mistress of the house as to the preparation of beef-tea from a peculiar jelly. John, his faithful servant, who was with him, came to me and said, ' The Colonel is wanting you quick, sir.' I went in, instantly saw a change, and took his lifted hand.

"After looking me earnestly in the face, ' Chaplain,' said he, ' I cannot distinguish your features ; what more you have to say to me, say now.' (I had, of course, remembered his dying condition, and conversed accordingly.) I said, ' Colonel, do you trust in God ? ' He answered with ready firmness and cheerfulness, ' *I do.*' ' And in the Lord Jesus Christ, your Saviour ? ' ' *I do.*' ' Then,' said I, ' there is no *need* of saying more.' I said a few words of prayer over him, with a blessing, after which his own lips moved in prayer, and he added audibly, ' Amen.' Then I said, ' Now what shall I say to your mother ? ' He answered, with his whole face lighted up, ' My mother ! Tell her *I do love my mother* (he emphasized every word). Tell her *I do trust in God, I do trust in the Lord Jesus.* Nothing else.' No more did he say then. He was soon sinking. The *last* was a few minutes later, and about fifteen minutes before his death, when he said, ' O, my dear mother ! ' About twenty-five minutes past twelve he died ; so peacefully that we could hardly tell the time.

"He died, as he had lived, a brave, gallant, noble man, a hero and a Christian ; cheerful to the last, considerate, happy. When he breathed his last, every face, of soldiers as well as officers, was wet with tears.

"Colonel Andrews had sent him word of our success in the battle. ' It is a glorious time to die ! ' was his joyful exclamation.''

" So died," writes Colonel Andrews, " one of the most faithful, brave, unselfish, and devoted officers of our army. He was, I think, the officer most beloved and respected throughout the regiment, by officers and men. His conduct as an officer and as a man was noble. On the battle-field he appeared to me to retain his self-possession most completely, and to have his soul bent upon doing his best to uphold the honor of his country's flag. He showed no consciousness of danger, although there was nothing rash in his conduct. He was uniformly kind to every one. How we all feel here in the regiment you can perhaps imagine. It is not the same regiment. His friends have every consolation possible. His memory is their pride."

Lieutenant Henry V. D. Stone wrote of him at this time : —

" Dear Colonel Dwight! he was the best man in the world ; too brave for an officer. He was always in the front, cheering on the men, and all the men loved him as they never loved any other.

" I wrote the telegram sent by Colonel Dwight from the field, and I was sent with Kent and others to take him from the field to the house where he died." *

" Make haste to join me," he said, by telegram, as he felt his life fast ebbing away ; and every effort was made to reach him, only to learn that it was *too late.* At his own request, urged in the dying hour, Chaplain Quint, who had watched him through suffering and through death, accompanied his body to Massachusetts, and saw it borne in safety to his home in Brookline.

* In a spirit no less heroic than that of his beloved Colonel, this " modest and brave officer " fell in the battle of Gettysburg, on the 3d of July, 1863, at the early age of nineteen years and eleven months.

Changed as his countenance was by death, there still rested upon his lips the same sweet expression of content which they had been seen to wear when he said, " The last year has been the richest of my life." His silent presence brought with it no suggestion of the horrors of the battle-field, but only the thought that, as he lay there alone between the two armies, " angels came and ministered unto him."

His family, on hearing of his death, had thought only of laying him quietly and without unusual ceremony in the beautiful cemetery of his native town ; but on learning his request for a soldier's burial, their one desire was to carry out his wish as perfectly as possible.

At the call of the Governor of the State a detachment from six companies of the Massachusetts Forty-fourth, under the command of Lieutenant-Colonel Edward C. Cabot, acted as military escort on the day of his burial. On that day, Thursday, September 25, even the agonizing sense of loss gave way for the time to gratitude, that it was one of autumn's brightest, and that everything conspired to enable his friends to do for him even as he would have done for any brother soldier who had asked it at his hands.

He had said that he did not like display, and it was felt, at the time, that nothing like display entered into the occasion. The ceremonies, in all their details, seemed an honest and tender expression of heartfelt feeling in contrast to an unmeaning pageant.

To some who witnessed the scene, the most striking feature was the expression of grief that was visible upon the countenances of all who crowded the road as the procession moved. Others were most impressed by seeing men advanced in years and high in station, to whom he had looked up with deferential respect, now come forth to do him reverence.

From the home made desolate by his death, with "wail of saddest music" he was borne, "in slow procession, winding through the ways once so familiar to his feet" * to the church where he had been a devout worshipper, and where he had learned to love the sublime burial-service which now fell with soothing power upon hearts bowed with the deepest sorrow. No more sincere mourners were there present than the children of the neighborhood, whose young hearts he had won by the overflowing love and kindness of his nature, and who now brought him the tribute of their sobs and tears.

One of the most affecting incidents of the day was the arrival, at a late hour, of the band of the Massachusetts Second, which had been recently discharged from service. These men, who in the army had experienced his kindness and his care, hastened from various distant points to the scene, anxious to follow him to the grave. They arrived in season to join the procession on its way from the church to the Brookline cemetery, where the concluding religious services were held.

Chaplain Quint then spoke, from the inspiration of the occasion, words eloquent with love and grief, which he found it impossible afterwards to recall. Some of them remained imperfectly in the memory of those who heard them as follows : —

* See Appendix X.

20

" Out of the din of battle, out of the smoke-shroud of death, out of the cheers of victory, I bring the tears of the Second Regiment of Massachusetts braves, for one of the noblest, the bravest heroes of them all.

" Yon throng of neighbors is the tribute to him as a generous, honorable, beloved man.

" The words of his revered professional associates have borne tribute to his ready insight, his strong reason, and his cultivated mind.

" But five hundred miles away, near the battle-ground stained with their and with his blood, where, before I left in charge of this sacred trust, the dead faces lay upturned to the sky, the wounded lay helpless, the dying lay gasping, do they weep, who, in the roughest shock of battle, were like iron.

" From them have I come these many miles, to them shall I instantly return when the work they have given me to do is ended."

Chaplain Quint then spoke of the devotion of his friend to the regiment to which he was wedded, and which he had helped to make the brave and veteran corps it was ; and of the bright faith and Christian peace in the enjoyment of which he suffered and died.

In closing, he took leave of the lifeless form which lay shrouded by the American flag before him, saying : —

" My comrade in the camp and in the field, in heat and in cold, in hunger and in thirst, by day and by night, in many a weary march, in many a wakeful bivouac, farewell until the reveillé of the resurrection morn."

With the chant, " Blessed are the dead who die in the Lord," and the concluding prayers of the burial-service, followed by the military honors belonging to his rank, and the music of the Star Spangled Banner, to which his heart had leaped even in the hour of death, these interesting exercises closed.

Some weeks later his body was tenderly removed to a cemetery of an adjoining town, of which he had once said, " My favorite spot, Forest Hills."

The only one of his brothers who was absent on the day of his burial was Captain Howard Dwight, then of the Fifth Missouri Cavalry, in the Department of the West.   He had the trial of learning at a distance from his home, amidst labors arduous and severe, the loss he had sustained.   Then he wrote : —

" . . . . I cannot think of it as real yet ; the void it makes in the home that is almost constantly in my mind is so great.   I had seen by telegram in one of the papers that Wilder was wounded, but, somehow, had not for a moment felt it possible that he could be lost to us.   To me he has ever been the most affectionate brother, and truest friend when I have most needed aid.

" It is a great comfort to me, however, to reflect that his death was one which had no horrors for him, and to the possibility of which he looked forward so cheerfully ; and I glory in his career as a soldier, though the end is so hard to bear.   I need not assure you how fully you and father and all at home have my sympathy in this affliction, and how much I regret that I cannot be at home to be of some use or comfort to you.

" I feel that I can do nothing better, however, than, where I am, to imitate, as closely as I may, the bright example that Wilder has given me."

*   .   *   *   *   *

Alas ! too closely did he follow him in the path of danger and of death.   Six months later, the grave

which had so recently closed over the body of Wilder
was opened anew to receive the body of Howard.

Animated by the same spirit, they fell in the same
cause, giving their lives to their country.

And now, under " the shadow of a great rock," " in
the hope of a joyful resurrection," —

> " They sleep beneath the sod,
> With all the stars of God
> To watch their grave."

We close this record with the following treasured
words from Mr. Justice Hoar's reply to the Suffolk
Bar at the first meeting of the Supreme Court after
the death of Wilder Dwight : —

" Tender and loving son, firm friend, true soldier, Christian hero, we give thee up to thy fame ! For you, life has
been enough.

> ' Goodness and greatness are not means, but ends.'

For us, there is left the precious legacy of his life. Brethren,
it is well that we should pause, as we are entering upon our
stated and accustomed duties, to draw inspiration from such
an example. For who can think of that fair and honorable
life, and of the death which that young soldier died, without
a new sense of what is worthiest in human pursuits, — a
stronger devotion to duty, a warmer ardor of patriotism,
a surer faith in immortality ! "

APPENDIX.

APPENDIX I.

ON Major Dwight's arrival in Brookline, while a prisoner on parole, in June, 1862, the wish was expressed by some of the citizens that he would meet them at the Town Hall.

To the friend by whom this wish was communicated to him he addressed the following letter : —

"BROOKLINE, June 9th, 1862.

"DEAR SIR, — The honor of a public meeting or reception by my friends in Brookline is one that I must decline. I appreciate only too deeply the kindness and friendship which prompt the offer. Such a meeting will be, or seem to be, a formal honor paid me by the town. I have done nothing to deserve it, and ought not to receive it. I cannot seem, by its acceptance, to claim, or admit the claim, of any personal merit or distinction.

"The Second Massachusetts Regiment, to which I belong, succeeded, I hope, in doing its duty under trying circumstances. It is at this moment in the field recovering the ground which it honorably yielded. But I am here, with empty hand, incapable of bearing arms with it.

"I wait only to be free again to return. Now is not the time when I can feel it fit that I should be the object of public praise or congratulation.

"Other reasons, which I need not state, unite to lead me to the conclusion that it is my duty to decline the honor which you so generously offer.

"Very respectfully, your obliged friend and servant,
"WILDER DWIGHT,
Major Second Mass. Vols.

"THOMAS PARSONS, ESQ., Brookline."

A number of his fellow-townsmen then united in requesting his acceptance of a sword as a token of their regard.   In reply he wrote as follows : —

"BROOKLINE, June 11, 1862.

"GENTLEMEN, — Your gift of a sword gives me more pleasure than I can well express.   It comes to me at a time when any recognition by my friends has a peculiar value.

"I welcome it as an expression of your confidence and good-will, and am impatient to be free again to use it more fortunately, I hope, than the one it replaces.

"It is my earnest prayer that I may be able to bring it back to you with honor.

"Your obliged friend,

"WILDER DWIGHT,
Major Second Regt. Mass. Vols.

"To THOMAS LEE, B. F. BAKER, J. S. AMORY, and others."

At this time he had the gratification of receiving a sword from members of the Class of 1853, for whom, ever since his college days, he had cherished a cordial friendship.   His first sword, the compelled surrender of which at Winchester was, to him, the most painful circumstance attending his capture, was presented him upon the occasion of his appointment as Major of the Second Massachusetts Infantry, by his friend and former associate, Judge Gray.

APPENDIX II.

THE following is extracted from a letter written, after the death of Wilder Dwight, by one * who was his chosen friend at Exeter, and who, when the time of his own departure drew near, was moved by faithful memories of the past to pay this affectionate tribute to the companion of his boyhood : —

" . . . . Doubtless, of later years, Wilder had nearer friends than myself, who knew far more than I of what his manhood promised and achieved. But hardly any one knew him more intimately in the golden hope and brightness of boyhood and youth.

" From the day he entered Exeter Academy, sixteen years ago, we were on the closest terms of friendship. We belonged to different classes, but that did not separate us out of school hours. We walked and talked and read together ; and in our vacations and during the year he spent at West Point our letters were frequent and full. I have no pleasanter memory of the dear old Exeter days than their associations with him.

" Then, as always, he had the rare combination of both intellectual and moral clearness of vision, common sense, and conscience. He was, besides, earnest, kind, cordial, and so even his elders were indebted to him for wisdom to discern and courage to do the right. I see now the bright, happy face, and hear the hearty laugh of those days of our boyhood, and that memory will never vanish.

* Rev. Theodore Tebbets, formerly pastor of the First Church, Medford, Massachusetts. He died on the 29th of January, 1863, leaving a memory which is enshrined in the hearts of all who knew him.

" . . . . For the last five years I had met him but three times, but I knew what he was doing, and rejoiced in learning of his unexampled but deserved success ; and I have had ample evidence, in the touching testimonials that have been publicly offered to his memory, that all the beauty and force, all the sweetness and power, of his boyhood's character were still the traits of his noble manhood. . . . ."

APPENDIX III.

MEETING OF THE BAR.

ON the morning of the 24th of September, 1862, the members of the Bar assembled in large numbers in the Law Library in obedience to the following call : —

" The members of the Suffolk Bar are requested to meet in the Law Library on Wednesday, the twenty-fourth day of September, at half past nine, A. M., for the purpose of taking measures to express their respect for the memory of their late associate, Lieutenant-Colonel Wilder Dwight.

" SIDNEY BARTLETT,
BENJAMIN R. CURTIS,
JOSIAH G. ABBOTT,
RICHARD H. DANA, JR."

Mr. Bartlett was called to the chair, and Mr. C. F. Blake was chosen Secretary of the meeting.

Mr. Abbott, Mr. F. E. Parker, and Mr. Gray were appointed a committee to prepare resolutions, and reported the following : —

" *Resolved*, That while we bow with submission to the Divine Will, that has taken from us our friend and associate, Wilder Dwight, we render thanks for the example of his manly life and the consolation of his heroic death.

"*Resolved*, That in the brief period during which our brother practised at this bar we had learned to respect his judgment, to admire his accomplishments, and to expect from his sound sense, and his rare aptitude for the sudden dangers of the trial and the argument, the attainment of the highest honors of the profession.

"*Resolved*, That we remember with pride that he was the first citizen of the Republic to tender to the President a regiment for the war, and the first member of this bar to devote himself to the support of the Constitution and the Flag ; and that amid the perils of the battle and the hardships of the camp he won the name of a true soldier, trusted by his superiors, beloved and respected by his men.

"*Resolved*, That we commend to the young men of Massachusetts the life and death of Wilder Dwight as a noble example. His short life was long enough to afford us a pattern of virtue, of courage, of high resolve, and of lofty achievement. It is fortunate for his country that he has lived. He has not died too soon to leave a memory precious to his companions, and worthy to be perpetuated.

"*Resolved*, That these resolutions be presented to the Supreme Judicial Court, with a request that they may be entered upon its records ; and that a copy of them be transmitted to the family of our brother as an expression of our profound sympathy."

Mr. Abbott then moved the adoption of the resolutions, and spoke at some length in their support.

He was followed by Mr. Josiah Quincy, Jr., who said that nearly thirty years had passed since he attended a meeting of the Suffolk Bar, but that he could not refrain from returning to express his sense of the rare qualities of the citizen and soldier whose memory they had met to honor. He had known Colonel Dwight in Europe under circumstances which had impressed him with the varied acquirements and bright social qualities of his young countryman. And an intimate intercourse in America had increased that estimate of his character and capacity. Mr. Quincy concluded by reading a portion of a letter from his son, a captain in Colonel Dwight's regiment. Both the young men had left the Suffolk Bar at the same time to defend the Constitution of their country before the high court of final appeal where the Judge of Nations is arbiter.

An extract from this letter, written after General Banks's retreat from Virginia, in May, 1862, is as follows: "Our Major (afterwards Lieutenant-Colonel) Dwight has won for himself the heartfelt admiration of the regiment. His indomitable pluck and perfect *sang-froid* were beautiful. I watched him on Saturday and Sunday with wonder and delight. Bullets and death he utterly despised and ignored. In short, he is a genuine hero."

Mr. Dana then addressed the meeting as follows: —

"MR. CHAIRMAN, — The sight of so many of our brethren reminds me that the last meeting I had the privilege of attending was when we came together to mourn the sudden extinguishment of that dazzling luminary of the forum, the bar, and the platform, which had so long cheered and infatuated us all.

"Rufus Choate died in the fulness of his years and fame. That light went out as it was declining to its evening. To-day we meet to mourn one who has fallen in the flush of youth, — a star but little risen above its eastern horizon, not yet a familiar sight, not yet recognized by all as an influence. This is a contrast, Sir; but, alas! how much deeper is the contrast in the place and manner of their death!

Rufus Choate died, indeed, on foreign soil, and under a foreign flag, but beneath a friendly roof, with kindly attentions, and in the quiet of profound peace. Our young brother fell in the midst of the uproar and carnage of a field of battle ; not on foreign soil, but on the soil of the old thirteen States, beneath our own flag, almost under the shadow of the Capitol, not by the hand of foreign foes, but of vindictive and infuriate brethren, who have struck hands — parricidal hands — against our common parent, against those who had been, and desired still to be, their brethren.

"Who would have dreamed, sir, when so little while ago Wilder Dwight stood among us at the funeral solemnities of that leader of our bar, so eager to show every mark of love and admiration, but not claiming a place among those who spoke, — who would have dreamed, in that hour of a peaceful and united Republic, that we should be bringing him home with bell and burial from the field of a battle of the greatest proportions, fought in the deadly struggle of civil war !

" But, sir, I desire to speak more particularly of the personal qualities of our brother. I cannot say, with Mr. Abbott, that I knew him intimately ; but I knew him very well. If we may approach with that freedom which all analysis implies, within the sacred precinct which the shadow of death forms around its victims, — if we may touch so freely one whom an heroic death has canonized, — I would say, as an honest judgment, that his most marked characteristic was what one is tempted to call a talent for success. He had that combination of qualities which led to success in whatever he undertook. His best friends may well admit that you can find, among the youth of this city, some who excelled him in that variety of acquirements which makes the accomplished and versatile man of society. Neither his tastes nor his powers lay in that direction. He had learned in the schools and at college that for which colleges and schools are most valuable, — the use of the instruments which men must employ in life. His love was for that kind of intelligent labor which looks to specific results.

"I spoke of his talent for success. I mean that he had those qualities which operated like a specific power in that direction. He had an intuitive knowledge of himself, and an instinctive knowledge of other men. He adapted his means to his ends. He knew what he was suited to do, and he had a power of will, a faculty of concentration, and patience, perseverance, and confidence, which insured success. He allowed no waste. He was as far as possible from anything desultory. When this war broke out, he determined to become a soldier. His friends knew he would make himself one. He determined to offer the first regiment of three years' men to the army, and he did so. He went to Washington to obtain advantages and opportunities most difficult to secure ; but we felt that he would succeed, and he did succeed. I remember seeing him at the State-House, seeking to accomplish certain things for his regiment then most difficult of attainment. He had the cheerful and satisfied look of one who had succeeded, yet he had but begun. A common friend whom I met — a member of the Governor's staff — said to me, 'It is hard to do, but it is Wilder Dwight, and he will carry it through'; and he did. When he was made prisoner at Winchester, and the Rebels were taking all their prisoners to Richmond, he determined not to go to Richmond, and he did not go, but was paroled. Some of us know the sagacity and perseverance by which he gained his point. And after returning to his regiment, and receiving that ovation which has been so touchingly described by Mr. Abbott, when rough men cried and hugged him in their arms, he set about getting himself exchanged ; and that, too, he accomplished speedily.

"But, sir, there is one enemy whom no man can conquer, the last enemy, to whom we all, to-day or to-morrow, must yield. Him that enemy, to our limited human conceptions, seems to have attacked too soon and too early. But in his short life he has helped to teach us many lessons. One lesson, suited to the needs of the hour, is that the best man makes the best officer. As a general rule, — there are many noble exceptions, — but as a general thing, the educated man is the best in command. I do not mean by the educated man, the man with an overloaded memory, but the man of developed powers, enlarged horizon, intellect trained to comprehending and explaining, and, above all, with that training of the inner man which gives him, from youth up, a sense of his own dignity, a power of maintaining it, and a respect for the rights and feelings of others, that training to high notions of honor, that amenability to the point of honor, which — I would say it in the confidence of these walls — is the spot where has lain the deficiency of our public men, where has been the defect with too large a part of our armies. To Wilder Dwight the point of honor was paramount. He might fall in battle, or perish by disease, he might risk or surrender forever all that life can promise, but he would not, could not, do anything questionable in the light of true honor.

"Of his professional prospects when he left us for the army we have the highest evidence, in the opinion formed of him by the Court and his seniors at the Bar. Of his extraordinary personal gallantry in the field, noticeable in a regiment of gallant men, others have shown to us the conclusive and most gratifying proofs.

He is gone! He is gone, with Abbott and Lowell and Putnam and Stearns, with Chandler and Perkins and Cary, with — no, sir, I will not complete the bright catalogue ; these names call back too many sad memories — with that noble army, that glorious company, that goodly fellowship, of the educated young men of Massachusetts, who have offered their lives to this sacred cause, and whose offer has been accepted."

Mr. Parker then said : —

" The remarks to which I have just listened induce me,
contrary to my previous intention, to bear, in few words,
my testimony of affection and respect to the memory of
Lieutenant-Colonel Dwight.   When I first knew him, he
was at school, and I had the opportunity of observing him
as he grew from a promising boy to an admirable man.   It
has just been said that his distinguishing quality was his
talent for success ; and to a distant observer this was no
doubt true.   But to those who knew him familiarly, the
nature of the success which he sought was more remarkable
than his faculty of attaining it.   When he left college, and
was to choose his path in life, it was in his power to take
that path which led by easy and rapid steps to leisure, social
position, and abundant wealth ; and not only was it in his
power to choose this path, but it was the one selected for
him, and to turn from which needed a strong exertion of
the will.   Just that life was offered to him which is to a
young man most tempting from its material advantages, and
to which public opinion in this community, at that time,
pointed as promising the most brilliant prizes of life.   But
he had the elevation of purpose to prefer the honorable toil
of our profession, because it required intellectual effort and
promised the noble reward of intellectual success.   He entered upon the study of the Law with the ardor and energy
of a strong nature ; and I remember how he regretted his
year of foreign travel to which Mr. Quincy has just alluded,
because it placed him farther from the attainment of the
main purpose of his life.   How steady was his progress to
the attainment of that purpose, and how rapid his steps up
the difficult ascent, you have heard from those best placed
to observe and best able to appreciate.   At the breaking out
of the war he had everything which a man of high ambition
most desires : he had youth and health, fortune and friends,
a profession in which he delighted, the practical talents

21

which smooth the way in it, and the confidence in himself which made labor light. But when the trouble of our country came, he thought that all advantages and successes which did not aid her were to be trampled under foot. He gave up to his country, without a moment's hesitation, all that he had gained and all that he was. More than this, he looked the dangers of his new profession in the face, not fascinated by its glitter, nor drawn from weightier thoughts by the sound of martial music, but deliberately, for the defence of the law, and the support of a cause which he solemnly considered to be just. When he left us for the last time, he believed, and to his intimate friends expressed his belief, that he left never to return. It is this elevation of purpose which separates Wilder Dwight from common men, and gives him his true title to immortality."

Mr. Gray then spoke as follows : —

" I feel that the relation which I held to Wilder Dwight makes it fit that I should add a few words ; though I would have preferred to leave it with those who speak with more weight of authority, or whose words are more expressive. To all that has been said in his praise I heartily assent, and would repeat it more forcibly had I the power.

" My acquaintance with him began when, introduced by the gentleman who has just spoken, he applied to enter my office as a student when I was about to form a connection in practice with the present Mr. Justice Hoar. I had occasion to hear all his arguments upon questions of law before the Supreme Court. And after he had become my partner, it was in his room that the first steps were taken toward getting up the Second Massachusetts Regiment, of which so much has been already said. And I can truly say, that from the beginning of our acquaintance, my love, my respect, and my admiration for him went on increasing to the end.

" If I may be permitted to judge from the assistance I derived from him, first as a student and afterwards as an associate, and from having been present at the argument of nearly all the questions of law which were argued before the full bench of the Supreme Court while he was at the Bar, I should find it hard to name one of his age who was better grounded in the principles of the Law. And I think I may say, that I have never known any young man who combined in such just and equal proportions the theory to be learned from the books with a readiness of practical application to the facts of cases as they came up.

" It has been said here to-day that his judgment was uncommonly mature for his years ; and that is true. But it is not all. He did not rest satisfied with what he had attained. As he grew older he improved, not only in experience and in soundness of judgment, but in breadth of view and height of aim, and in generous consideration of the efforts of others not so high in their aims or so fortunate in their faculties as himself. He had no mean spirit of rivalry. He ran not to pass others in the race, but to reach the goal ; and he would have run the same race if no others had run with him.

" In everything that he undertook he was moved by the same spirit. His character is, perhaps, shown more clearly by a few illustrations from his life than by any abstract comments or opinions.

" I remember when he was at home on parole, after he had been taken prisoner in the retreat of the Shenandoah Valley (and it should be remembered that from the time he entered the army he never took a day's furlough, or was absent from his regiment except from some exigency of the service), that he was speaking of the descent of a hill with his regiment under a very heavy fire, and was asked about his thoughts and feelings then. ' If you wish to know,' he answered ' (as we are all friends here), I had written a letter to one of you commenting pretty freely upon the campaign, and perhaps on some individuals; and I thought if I should be killed I should not like to have it fall into the enemy's hands. So I took it out of my pocket, and as we marched down the hill I tore it up.' This shows how he always kept in view his whole duty, the smallest things as well as the most important.

" To those who really knew him, his warmth of feeling was not less remarkable than his purity of principle and his strength of character. None but his intimate friends knew how much of his time was taken up in acts of kindness and charity. From the time he became a soldier, he was devoted to the care of his men, both as a matter of military judgment and of right feeling in this, as in other things, showing how his intellect and his heart worked together. His men's appreciation of his kindness has been shown by the instances which have been recited by others. But it is very striking how in each principal act of his military career the same spirit was manifested. At Winchester he was taken prisoner while caring for a wounded soldier. At Antietam he received his death-wound while suggesting to his Colonel that the men had been halted at a place where they were too much exposed to the enemy's fire. And I see in a newspaper this morning (and I believe it because it accords with what I have often heard of him), that when he was lying on his death-bed, his attention was principally directed to the other wounded men about him, and his indignation strongly expressed to a surgeon who neglected them.

" If I were conversing with any one of you as man to man, I could go on all day with illustrations of his character. But I feel, even in addressing a circle of this size, that I cannot well collect my thoughts or express myself with sufficient distinctness.

" Let me, before closing, but mention a parallel which came to my mind on the morning of the news of his death, while talking of his many noble qualities with an older friend of his, one nearer his own age than myself.

" We had been speaking of his patriotic feeling, his broad and sound views of politics and government, his zeal and labor in learning the art of war, the love his men bore him, and his deference to those of military education or experience.

" Indeed, with all his resolution in carrying out his plans, he had really a modest opinion of his own abilities. When he undertook anything he did all he honorably could to carry it through, and his manner sometimes implied a self-reliance which he did not really have. At the time of getting up his regiment, he had no thought of any higher office for himself than a captain's, and he would have taken a sergeant's place if it had been assigned to him. After all his friends and those who knew most about the regiment had assumed that he would have a higher place in it than any other civilian (it being understood that he had procured two graduates of West Point for the highest officers), he had hardly entertained the idea seriously, and his friends know what misgivings he had about accepting the post of major, when tendered to him by his superior officers.

" He never did anything for vainglory. But he never shrunk from putting himself forward, at any personal risk, when there was an object to be gained. In the charge of Gordon's and Crawford's brigades at the crisis of the battle of Antietam, under the last order of General Hooker, as he left the field wounded, the Second Massachusetts and another regiment of Gordon's brigade advanced with their lines at a slight angle, so that their converging fire almost destroyed the opposing Rebel regiment, and they charged directly over it. Colonel Dwight dismounted, took the papers from the body of the Rebel colonel, seized the Rebel colors, remounted, and rode up and down the line, under the hot fire of the enemy, waving the flag to encourage the men.

" As we talked of him, I recalled and quoted the historian's description of the motives of a noble Roman youth,

who left civil life for the military service of his country,—
as contrasted with the idleness and luxury of many military
men. ' *Sed noscere provinciam, nosci exercitui, discere a pe-
ritis, sequi optimos, nihil appetere jactatione, nihil ob formidi-
nem recusare, simulque anxius et intentus agere.*' When I
went home I opened the book to see whether I had not
remembered this more aptly than it was written ; and found
the very next sentence so strikingly applicable, that I ven-
ture in this educated audience to quote that too. ' *Non sane
alias exercitatior, magisque in ambiguo, Britannia fuit : truci-
dati veterani, incensæ coloniæ, intercepti exercitus : tum de
salute, mox de victoriâ, certavére.*' It was at that moment,
when the Republic was safe, and about to be victorious, that
Wilder Dwight fell.''

Mr. Ellis followed with these remarks :—

" Mr. Chairman,— To such testimony from teacher, partner, comrade, and friends nothing can be added. But,
considering who those are who have thus spoken, I may be
pardoned for trying to utter a word which it is fit should be
said for the Bar.

" We have lately had taken from our midst the fairest
lives that peace can produce, and only wept in silence.
But in an hour like this we must give utterance to our
feelings ; for, whether it be true or not, it surely is to be
expected that the value of States and institutions, results
of the labors of races for ages, is best known to those whose
lives are passed in study of the laws ; and that they feel
more than any others how sacred is the call of duty which
governs those who take up the sword to defend them.

" The brethren of the Bar, attesting their sense of the
worth of the friend whom they mourn, and his merit in going
forth, express their feeling at the conduct of others who
have gone from amongst them to fight, or to die, for their
country.

" Deliberately, solemnly, they now record their judgment,

that he did the highest duty man could do, and died the best death man can die."

The resolutions were unanimously adopted, and the Attorney-General was requested to present them to the Court. The meeting then adjourned.

PROCEEDINGS IN COURT.

On the first day of October Term of the Supreme Judicial Court for the County of Suffolk, Mr. Justice Hoar presiding, Mr. Abbott offered the resolutions adopted at the meeting of the Bar, and moved that they be entered upon the records of the Court. He introduced his motion with the following remarks :—

" MAY IT PLEASE YOUR HONOR, — In the absence of the Attorney-General, the constituted organ of communication between the Bar and this Court, and because, I suppose, I was, out of the Bar and in the Bar, perhaps as near and dear a friend of the deceased as any other one, I have been requested by my brethren to present these resolutions to your Honor ; and the occasion may make it fit, with the permission of your Honor, before I make the formal motion to enter these resolutions upon the records, that I should say a few words in reference to our departed friend.

" I would not trust myself to enter now, even when the freshness of grief has been softened by time, into any lengthened, any careful, analysis of his character and his qualities ; but, sir, occupying the position in reference to him which I did, — a position of great intimacy, remarkable, I may say, between a person so young as he was — for, with all he had accomplished, he had not reached the age of thirty years — and a person of my years, I may be permitted to say, not in

words of exaggeration, but in simplest words, and words
which utter but the simplest truth, what I know of him.
And if I were to characterize his peculiar qualities, I should
say, more in this than in anything else, was he remarkable,
that for a person so young, for a person who from his years
could have had so little knowledge of the affairs and conduct
of life, he was most mature, — most mature in judgment and
in experience.   I do not mean that he was one of those
most disagreeable of all persons, an old young man ; for,
though mature in judgment and in experience, he retained
all the grace and the freshness of youth, which you and I,
sir, as we recede farther from these days of youth, learn most
to prize and to value.   In addition, sir, he had common
sense.   He had a rare combination of common sense and
good judgment, — a combination of those qualities which
would enable him, or any one else who may be the fortunate
possessor of them, to decide at once what he can do and
what he cannot do ; to see what is within his grasp
and what is within his power, and what is not, so as to
make his efforts tell, and not be constantly striving after
what is not within his power.   That common sense, that
clear, good, sound judgment, in a person so young, combined with great energy and great force and power of will,
enabled him to be more practical, more successful, in doing
whatever he undertook than almost any man who had lived
so few years.   Practically he was a man who accomplished
all things he undertook, and did well what he undertook,
because his good sense, his common sense, his good judgment, his clear head, enabled him to see what he could do,
and to know what he could do, and what he could not
do.

"In reference to his qualifications and his ability as a
lawyer, your Honor and your associates have some knowledge, because, although so young, he had often had the
pleasure of appearing before your Honor sitting at *nisi prius*,
and before your associates sitting as a Court of Law.   For

myself, after more than a score of years spent in courts, almost living in them, and knowing something of the practice of the law, and the way it should be practised, I can only say, without being invidious to my friends around me, I never knew so young a person in the whole of my acquaintance, or in the whole length and breadth of the Commonwealth, whose future had more promise than the future of Colonel Dwight. I can say in reference to my appreciation of him, and what I know you will appreciate, as the highest evidence, in my judgment, of his qualifications as a lawyer, that I have come up before you and your associates — the tribunal which I most respect above human tribunals — depending entirely upon briefs furnished by my associate, this young man. I have trusted — beginning with the first cause he ever had occasion to try after being admitted to the Bar — trusted, what I should rarely do, the entire preparation of causes to him, and sat down to the trial of them without any personal attention to the preparation myself. That, sir, is the highest possible testimony I can give as to my own belief as to his qualifications and his prospects.

"As a man, you knew him. He was just, he was true, he was manly, he was generous. He was unselfish ; always ready to devote himself to others ; ready to do more for others than for himself.

"One single word as to his military career. You know with what alacrity he sprang, at the first news of the breaking out of the great Rebellion, to the defence of his country. I recollect perfectly well, and shall never forget it, that being engaged at that time in this court in the trial of a somewhat important case, and, as you know, coming in early in the morning and remaining until night, he came to me before court in the morning with the announcement that he desired to ask my opinion, although he had made up his mind upon the matter. I think it was the very day after the news had arrived of the first gun fired in this war which has so long desolated the land ; and the question was whether he should offer his services to his country, — whether he should join with others in the defence of that Constitution and those Laws under which he and his had lived and prospered. And, sir, now in full view of all that has come to pass, I am glad that I gave my advice to him to do as he had done. I could not hesitate, having, as I told him, the very night before given the same advice to three of my sons. We know with what energy, with what power, with what earnestness of purpose, he joined in the work of organizing and taking to the seat of war the regiment with which he was connected. To him, more than to any other man, it is undoubtedly owing that the Commonwealth then had a regiment sent to the war of which she had a right to be proud, a regiment that has never retreated without orders, which has always done its duty, and its whole duty.

"I know how he was thought of, because I have the testimony of one who was with him from the time the first soldier joined the regiment down to the time he laid down his life, a few weeks before Colonel Dwight's death. You will permit me to read here something I received from the one I refer to, who was with him in the first fight of the regiment at Winchester, where this regiment, and mainly by the efforts of the then Major Dwight, saved the army-corps of General Banks, marching sixty-three miles in thirty-six hours, and fighting a large part of those hours. This account is from one who was with him in the rear-guard : ' His courage and coolness are worthy of all praise. He walked about, apparently as unconcerned as if lounging on Washington Street. His devotion to the wounded is sublime. He is my hero of the fight. The men never tire of talking of him, and praising him.'

"I could desire that some account might have been given by an eyewitness of his reception by his regiment, and by men of other regiments, on his return from his short captivity, coming upon them unexpectedly. The account is most thrilling and most affecting. Although the war is reaching to our borders, we can have no conception of the way that men, who have shared the hardships of the march and the dangers of the battle-field, are knit together in soul and mind and heart ; and these soldiers were men of New England, cold and undemonstrative, unapt to show their feelings, however strong ; yet you would have supposed that it was the return to a regiment of Frenchmen, so demonstrative were they on that occasion.

" His conduct was the same on that last sad day when he was called to lay down his life. He showed the same bravery as a man, the same skill as a soldier, the same steadfastness of soul, when he was looking death full in the face. He showed himself, as he was, in addition to all his other qualities, a good and true Christian, — a man who, I know, always believed, always had faith in the Christian religion ; and I may be permitted to say, that, while he laid upon the battle-field penning a note to the one he loved most and dearest on earth, he wound up by saying, and in so doing well rounded off his life : ' All is well with those that have faith.'

" In conclusion, sir, I can say of him, and can say of him from knowledge, because I knew him most intimately and loved him most dearly, that in all the relations of life, as a son, as a brother, as a friend, as a citizen, he was most dutiful, most loving, most true, most manly, and most generous.

" I now move you, sir, that you will please to direct these resolutions to be entered upon the records of the Court.

Mr. Justice Hoar responded : —

" GENTLEMEN OF THE BAR, — The Court receive with sat isfaction the tribute to the worth of your departed associate, which the resolutions you have now presented so truthfully and appropriately set forth. According to your request, I direct them to be entered upon the records of the Court, as an enduring memorial of the estimation in which his professional character was held by his brethren, and of the impression made upon them by a life so honorably spent, so nobly closed.

"Although the connection of Mr. Dwight with this bar was a short one, it was long enough to exhibit the thoroughness of his training, the clearness and strength of his intellect, his diligence as a student, the soundness of his judgment, and the manliness of his character. I feel that I may speak for my brethren as well as myself, when I say that he has attracted the notice of the Court as one of the most promising young men practising at this bar, — of uncommon accomplishments and capacity, devoted to his chosen profession with a zeal and fidelity which must have insured distinction and success.

"Perhaps this is all which a just expression of sympathy and respect, and the proprieties of the place and the occasion, require now to be said. But, gentlemen, when I think that we are never again to see that bright, young face in these scenes in which it was so familiar and so pleasant, that we are here paying the last sad honors to his memory, I feel that you will pardon me for adding a few words prompted by personal affection for one whom, as pupil, associate, and friend, I have known so intimately and loved so well.

"You have spoken of him in terms of high praise; but he deserved it all. The honors you have paid to him have been usually reserved for the leaders of the bar, for the elders and sages of the law; but his few years bore the fruit of long life. And if it is ever permitted to be careless of measuring the language of eulogy, to give full utterance to our love and admiration, is it not when the bright promise of youth is thus suddenly cut down? As we advance in life, the attainments of the best of us are subject to many limitations and deductions. But the future of honor and usefulness that opened before him was unlimited ; and what achievement or performance was ever equal to a great hope ? He had, of course, not been engaged in many important causes, but he had been in some, and his manner of dealing with them was such as to excite the interest and respect of his associates and antagonists. Though a beginner, and never intrusive, he seemed to attach himself by a natural affinity to the society of able men, and I suppose no man of his age was on terms of intimacy and friendship with so many of those who hold the front rank in the profession. Yet he was the genial and sympathetic companion of the large circle of his own age, among whom his strong sense, ready wit, energy, cheerfulness, and cordial good fellowship made him a natural leader. To those who knew him slightly he may have seemed exacting and imperious ; but to one who knew him well, it was evident that this decision and readiness to act was only the ' assurance' (if I may so use the word) which springs from clear perceptions, conscious power to produce results, and a resolute will, — a quality often found attending great powers. He saw what ought to be done, he knew he could do it, and he did it. He was ambitious, but with no vulgar ambition. He had large views of life, its objects, and its possibilities ; and for these with thoughtful and diligent preparation he reserved himself, seeking no sudden notoriety, and aspiring to no place or honor but those which are awarded to substantial service. It was characteristic of him, that with every advantage for an early entrance upon active life, he delayed entering upon the practice of his profession until after a period much more than that usually allotted to preparatory study. Of a family among the most respectable in our Commonwealth, from a refined and cultivated home, his mind enriched with the learning of the University and matured by foreign travel, he came to the practice of his profession, undoubtedly with the purpose to seek eminence in it, but to seek it only in the lofty path of usefulness and honor. He was intrinsically modest, and, coupled with such energy and force of will, it was a beautiful trait of his character.

"You have alluded, sir, in presenting the resolutions, to his military career. When he had first determined to offer his services to the government, to give his time and his talents to the cause of the country, with that practical skill and sagacity which always attended his actions, he set about making his services efficient for the purpose which he had in view, and he determined to raise a regiment, and as the beginning, to provide a sufficient fund for the purpose ; and he set on foot a large and successful subscription. Next he looked for officers skilled in command, fitted by education and character and capacity for the purpose, and he associated himself with such in organizing the regiment. But for himself it required some urging to induce him to take a place among the field-officers. He said to me that if he could be a captain or a lieutenant, with his inexperience in military matters, it ought to be as much as he should undertake. He was appointed major of the regiment, and I remember, when the regiment was nearly ready to start, the great amount of labor which its preparation involved being done, I said to him, just as he had received his commission, ' I was glad that I had a friend appointed to that particular place, so that now I might ascertain — what I never knew — what the duties of a major were.' Said he, ' They are, theoretically, nothing ; practically, everything.'

"His views of the war and its objects were such as you would expect from his unselfish character. He gave himself to that duty, when he embraced the military profession, with the same singleness of purpose and entire devotion with which he had given himself to the other duties of life. Whatever his hand found to do, he did it with his might. ' *Et sive ad rem militarem, sive ad juris scientiam, sive ad eloquentiæ studium inclinasset, id solum ageret, id universum hauriret.*'

"From such a character as his what had we not to hope ? What a future was before him !

'For can I doubt, who knew thee keen
   In intellect, with force and skill
   To strive, to fashion, to fulfil,
I doubt not what thou wouldst have been.'

"I hold in my hand, brethren, something that I cannot forbear to read to you, and which brings to my own mind, with a vividness that I cannot express, that cheerful, bright presence, which was always an encouragement and a stimulant. After he had received his mortal wound, which he knew to be mortal, and had opened his eyes from a period of exhaustion to find the familiar face of his friend, the Chaplain of the regiment, bending over him, 'with a firm look and a natural smile, he said, "It is all right, all right." ' The narrator proceeds, 'I replied, "I thank God you feel so cheerful," when he added,' (and you notice the brisk and rapid manner of the soldier, but how characteristic of him whom we so well remember,) ' " Now, Chaplain, I know I am done for, but I want you to understand I don't flinch a hair. I *should* like to live a few days, so as to see my father and mother. They think a good deal of me, especially my mother. Too much. (This was said smilingly.) But apart from that, if God calls for me this minute, I am ready to go." '

"Tender and loving son, firm friend, true soldier, Christian hero, we give thee up to thy fame! For you, life has been enough.

'Goodness and greatness are not means, but ends.'

For us, there is left the precious legacy of his life. Brethren, it is well that we should pause, as we are entering upon our stated and accustomed duties, to draw inspiration from such an example. For who can think of that fair and honorable life, and of the death which that young soldier died, without a new sense of what is worthiest in human pursuits, — a stronger devotion to duty, a warmer ardor of patriotism, a surer faith in immortality!"

APPENDIX IV.

AT a meeting of members of the Class of 1853, of Harvard College, at the Parker House, on the evening of September 23, 1862, called to take notice of the death of Lieutenant-Colonel Wilder Dwight, a member of the same, it was unanimously

"*Resolved*, That in the death of Lieutenant-Colonel Dwight the University has lost a graduate who, in his life and services, and still more by the promise of future usefulness and distinction (so prematurely disappointed), has reflected new honor on the places of his birth and education.

"*Resolved*, That we recognize in his military career and death the same activity, earnestness, and practical ability which ever distinguished him, and which have been the subject of honorable mention by his commanding officer, Colonel, now General, Gordon, in his official report, when he wrote of ' this promising and brave officer, so cool upon the field, so efficient everywhere, so much beloved in his regiment, and whose gallant services on the night of the 24th instant will never be forgotten by them.'

"*Resolved*, That we attend his funeral, and transmit a copy of these resolutions to the family of the deceased, as a token of our most respectful sympathy in their affliction."

The above resolutions were transmitted to the family of Colonel Dwight, accompanied by the following letter: —

" WILLIAM DWIGHT, ESQ.,

" DEAR SIR, — The resolutions which I have the honor of transmitting to you herewith are not valuable as coming from a body of any importance, or whose notice is supposed to add anything to the distinction of Colonel Dwight's name, but must be taken as an expression of the feelings of private friends, who knew him before his entrance into professional and public life, and who watched his course with an interest which strangers could not feel.

" Allow me, sir, to add my own regrets at the loss of a friend with whom I always held the kindest relations, and for whose unsullied integrity and great abilities I always entertained a profound respect.

" In behalf of the Class Committee.

" Very respectfully your obedient servant,

" SAMUEL S. SHAW."

22

APPENDIX V.

A DIRGE.

READ AT THE CLASS SUPPER OF THE CLASS OF 1853, COMMENCEMENT EVENING, 1863.

MOURN for the young!
  Mourn for the brave!
He sleeps beneath the sod,
With all the stars of God
To watch his grave.
He gave himself for us
In battle glorious, —
And shall he go unsung?

Mourn for the young!
Mourn for the brave!
About his gallant head
Did battle-banners wave;
About his dying bed
The bullet sung;
The cannon's thunder rung
The triumph in his ear.
The spirit is with God;
The body with the clod;
But memory with us here.

Vanished like a vanished flame, —
That comprehensive wit,
That nobleness of aim,
And force to compass it.

Glory claims him hers, and we
Must lay him down.
There is none left like thee,
King jewel of our crown!
But when a hero dies,
Thank God! the cause
Of country, freedom, laws,
Lives by the sacrifice!

Mourn for the young!
Mourn for the brave!
The slow vine creeps around
The soldier's grave.
Long be votive garlands flung
Upon the sacred mound!
And when a hundred years
Lose record of our tears,
Still will the voice of fame
Exult to name his name;
And every spring the clover and the sorrel
Make haste to bloom for crown and laurel!

E. J. CUTLER.

APPENDIX VI.

THE following is extracted from a notice of Wilder Dwight which appeared in the Boston Courier immediately after his death. It is inserted here as containing an admirable analysis of his mind and character.

" . . . . He possessed powers of a most uncommon order, and which seemed destined to raise him to an exalted position in the profession of the law. . . . .

" His success at the bar was very rapid ; and few young men had so high, and none a higher, position in the profession than he had when he left it for the field.

" He had studied law with great assiduity, and his knowledge of the science was not only extensive and exact, but also, systematic and practical. His perceptions were quick, his memory good, and his reasoning powers singularly acute and vigorous. He frequently, during the four years he was in practice, appeared before the Supreme Court in banc, and many of his arguments there displayed learning, research, and vigorous practical logic, which would have done credit to many of the leaders of his profession. But of his abilities there was only one opinion among his brethren. We never heard a young lawyer, who was acquainted with him, in naming the promising young men of the Bar, fail to mention Mr. Dwight amongst the very first.

" Mr. Dwight's literary acquirements were also of a superior kind. In the history and literature of his profession he was exceedingly well versed, and his knowledge of the lives and characters of the great ornaments of the Bar, both in England and this country, was very great.

" He had also read, in general literature, much more than young men are apt to do in these days, not being satisfied, as too many are, with skimming over the pages of the Edinburgh Quarterly or North American, and to rest with the smattering information which the periodical publications afforded him. His quick perception and keen discrimination enabled him, undoubtedly, to succeed with much less study and much less profound learning than persons of slower and less pointed intellects could ; but he was too wise to trust very much to these, and his acquirements were anything but superficial. His style, both in writing and speaking, was singularly concise and sententious ; and in discussing any subject, his thoughts and arguments came so rapidly, pointedly, and tersely from his lips as greatly to embarrass his opponent. His temper was quick, and often overbearing ; and had he lived, this would have been, at times, very uncomfortable to his opponents ; but in private life it interfered little with the extreme good nature and generosity of his disposition ; and we think his personal friends seldom had reason to complain of unkindness or irritability from him. His courage, moral and physical, was undaunted, and was strengthened by the self-confidence and reliance naturally arising from his knowledge that he possessed unusual mental powers and resources ; and we know no one who possessed, to a greater degree, the pluck which the English so much admire. . . . .

" The remembrance of most members of the Bar, however high their position, soon becomes reduced to traditions among their successors. Still less can it be expected that the reputation of young barristers will survive. But if at the Bar he be forgotten, and among the crowd of the fallen brave of this war his name be lost, it will be long, very long, before, among his friends and associates, mention ceases to be made of Wilder Dwight.

"C. H. H."

The value of the tribute quoted above is enhanced
by the fact that the writer was not restrained by the
partiality of intimate friendship from recognizing the
easily besetting fault against which nearly a life-long
struggle was maintained.   In justice to the memory
of Wilder Dwight, however, it should here be said,
that those who saw him most intimately when he
was last at home, after a year's service in the army,
were impressed by the conquest which, in this respect,
he had achieved.

He had, in anticipation, laid down his life for his
country, and with that act of self-surrender he seemed
to have cast behind him everything which could, in
any way, mar the beauty of the sacrifice he so freely
offered.

APPENDIX VII.

IN the autumn of 1861, while the Second Massachusetts Regiment was at " Pleasant Hill Camp, near Darnestown," and at " Camp near Seneca," in Maryland, it was near the farm of Mr. Desellum for many weeks.

During that period he visited the camp frequently for the purpose of taking to it the produce of his farm.

In this way he became acquainted with Colonel Dwight, and so much attached to him, that, on hearing of his death, he sent to his family the following tribute to his worth : —

" . . . . I cannot describe my feelings when I received the sad intelligence that the kind, the brave, the noble Colonel Wilder Dwight was no more. I have not language to convey my sorrow, nor the worth of the deceased. Regarding Colonel Dwight, after a year's acquaintance, as one of the noblest of men, — which I can conscientiously say without flattery, — it gives me great satisfaction to bear my humble testimony to his distinguished memory and merit. My first impression of Colonel Dwight was, that he was a reliable gentleman ; subsequent intercourse confirmed my opinion. At all times I found him kind and courteous, uniting politeness and simplicity with the dignity of a gentleman. I saw in him a master-mind, quick in perception, eager for information. I noted his quick movements, invincible determination, restless desire to combat or overcome obstacles.

" I had opportunities to see the Colonel's true character ; being only a private and obscure citizen myself, there was no necessity for him to disguise (which he never did) his true character. My frequent interviews with him have made an impression of his worth that can never be forgotten.

" Far away from home, amidst the varied temptations to indulgence of a camp life, his moral character remained untarnished. He was ever watchful of the morality and discipline of his regiment, — his own *personal example* always conspicuous, — no trifling jests or conversation were indulged in by him.

" His active and well-trained mind was continually investigating and digesting all the information within his reach. I never found him idle.

" Space will not permit me here to detail what I know of Colonel Dwight's vigilance in guarding and collecting information while in camp on the Seneca Creek last fall. Ceaseless application and untiring devotion to his country were predominant.

" Of his arduous duties in camp, his devotion and attention to the wants and comforts of his men, I have been an eyewitness.

" He was brave, almost to temerity. How effectual was his example is best seen in the intrepidity, courage, and devotion of the Second Massachusetts Regiment.

" I never had a conversation with the Colonel on sacred subjects, but his strict morality impressed me with the belief that he fully appreciated the doctrines of the Gospel.

" His last words, the language of the dying patriot, show that the ruling passion was strong in death. The battle of Antietam, in magnitude and results, will be referred to till the end of time. Who does not envy the death of a patriot on such an occasion ? " . . . .

APPENDIX VIII.

EXTRACT from a letter written during a visit to Maryland and Virginia in the spring of 1866 : —

"HARPER'S FERRY, May, 1866.

" . . . . Finding myself in the immediate vicinity of Maryland Heights, I was bent upon visiting the spot where the Massachusetts Second encamped during the summer of 1861, when Wilder wrote so enthusiastically of the scenery.

" I was misdirected, by a man at the hotel, to the very summit of the Heights. I had Wilder's letter with me, describing the situation of the camp. With that as my guide, I was quite sure, on reaching the top of the mountain, that far beneath me lay the farm upon which was the camp of the Second. There was the ' broad table-flat,' not, as when he described it, ' white with tents and alive with armed men and vocal with martial music,' but with its old farm-house and out-buildings looking so solitary and so peaceful that it seemed impossible it could ever have been the seat of war.

" I had been misdirected quite away from the proper path, yet, I could hardly regret it, as I remembered how often Wilder had written of his rides on horseback to the top of the mountain, first ' over a rough path cut by the Rebels two months before,' and afterwards ' over the road cut by the immortal Second,' the very road which I had been pursuing.

" I descended to the farm, which was now my goal, by a shorter path, on foot. It was very steep and rough, yet there was a certain pleasure in the wild and strange experience.

" ' You might enjoy,' Wilder wrote, ' the tangled pathway through the woods ; you would certainly find a thirsty pleasure at the spring of pure water which pulses from the heart of the mountain.' And now I reached the spring which I recognized as the one at which Wilder had often been refreshed. After drinking the water, I stepped upon the plateau. Here was the farm upon which the Massachusetts Second encamped in July, 1861. A more delightful spot cannot be imagined.

" I met the farmer just coming out from his barn. I said to him, ' Did you occupy this farm in July, '61, when the Massachusetts Second encamped here ? ' ' Yes, I did,' said he ; ' why ? were you here then ? ' ' No,' I replied ; ' I asked because my son was, at that time, the Major of the regiment.' At this the man took my hand and grasped it with all his might, as he said, ' You are not Major Dwight's mother, are you ? ' The tears filled his eyes ; he tried to speak, but his voice was choked, as he said, ' The Major lived here a good while, he took his meals with us in this house all the time the regiment was here.' He took me on to the piazza of the house, and gave me a seat. He sat down beside me, but seemed unable to say another word. I talked to him, and read to him from Wilder's letter what he said of the ' friendly supper ' he had given them on the first night of their arrival. Soon the man said, ' I 'll go call my wife ; she can talk to you about him better than I can.' Almost immediately a brisk little woman made her appearance, with both hands extended to take mine. ' O ! I did love him ! ' she said ; ' everybody loved him, — the servants, the children, the officers, the soldiers, — he was beloved by all. His kind sympathy for me I shall never forget. When we were overrun here by the army, and our house was taken as a hospital, and we were turned out of it into one of the out-buildings, he showed such sympathy and kindness for me ; he would have stayed the torrent if he could.' I said to her, ' I am thankful that I have found this spot.

I think he never was so happy anywhere during his army life as he was here; he enjoyed the scenery so much.' 'O! he had a fine imagination,' she replied; 'he would sit at the western window of that room at sunset, and look out upon the view, and draw inspiration from it; and then he would talk and look so happy and seem to enjoy it so much. And such a smile as he had! I never met him all the time he was here that he did n't give me that smile. I used to say to him, 'Major, you shed sunshine wherever you go.' She took me in to her best room, that I might sit at the window which he enjoyed so much. Then she led me to the porch on the western side of the house, that she might show me the seat he used to occupy there; where, she said, he often wrote his letters to me.

"She gave me several characteristic anecdotes of him, illustrating his kindness and sympathy for her. She said she wished she had known I was coming, that she might have recalled more incidents connected with him to tell me. 'I shall think of a great many more when you are gone,' she said. 'I am too much excited to remember them all now, — so suddenly.' Her husband kept out of the way while we were talking of Wilder. 'He never can bear to speak of a friend who has died,' she said; 'but I feel so differently. I love to talk of the Major.'

"Among the many illustrations which this journey has furnished of Wilder's 'remarkable power of impressing himself upon all with whom he came in contact,' no one has affected me more deeply than this visit to good Mr. and Mrs. Unsel, of Maryland Heights." . . . .

APPENDIX IX.

THE following tribute to Colonel Dwight appeared, on the occasion of his death, in The Examiner, a paper published in Frederick City, Maryland. It was written by the Rev. George Dhiel, D. D., of Frederick, at whose house, among others, Colonel Dwight, with Chaplain Quint, was warmly welcomed on his way to Antietam.

It is the more valuable as showing the power Colonel Dwight possessed of winning the love and respect even of comparative strangers.

"DEATH OF A GALLANT OFFICER.

"Lieutenant-Colonel Wilder Dwight, a brave and faithful officer, was mortally wounded in the battle of Antietam, on Wednesday, the 17th ultimo, at eleven, A. M., and died at the house of Mr. Jacob Thomas, near Boonsboro', on Friday afternoon following. His remains were brought to Frederick the same evening, and the next day, in the charge of his brother, Colonel William Dwight, together with several officers of his own regiment, were taken to Boston for interment. Lieutenant-Colonel Dwight was a young man of great merit and superior accomplishments. The son of wealthy parents, he enjoyed from early life the advantages of the best society and education that the city of his residence, the Athens of America, could afford. He was graduated with distinguished honors at Harvard University. After spending some time in Europe, he studied law in Boston. In due time he was admitted to practice in the several courts of the city, and soon took his place in the very first rank among the young men of the Boston Bar.

"Upon the breaking out of the Rebellion he felt it his duty to offer his services in the cause of his country. He was chosen Major of the Second Regiment Massachusetts Volunteers, and during the last summer was promoted to a lieutenant-colonelcy. Connected with General Banks's division, during the last winter he spent several months in this place, and endeared himself to all who made his acquaintance.

"Gentle, noble, generous, and self-sacrificing, he was eminently distinguished for his social excellences, and respected by all.

"His untimely death in the hour of victory and the full pride of manhood is sad indeed, and has filled with sorrow a large circle of friends in this city.

"D."

APPENDIX X.

THE following lines appeared in the Boston Daily Advertiser on the morning of the day of Captain Howard Dwight's burial.

HOWARD DWIGHT.

DIED MAY 4, 1863.

Another wail of saddest music heard, —
Another slow procession winding through
The ways once so familiar to his feet, —
Another flood of tears to overflow
The cup e'en now filled to the brim with grief,
And we have paid our last respects to him,
The second offering of a stricken house.
Father! God give thee strength to bear the stroke ;
And mother! pray thee Heaven may stay thy faith ;
So that when side by side these brothers lie,
Your two brave children, loved and praised by all,
Ye'll say with us, 't is well such men have lived,
To die examples for those left behind.

F. B.

May 22, 1863.

APPENDIX XI.

WITHIN the rock which overhangs the grave of Wilder and Howard Dwight is inserted a simple tablet of bronze, bearing a double inscription; the dividing line being two swords, *in relievo*, suspended by their knots; their hilts wreathed with laurel. Leaves of the laurel and of the oak form the edge of the tablet. The inscription is as follows:—

HERE LIE THE BODIES OF
WILDER DWIGHT, LIEUTENANT-COLONEL OF THE SECOND REGIMENT
OF MASSACHUSETTS VOLUNTEERS, AND
HOWARD DWIGHT, CAPTAIN AND ASSISTANT ADJUTANT-GENERAL
IN THE SERVICE OF THE UNITED STATES.

WILDER,	HOWARD,
SECOND SON OF WILLIAM AND ELIZABETH A. DWIGHT, WAS BORN IN SPRINGFIELD, APRIL 23, 1833. HE WAS MORTALLY WOUNDED IN THE BATTLE OF ANTIETAM, AND DIED AFTER TWO DAYS, NEAR THE FIELD OF BATTLE, SEPTEMBER 19, 1862. IN THE THIRTIETH YEAR OF HIS AGE. AS HE LAY WOUNDED AND ALONE UNDER THE FIRE OF THE ENEMY, HE WROTE, WITH OTHER WORDS OF COMFORT, TO HIS MOTHER THESE WORDS: "ALL IS WELL WITH THOSE WHO HAVE FAITH."	FOURTH SON OF WILLIAM AND ELIZABETH A. DWIGHT, WAS BORN IN SPRINGFIELD, OCTOBER 29, 1837. IN THE CAMPAIGN AGAINST PORT HUDSON HE WAS SURPRISED AND KILLED BY GUERILLAS, NEAR THE BAYOU BŒUF, LOUISIANA, MAY 4, 1863. IN THE TWENTY-SIXTH YEAR OF HIS AGE. BEFORE DEATH CAME, HE HAD CHEERFULLY DECLARED HIMSELF WILLING TO DIE FOR THE CAUSE TO WHICH HIS BROTHER HAD GIVEN HIS LIFE.

"NO MAN CAN SUFFER TOO MUCH, AND NO MAN CAN FALL TOO SOON,
IF HE SUFFER OR IF HE FALL
IN DEFENCE OF THE LIBERTIES AND CONSTITUTION
OF HIS COUNTRY."
"THEY REST FROM THEIR LABORS,
AND THEIR WORKS DO FOLLOW THEM."